VIDEO SIGNAL COMPRESSION AND STANDARDS

VIDEO SIGNAL COMPRESSION AND STANDARDS

A Review

Selvaraj Saravanan

**Maamallan Institute of Technology,
Jeppiaar maamallan nagar, Sriperumbudur,
Kanchipuram District, India.**

PARTRIDGE

A Penguin Random House Company

To order additional copies of this book, contact
Partridge India
000 800 10062 62
orders.india@partridgepublishing.com

www.partridgepublishing.com/india

CONTENTS

DEDICATED TO MY LORD MURUGA

EPIGRAPH

The primary objective of the study is to increase the performance in terms of PSNR and compression ratio of Video signals during compression. The study aims to examine the power requirement of H.264 using the modified algorithms. The power consumed by the memory is more compared to other part of H.264.Hence reduction of memory requirement is an objective. The performance is evaluated in terms of speed. The speed will be increased by reducing logic cell needed. So, the major objective is to decrease the logic cells and memory needed in H.264 for video compression. The secondary objectives are

- ❖ To check No. of received frames and quality of perceived video.
- ❖ Measuring Channel throughput.
- ❖ Measuring Hardware speed with quality.
- ❖ To check whether it is good enough for both gray scale and colour images.
- ❖ Examine the support of progressive transmission.
- ❖ Extendibility to achieve lossless coding.
- ❖ To measure the Trade-off between quality and compression ratio

The study also aims to briefly examine the salient features of the H.264 blocks compared to other video coding standards.Just a few years ago, digital video was only used in professional studios. This was so large because large amounts of storage and processing power were needed and the computers required manipulating video where prohibitively expensive. The personal computer industry has seen an incredible increase in available processing power which has enabled the introduction of desktop video and video based interactive multimedia services.

In the present era of multimedia, the requirement of video storage and transmission for video conferencing, video retrieval, video playback etc., various digital video coding techniques have been developed. However with the increasing presence of high definition video content resulting in continuous advances in video capturing and display technologies, the H.264/ AVC video coding standard offers significantly improved compression efficiency and flexibility compared to previous standards.

The H.264 video coding standard promises increased visual quality and reduced bandwidth. In this context, the research project introduces H.264 video compressions technique including CAVLC, deblocking filter, transform and quantization, etc.

This book focuses on study and implementation of High performance and Low power architecture for H.264/AVC in video compression. Different transform methods are applied to obtain highest compression in video. Recent years have witnessed the success of DCT and are standardized. Hence many types DCTs are proposed in this book. The proposed architecture can obtain highest compression ratio compared to previous results. Finally DWT technique is proposed, implemented and evaluated. The results are quite satisfactory and good. The work in this book explores the DWT based video coding by novel DWT, MC, OPCM video coding framework, which adopts the EBCOT as the coding engine for both intra (or) interframe mode.

The increasing deployment causes the quality of supported video to become a major issue. The present work highlights the above requirements and analyzes the performance of video compression in H.264. In this thesis, we also investigated many performance measures like PSNR. As a result, the need for better compression technology is realized.

FOREWARD

Video coding today is used in a wide range of applications ranging from multimedia messaging, video telephony and video conferencing over mobile TV, and wireless and Internet video streaming to standard- and high-definition TV broadcasting. Over the past 50 years, digital signal processing has evolved as a major engineering discipline. The fields of signal processing have grown from the origin of fast Fourier transform and digital filter design to statistical spectral analysis and array processing, image, audio, and multimedia processing, and shaped developments in high-performance VLSI signal processor design. In particular, the Internet and wireless networks gain more and more importance for video applications. With telecommunication we can serve our society in much desired needs and – astonishing to many people – we can do it while saving cost, preserving nature and improving the quality of life as well as lifestyle, all at the same time. The range of bit rates and picture sizes supported by H.264/AVC is correspondingly broad, addressing video coding capabilities ranging from very low bit rate, low frame rate, "postage-stamp" resolution video for mobile and dial-up devices, through to entertainment-quality.

The entire H.261 specification was only 25 pages long, and only 17 of those pages were actually required to fully specify the technology that now lies at the heart of all subsequent video coding standards. H.264/AVC, which was recently, completed as a joint project between the ITU-T video coding experts group (VCEG) and the ISO/IEC moving picture experts group (MPEG).

In contrast, the H.264/AVC and MPEG-4 Visual and specifications are more than 250 and 500 pages long, respectively, with a high density of technical detail (despite completely leaving out key information such as how to encode video using their formats). They each contain areas that are difficult even for experts to fully comprehend and appreciate.

.

PREFACE

The rapid advancement in computer and telecommunication technologies is affecting every aspect of our daily lives. It is changing with the way we interact with each other, impact is created by the way we conduct business on the environment in which we live. With the recent advances in video capturing and display technologies (see Figure 1.2), the presence of High Definition (HD) and Ultra High Definition (UHD) video contents in various multimedia applications is quickly increasing. The fields of signal processing have grown from the origin of fast Fourier transform and digital filter design to statistical spectral analysis and array processing, image, audio, and multimedia processing, and shaped developments in high-performance VLSI signal processor design. This is made possible largely due to researches who achieve tremendous progress around the world in data compression technology, in particular for video data. Because there are a wide range of target applications from low-end to high-end under various constraints such as power consumption and area cost, an application-specific implementation may be pure software, pure hardwired, or something in between. To facilitate interoperability between decompression at the consumption end and compression at the video producing source, several generations of video coding standards have been defined and adapted.

Signal processing can be broadly defined as the application of analog or digital techniques to improve the utility of a data stream. Analog techniques are applied to a data stream embodied as a timevarying electrical signal while in the digital domain the data is represented as an array of numbers. A sequence of frames of pixels is a representation of video signal. There exists vast amount of redundant information that can be eliminated with video compression technology so that its transmission and storage becomes more efficient.

Image and video compression is a complex and extensive subject and this book keeps an unapologetically limited focus, concentrating on the standards themselves (and in the case of MPEG-4 Visual, on the elements of the standard that support coding of 'real world' material of video) and on video coding concepts that directly underpin the standards. The leading contenders are the International Standards known as MPEG-4 Visual and H.264. H.264/AVC, the result of the collaboration between the ISO/IEC Moving Picture Experts Group and the ITU-T Video Coding Experts Group, is the latest standard for video coding. H.264/AVC provides gains in compression efficiency of up to 50% over a wide range of bit rates and video resolutions compared to previous standards. There is therefore a need to develop low complexity implementations of H.264/AVC that offer the performance and flexibility advantages of the standard without an excessive computational cost.

Compared to previous standards, the decoder complexity is about four times that of MPEG-2 and two times that of MPEG-4 Visual Simple Profile. Its high compression ratio comes at the expense of more computational-intensive coding algorithms.

ACKNOWLEDGEMENTS

I take this opportunity to record my sincere thanks to all who helped me to successfully complete this work. This book is the outcome of many years of research and teaching in the field of signal Processing. Such a book would never have been possible without the constant support by colonel **Dr.Jeppiaar**, Chairman, Maamallan Institute of Technology.I am very thankful to Principal Dr.J.Abbas Mohaideen, for giving constant encouragement, enlightful comments and enough time to do this work. I am mainly concerned with passing on the knowledge I actually acquired myself.I extend my thanks to my friends Mr.A.Karthikeyan and Mr.R.Karthikeyan for their invaluable academic motivation and encouragement throughout the preparation of this book.The depth of technical knowledge presented in many chapters would have been impossible to achieve without numerous discussions with my colleagues. I want express my deepest gratitude to my parents Mr.G.Selvaraj and Mrs.S.Kamatchi and brother Mr.S.Gopalakrishnan for their love and support throughout my life.I owe much of the success of this work to my Wife, Mrs.S.Shanthi, for constantly encouraging and supporting me in every possible way through the years. Finally to my sons, S.Hemachandran & S.Ram Ganesh, who brings so much happiness to their dad every day.

Special thanks to the reviewers of this book.They are giving enough support and advice for content evaluation.I specially thank Mr.Cruz and Ann Minoza for the clarification of doubts and good communication through the entire publishing process.

INTRODUCTION

The digital video signal is free of noise and is very robust, but it occupies too much bandwidth for economical tape recording, let alone disk recording or transmission over the air. The first digital picture to travel across the Atlantic between London and Halifax, Nova Scotia was sent by cable in 1922. The scanning and reproduction of the two-level photograph were performed automatically but off-line, with punched paper tape being manipulated by the operators at both ends of the link. Fortunately, in most television pictures there is a lot of repetitive detail in plain backgrounds, blue sky, and common successive frames, which we can simply discard without the eye noticing that it has again been cheated. This process is called digital video compression. Video compression is done by the removal of redundant video data so that the video file can be transmitted or stored effectively.

If digital video signals could be processed in such a way as to enable them to be economically recorded on computer hard disks without any apparent loss of quality, then the possibilities for editing, painting, and animating would seem endless. Also, if digital video could be squeezed into the same bandwidth as that occupied by conventional analog signals, viewers could receive guaranteed studio quality pictures at home. Video compression involves using a pair of algorithms. One algorithm is used to encode the source video stream while a reverse algorithm is used to decode the video stream and display it at the same quality as the source video. Combination of these two algorithms are known as a codec (encode/decode, compress/decompress).

It was the computer industry that came up with the Joint Photographic Experts Group (JPEG) standard for compressing high-resolution digital still pictures, and it wasn't long before somebody thought it would be "cool" to show video on his computer too, so along came motion JPEG.

SELVARAJ SARAVANAN

The Moving Picture Experts Group (MPEG) was formed in 1988 to determine international standards for the digital compression of moving pictures, particularly to satisfy the growing interest in CD-ROMs. Motion JPEG and MPEG techniques are now used extensively for computer imaging and can be very cost-effective for disk recording, CDROMs, etc., but neither offer optimum results for broadcasting. Video compression systems are employed in many commercial products, from consumer electronic devices such as digital camcorders, cellular phones to video teleconferencing systems. Applications like these make the video compression hardware devices an inevitable part of many commercial products. VLSI technologies have been increasing processor speed and DRAM capacity dramatically with recent advances in microelectronic technology; smaller devices are now possible allowing more functionality on an integrated circuit (IC). Portable applications shift from conventional low performance products such as wristwatches and calculators to high throughput and computation intensive products such as notebook computers and cellular phones.

However, the advancements also have introduced a large growing performance gap between processor and main memory1) Recent growing mobile-market strongly requires not only high performance but also low-energy dissipation for expanding the battery life. 2) Recent VLSI technology have made it possible to integrate processor and main memory into the same chip, so that the chip boundary between main memory and cache can be eliminated.3) Another driving force behind design for low power is that excessive power consumption is becoming the limiting factor in integrating more transistors on a single chip or on a multi-chip module due to cooling, packaging and reliability problems.4) Furthermore bigger circuits let chip yields drop and result in higher costs and Bigger chips also have the consequence of longer wires which cause higher communication delays and need stronger more power consuming drivers.5) More functionality and higher capacity requirements go along with more complex, faster circuits and thus higher power dissipation.6) Real-time video systems process huge amounts of data and need a large communication bandwidth. Real-time video applications include strategies to compress the data into a Manuscript into a feasible size. Compared to the currently existing standards; H.264 has many new features that makes it the most powerful and state-of-the art standard. Network friendliness and good video quality at high and low bit rates are two important features that distinguish H.264 from other standards. The usual 8x8 DCT is the basic transformation in H.264. This eliminates any mismatch issues between the encoder and the decoder. The demand of multimedia communications on mobile and portable applications is growing nowadays.H.264 / MPEG-4 are designed as a simple and straightforward video coding, with enhanced compression performance, and to provide a network-friendly video representation. H.264/ MPEG-4 has achieved a significant improvement in the rate-distortion efficiency providing a factor of two in bit-rate savings compared with MPEG-2 Video, which is the most common standard used for video storage and transmission. H.264 offers between the range 2-to-1 and 3-to-1 improvement over MPEG-2 in compression ratio, resulting in significant savings in video storage capacity and network bandwidth. H.264 provides implementation of Internet efficiently based application because of its well considered scheme to harmonize with network protocols.

The H.264 standard enables use of a more flexible and efficient model for motion compensation. Use of multiple reference pictures and different block sizes are supported for motion compensation. The standard also specifies use of an improved deblocking filter within the motion compensation loop in order to reduce visual artifacts. It supports spatial prediction within the frames that helps reduce the residual energy of motion compensation. The standard also features a more complex and efficient context-based arithmetic coding (CABAC) for entropy coding of the quantized transform coefficients. In video compression, motion estimation plays a key role for reducing the complexity of the calculation. There are different impacts on the performance while using various search algorithms for motion estimation. Efficient algorithm can save more computing time and more search points.

LIST OF ACRONYMS & DEFINITIONS

<u>LIST OF ACRONYMS IN ALPHABETICAL ORDER:</u>

AVC   : Advanced Video Coding
AVS   : Audio Video Standard
ASIC   : Application Specific Integrated Circuit.
ASO   : Arbitrary Slice Ordering
ATM   : Asynchronous Transfer Mode
AVS   : Audio Video Standard
BER   : Bit Error Rate
CABAC   : Context Adaptive Binary Arithmetic Coding
CAVLC   : Context Adaptive Variable Length Coding
CAE   : Context-based Arithmetic Encoding
CBR   : Constant Bit-Rate
CIF   : Common Intermediate Format
CRC   : Cyclic Redundancy Check
DCT   : Discrete Cosine Transform
DPCM   : Differential Pulse Code Modulation
DWT   : Discrete Wavelet Transform
ETSI   : European Telecommunication Standards Institute
FCM   : Frame Coding Mode
FGS   : Fine Granular Scalability
GOP   : Group of Pictures
FMO   : Flexible Macro block Ordering
HD   : High Definition
HDTV   : High Definition Television
HEVC   : High Efficiency Video Coding
HRD   : Hypothetical Reference Decoder
HVS   : Human Visual System
IP   : Internet Protocol

ISO   : International Organization for Standardization

ITU-T   : International Telecommunication Union's-
                Telecommunication standardization sector [390]

JPEG   : Joint Photographic Experts Group

LSB   : Least Significant Bit.

MAP   : Maximum- A-Posteriori

MB   : Macro Block.

MBPAFF   : Macro Block Pair Adaptive Field Frame

MPEG   : Motion Picture Experts Group

MSB   : Most Significant Bit.

MSE   : Mean Square Error

MV   : Motion Vector.

NA   : Not Applicable

NAL   : Network Abstraction Layer

PCM   : Pulse Code Modulation

PES   : Packetized Elementary Stream

PSNR   : Peak Signal to Noise Ratio

QCIF   : Quarter Common Intermediate Format

QP   : Quantization Parameter

RBSP   : Raw Byte Sequence Payload

RTP   : Real Time Protocol

SC   : Start Code

SD   : Standard Definition

SMPTE   : Society of Motion Picture and Television Engineers

SSIM   : Structural Similarity Index Matrix

SVC   : Scalable Video Coding

TCP   : Transmission Control Protocol

VBR   : Variable Bit-Rate

VCEG   : Video Coding Experts Group

VCL   : Video Coding Layer

VHDL   : VHSIC Hardware Description Language

VLC   : Variable Length Code.

VLD   : Variable Length Decoding

VLSI   : Very Large Scale Integrated circuit

VO   : Video Object

VOP   : Video Object Plane

VQEG   : Video Quality Experts Group

WHT   : Walsh-Hadamard Transform

DEFINITIONS:

AC coefficient: Any transform coefficient whose frequency is in one or both dimensions is non-zero.

Backward prediction: Prediction from the future reference frame (field).

Bit stream: An order of series of bits that forms the coded representation of the data.

Bit rate: The rate at which the coded bit stream is delivered as the input of a decoder.

Block: An 8-row by 8-column matrix of samples, or 64 transform coefficients.

Byte: Sequence of eight bits.

Channel: A digital medium that stores or transports a bit stream.

Coded picture: A coded picture is made of a picture header, the optional extensions immediately following it, and the following picture data. A coded picture may be a coded frame or a coded field.

Coded video bit stream: A coded representation of a series of one or more sequences.

Coding parameters: The set of parameters which are user-definable that characterize a coded video bit stream.

Component: A matrix, single or block sample from one of the three matrices (luma and two color-differences) that make up a picture.

Compression: Reduction in the number of bits used to represent an item of data.

DC coefficient: The transform coefficient for which the frequency is zero in both dimensions.

Decoder: An embodiment of a decoding process.

Dequantization: The process of rescaling the quantized transform coefficients after their representation in the bit stream has been decoded and before they are presented to the inverse transform.

Encoder: An embodiment of an encoding process.

Encoding (process): A process which reads a stream of input pictures and produces a valid coded bit stream.

Field: For an interlaced video signal, a "field" is the assembly of alternate lines of a frame. Therefore an interlaced frame is composed of two fields, a top field and a bottom field.

Frame: A frame contains lines of spatial information of a video signal. For progressive video, these lines contain samples starting from one time instant and continuing through successive lines to the bottom of the frame. For interlaced video, a frame consists of two fields, a top field and a bottom field. One of these fields will commence one field period later than the other.

Frame rate: The rate at which frames are output from the decoding process.

Inter coding: Coding of a macro block or picture that uses information both from it and from macro blocks and pictures occurring at other times.

Intra coding: Coding of a macro block or picture that uses information only from that macro block or picture.

Level: A defined set of constraints on the values which may be taken by the parameters (such as bit rate and buffer size) within a particular profile. A profile may contain one or more levels. Levels are hierarchical. A bit stream compliant to a particular combination of level and profile, is compliant to all higher levels at the same profile. (91,375)

Luma; Y': is the value resulting from a weighted sum of 3 nonlinear (gamma pre-corrected) R,G,B components. It is often carelessly called luminance and given the symbol Y.

Macro block: The four 8 by 8 blocks of luma data and the two corresponding 8 by 8 blocks of color-difference data coming from a 16 by 16 section of the luma component of the picture.

Motion compensation: The use of motion vectors is to improve the efficiency of the prediction of sample values. The prediction uses motion vectors to provide offsets into the past and/or future reference frames or reference fields containing previously decoded sample values that are used to form the prediction error.

Motion estimation: The process of estimating the motion vectors during the encoding process.

Motion vector (MV): A two-dimensional vector used for the motion compensation that provides an offset from the coordinate position in the current picture or field to the coordinates in a reference frame of reference field.

P picture; predictive-coded picture: A picture that is coded by using motion compensated prediction from past reference fields or frame. A P picture can contain macro blocks that are inter-coded (i.e. coded using prediction) and macro blocks that are intra-coded.

Pan scan window: The portion of video displayed on a screen as a result of the view selection.

Pel: an alternate term for pixel.

Picture: Source, coded or reconstructed image data. A source or reconstructed picture consists of three rectangular matrices of 8-bit numbers representing the luma and two color-difference signals. For progressive video, a picture is identical to a frame, while for interlaced video, a picture may refer to a frame, or the top field or the bottom field of the frame depending on the context.

Profile: A defined subset of the syntax of the standard, with a specific set of coding tools, algorithms, and syntax associated with it. There are three profiles: simple, main and advanced.[376]

Quantize quantization: A process in which the continuous range of values of an input signal is been divided into no overlapping (but not necessarily equal) sub ranges, and a discrete, unique value is assigned to each sub range. A unique index is being generated to represent this value.

Rounding: The process of adjusting the bias before a division (or shift) operation.

Sequence: It is a coded representation of a series of one or more pictures. In the advanced profile, a sequence consists of a series of one or more entry-point segments, where each entry-point segment consists of a series of one or more pictures, and where the first picture in each entry-point segment provides random access. In the simple and main profiles, the first picture in each sequence shall be an intra coded picture.

Slice: A consecutive series of macro block rows in a picture, which are encoded as a single unit.

Variable bit rate: Operation where the bit rate varies with time during the decoding of a coded bit stream.

Variable length coding (VLC): A reversible procedure for coding that assigns shorter code-words to symbols of higher probability and longer code-words to symbols of lower probability.

Video sequence: The highest syntactic structure of coded video bit streams. It contains a series of one or more coded frames.

Zigzag scanning order: A specific sequential ordering of the transform coefficients from (approximately) the lowest spatial frequency to the highest. (377)

1

INTRODUCTION

1.1 GENERAL

With the rapid advance of VLSI technology, the attributes of parallelism, pipelining, concurrency, and regularity have become a new set of criteria in designing the hardware for digital processing. The VLSI fabrication technology advances, it becomes feasible to design the entire multimedia systems on a single chip—*system on chip*. However, the high power dissipation of the chip calls for extra cooling devices and expensive packages to dissipate the generated heat. It increases both the weight and cost of those systems thus the need for low-power design becomes essential. With highly sophisticated processing schemes at hand and further promising advances in video technology, efficient VLSI implementation is of great importance. Although conventional digital signal processors are highly optimized for processing speech and audio signals, they lack the required high performance for video signal processing.

Therefore, special architectural approaches are required for efficient hardware solutions delivering sufficient video processing performance at low cost. Power consumption has been introduced as a major design parameter due to the fast growing technology in mobile communications, which require portable power supplies.

The architectural requirements here include:

1. low-power and computational complexity at the mobile station (sensor node) for both encoding and decoding of video:
2. High compression efficiency:
3. Robustness to channel loss:

In the last ten years image and video compression research developed new techniques and tools to achieve high compression ratios even when high quality is required. These techniques involve several parts of the compression/decompression chain including transform stages, entropy coding, motion estimation, intraprediction, and filtering. At the same time image and video compression standards were already ready to identify the most relevant novelties and incorporate them. Current video coding paradigms fail to simultaneously address these demanding requirements satisfactorily. As network support for coded video has diversified, the costs for both computing power and memory have reduced, and advanced video coding technology has emerged, a need has arisen for high-quality video compression standard. Development of the international video coding standards such as MPEG-1, MPEG-2 and H.261 boosted a diverse range of multimedia applications, including DVDs, HDTV broadcasting, Internet video streaming, and teleconferencing. The sole purpose of MPEG-2 is to reduce these bit rates to something more manageable, and its success relies on data reduction primarily in two areas of the motion picture.

1.2 ORGANIZATION OF BOOK

This book is organized under 10 chapters. The first chapter gives an introduction to the study of video coding. It describes the relevance, general objectives, scope and limitations of the study and the methodology adopted. The second chapter presents a brief review of the relevant literature on the subject. In this chapter, video fundamentals,color vision and light intensity are explained.It also describes video compression, overview and color models.Specifically, the different video formats used by the industry are discussed.In the Third chapter, coding principles are explained and different transforms like DCT, DWT are explained in detail. The different coding methods are also discussed in this chapter. Chapter four explains standard video codec's like H.261, H.262, H.263, H.264, MPEG-1, MPEG-2 and MPEG-4 are explained. The architecture, levels and profiles, coding tools of that codec's are discussed. The open video codec's like Real video, Divx, WMV, Theora, AVS china, VP 8, and Dirac are explained in chapter 5.A specific version taken from each codec and explained about encoder and decoder, coding modes, tools and implementation are discussed.

Chapter 6 contains the comparison of both standard and open video coding standards are presented. Simulation results of researchers are also included for reference. In Chapter 7, short survey of H.264 blocks is discussed. The concepts and results of 20 research papers are presented. The Transform coding are explained in chapter 8.The concept, types, structure and graph of different transforms are explained. In Chapter 9, comparison of different transforms is discussed. Mainly, DCT, DWT and Walsh-Hadamard transforms are compared with simulation results. Chapter 10 explains the Quantization concept. The quantization types such as scalar quantization, vector quantization are explained in detail. All the chapters are arranged such that the reader can able to get clear idea about video fundamentals, compression, and codec's and transforms used in the video codec's.

2

LITERATURE REVIEW

2.1 VIDEO CODING BACKGROUND

2.1.1 Video Fundamentals:

Just as the visual system evolved to best adapt to the environment, video displays and video encoding technology is evolving to meet the requirements demanded by the visual system. If the goal of video display is to veritically reproduce the world as seen by the mind's eye, we need to understand the way the visual system itself represents the world. Video is a significant part of modern life, from movies and television shows, to news, sports, home videos and events. The largest category of growing Internet traffic is video to both personal computers, and TVs.

Video is a very rich source of information. Its two basic advantages over still images are the ability to obtain a continuously varying set of views of a scene and the ability to capture the temporal (or 'dynamic') evolution of phenomena. A number of applications that involve processing the entire information within video sequences have recently emerged. These include digital libraries, interactive video analysis, softcopy exploitation environments and Low-bitrate video transmission and interactive video editing and manipulation systems. These applications require eminent representations of large video streams, and efficient methods of accessing and analyzing the information contained in the video data.

VIDEO SIGNAL COMPRESSION AND STANDARDS

<u>Video Basics</u>
Resolution
Television broadcast
Standards
» NTSC — 525 lines
» PAL — 625 lines

Computer graphics
Standards
» VGA — 640x480
» SVGA — 1024x768

Multimedia standards
» CIF — 352x288
» QCIF — 176x144

Digital video standards
» CCIR 601 — 720x480
» HDTV — 1440x1152

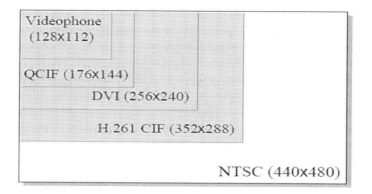

Figure 2.1: Image sizes(in picture elements)

The image sizes shown in figure 2.1.The Representation of a 2-dimensional image & 3-dimensional are shown in figures 2.2 & 2.3.

(R, G, B) 11, (R, G, B) 12, (R, G, B) 13, (R, G, B) *row, col*

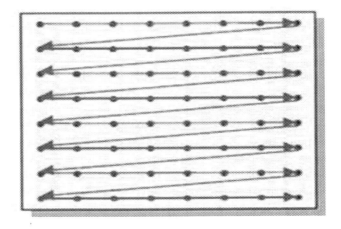

Figure 2.2: Representation of 2-dimensional image

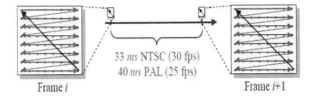

Figure 2.3: Representation of motion (3-dimensional images)

2.1.2 A Brief Overview of the Visual System

Visual system can lead to insight into how rendering video imagery can be enhanced for aesthetic and scientific purposes. The development of color video systems has been tailored to suit the characteristics of the human visual system, or HVS. The sensation of color is produced by different distributions of light of varying wavelengths. A camera captures color light and separates it into its red, green, and blue primary components, or *RGB* components. Output light intensity of a display device, e.g. a television, is non-linearly related to its input, generalized by

$$B = cv^{\gamma} + b \tag{2.1}$$

Where B is the intensity, c is a gain factor, gamma is the non-linear factor, and b is an arbitrary offset. To preserve linearity of the original *RGB* components and avoid correction systems in receivers, the color components are raised to the power $1/\gamma$ before transmission.

2.1.3 Color Vision

The human eye color perception is shown in figure 2.4.The Human eye Colour x Luminance perception and Human eye Colour x Luminance perception R (8 bits) G (8 bits) B (8 bits) are shown in figures 2.5 and 2.6.

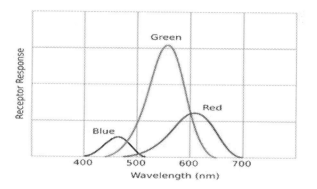

Figure 2.4: Human eye color perception

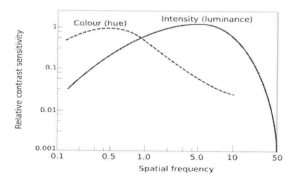

Figure 2.5: Human eye Colour x Luminance perception

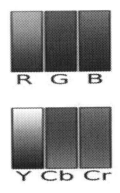

Figure 2.6: Human eye Colour x Luminance
perception R (8 bits) G (8 bits) B (8 bits)

Each color is coded separately Y (8 bits) Cb (4 bits) and Cr (4 bits).
    Y: Luminance
    Cb: Blue color
    Cr: Red color

Green color is presence of luminance and absence of Blue and Red color.

RGB color components are:
    1)   Converted to YUV
    2)   U and V components are subsampled by 2x2

The Conversion of color components is shown in figure 2.7.

Color Transformation

$$
\begin{bmatrix} Y \\ U \\ V \end{bmatrix} = \begin{bmatrix} 0.2990 & 0.5870 & 0.1140 \\ -0.1687 & -0.3313 & 0.5000 \\ 0.5000 & -0.4187 & -0.0813 \end{bmatrix} \begin{bmatrix} R \\ G \\ B \end{bmatrix} \qquad (2.2)
$$

    3)   U/V chrominance components are down sampled in coding

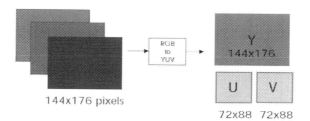

Figure 2.7: Conversion of color components

Factors Affecting Video Quality in a Compression System

• Quality of the input video
  – Amplitude, dc level, bandwidth, ringing, jitter
  – Noise, composite/component decoding artifacts
  – Prefiltering to eliminate the above problems

• Nature of the input video
  – Picture spatial and temporal complexity

Performance Tradeoff

The factors affecting the video quality are explained using the figure 2.8.

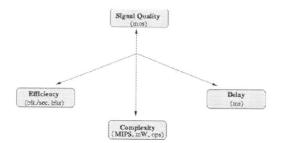

Figure 2.8: Factors affecting video quality

2.1.4 Overview

A picture is worth a thousand words. One of the primary challenges for a digital video compression system is how to remove the statistical and psychovisual redundancies in the videos with minimum impact to the perceptual quality.A typical digital video compression system is composed of functional modules, such as signal transformation, Motion Prediction (MP) and Motion Compensation (MC), quantization and entropy coding, to name a few (K.R.Rao and J.J.Hwang 1996). A simplified video compression system is illustrated in Figure 2.10 where both the preprocessing and postprocessing modules are not included.

With this in mind, the ITU-T VCEG and ISO/IEC MPEG bodies created the Joint Collaborative Team on Video Coding (JCT-VC) which is currently developing a new video coding standard,[32] the High Efficiency Video Coding (HEVC) standard, particularly for very high resolution videocontents. [33]. The Table 2.1 gives Video codecs and formatsand Table 2.2 gives the details of video codecs and Application.

Table 2.1:Details of video codecs and Application

Standard	Main Application	Year
H.261	Video conferencing	1990
H.262	DTV,SDTV,HDTV	1995
H.263 H.263+ H.263++	Videophone	1998 1999 2000
H.26L	VLBR video	2002
MPEG-1	Video CD	1992
MPEG-2	(Generic) DTV,SDTV,HDTV	1995
MPEG-4 Version 2	Interactive video(Synthetic and natural	1999 2000
Mpeg-7	Multimedia content Description interface	2001
MPEG-21	Multimedia Framework	2002
JVT H.264 MPEG-4 Part 10 Video fundamentals	Image Advanced (AVC) Video coding	2000 2003

Table 2.2: Video codecs and formats

Timeline of Standardized video coding			
Year	ITU-international telecommunication, union telephone,radio,tv	ISO-international standardization organization,photography,computer,consumer	Proprietary formats
1984	H.120		
1990	H.261-video conferencing		
1993		MPEG-1-video CD	
1994	(H.262)	Mpeg-2-Digital TV,DVD	
1995	H.263-Improved video conferencing		Real audio
1997		ATSC-US,HDTV	Real video windows media
1999		MPEG-4	
2002	AVC/H.264)	AVC (MPEG_4 part 10)	

2.1.5 Video Formats Used by Industry

ITU-R

According to ITU-R 601 (earlier ITU-R was CCIR), a color video source has three components: a luminance component (Y) and two color-difference or chrominance components (Cb and Cr or U and V in some documents). The CCIR format has two options: one for the NTSC TV system and another for the PAL TV system, both are interlaced. The NTSC format uses 525 lines per frame at 30 frames=s. The luminance frames of this format have 7203480 active pixels. The chrominance frames have two kinds of formats: one has 3603480 active pixels and is referred as the 4:2:2 format, whereas the other has 3603240 active pixels and is referred as the 4:2:0 format. The PAL format uses 625 lines per frame at 25 frames=s. Its luminance frame has 7203576 active pixels per frame and the chrominance frame has 3603576 active pixels per frame for the 4:2:2 format and 3603288 pixels per frame for the 4:2:0 format, both at 25 frames=s. The a:b:c notation for sampling ratios, as found in the ITU-R BT.601 [ITU-R BT.601] specifications, has the following meaning: 4:2:2 means 2:1 horizontal downsampling, no vertical downsampling. (Think 4 Y samples for every 2 Cb and 2 Cr samples in a scanline.) 4:2:0 means 2:1 horizontal and 2:1 vertical downsampling. (Think 4 Y samples for every Cb and Cr samples in a scanline.)

Source Input Format

Source input format (SIF) has luminance resolution of 360×240 pixels per frame at 30 frames=s or 360×288 pixels per frame at 25 frames=s. For both cases, the resolution of the chrominance components is half the luminance resolution in both horizontal and vertical dimensions. SIF can easily be obtained from a CCIR format using an appropriate antialiasing filter followed by subsampling.

Common Intermediate Format

Luminance resolution has 352×288 pixels per frame at 30 frames=s and the chrominance has half the luminance resolution in both vertical and horizontal dimensions. As its line value, 288, represents half the active lines in the PAL television signal, and its picture rate, 30 frames=s, is the same as the NTSC television signal, it is a common intermediate format for both PAL or PAL-like systems and NTSC systems. In the NTSC systems, only a line number conversion is needed, whereas in the PAL or PAL-like systems only a picture rate conversion is needed. For low bit rate applications, the quarter-SIF (QSIF) or quarter-CIF (QCIF) may be used because these format have only a quarter number of pixels of SIF and CIF formats, respectively.

ATSC Digital Television Format

The concept of digital television consists of SDTV (standard-definition television) and HDTV. Recently, in the United States, the FCC (Federal Communication Commission) has approved the ATSC recommended DTV standard [atsc 1995]. The DTV format is not included in the standard due to the divergent opinions of TV and computer manufacturers. Rather, it has been agreed that the picture format will be decided by the future market. The ATSC recommended DTV formats including two kinds of formats: SDTV and HDTV. The ATSC DTV standard includes the following 18 formats: It is noted that all HDTV formats use square pixels and only part of SDTV formats use square pixels. The number of pixels per line versus the number of lines per frame is known as the aspect ratio.

VIDEO SIGNAL COMPRESSION AND STANDARDS

Video Sampling

Digital video cameras perform two kinds of sampling – sampling in the temporal domain given by the number of pictures per second (frame rate), and sampling in the spatial domain given by the number of points (pixels) in each of the pictures (picture resolution). The frame rate is most often expressed in frames per second (f/s or frame/s) or, alternatively, in Hertz. Today's common frame rates have their origins in analogue television systems.

The National Television Systems Committee(NTSC) standardized the NTSC system, which is in use in Canada, Japan, South Korea, USA and some other places in South America, working with 29.97 f/s (denoted commonly as 30 f/s). In the rest of the world Phase Alternation by Line (PAL) and S'equentiel Couleur A' Me'moire (SECAM) are used, operating at a frame rate of 25 f/s. In some low-rate and low-resolution applications the frame rate is reduced before the actual transmission to save data rates.

Compression Impairments

Blocking: appearance of underlying block structure
Error Blocks: a form of block distortion

- One or more blocks bear no resemblance to the current or previous scene and often contrast greatly with the adjacent blocks Edge busyness: distortion concentrated at edges of objects
- Characterized by temporal and spatial features Mosquito noise: edge busyness associated with movement
- Characterized by moving artifacts or blotchy noise patterns superimposed over the objectsQuantization noise: snow or salt & pepper
- Similar to random noise but not uniform over the imageBlurring: distortion of the entire image,
- Characterized by reduced sharpness of edges and spatial details Jerkiness: smooth, continuous motion now perceived as a series of distinct images

Compression ratio

In order to evaluate the performance of a compression method, one of the two major criteria is bit-rate, which is expressed in terms of bit per pixel (bpp). It is dened as the average number of bits required by the compressed image for each pixel of the image.

Thus

$$b_{pp} = \frac{size\ of\ compreesed\ image\ in\ bits}{no\ of\ pixels\ in\ the\ image} = \frac{k}{MN} \qquad (2.3)$$

Sometimes, the amount of compression is also de_ned as compression ratio (CR),Where

$$CR = \frac{size\ of\ original\ image}{size\ of\ compressed\ image} = \frac{MNb}{K} \qquad (2.4)$$

Another criterion is the quality of the reconstructed image. The amount of compression, the quality and the computation time are closely interrelated and one of them may be more important than others depending on the specific application. A compression algorithm can be thought of as means to other the best trade of among these three. The measurement of visual quality of the reconstructed image or video is very important. There are two types of quality (visual) assessments: the subjective assessment, and the objective assessment. Each of these has its own merits and demerits.

2.1.6 Performance Indicators

The performance of error resilience methods can be evaluated by measuring the end-user distortion in the presence of transmission errors with given characteristics and by analyzing the cost determined by increasing the rate and/or complexity. In this section, metrics are presented that are used throughout this book for performance evaluation. DistortionTo evaluate the distortion within the nth video frame F_n with respect to a reference (distortion-free) frame R_n, the mean square error (MSE) can be used:

$$MSE[n] = \frac{1}{M.N.|C|} \sum_{c \in C} \sum_{i=1}^{N} \sum_{j=1}^{M} \left[F_n^{(c)}(i,j) - R_n^{(c)}(i,j) \right]^2 \qquad (2.5)$$

where $N \times M$ is the size of the frame and C is the set of colour components, for RGB colour space $C = \{R, G, B\}$. The number of colour components corresponds to the cardinality $|C|$ of the set. Row index i and column index j address the individual elements of the colour component matrix. For image distortion, the MSE is most commonly quoted in terms of the equivalent reciprocal measured Peak Signal to Noise Ratio (PSNR) defined as:

$$PSNR[n] = 10 . \log_{10} \frac{\left(2^q - 1\right)^2}{MSE[n]} \ [dB] \qquad (2.6)$$

where q represents the number of bits used to express the colour component values. In YUV colourspace the two chrominance parts are usually smoother than the luminance. PSNR measures the pixel error between an original and image that has been compressed and decompressed. The PSNR averaged over the whole video sequence can be defined in two ways – as an average PSNR over the PSNR[n] of all its frames, or as

$$PSNR = 10 . \log_{10} \frac{\left(2^q - 1\right)^2}{\overline{MSE}} \ [dB] \qquad (2.7)$$

where MSE is average MSE defined by

$$\overline{MSE} = \frac{1}{F} \sum_{n=1}^{F} MSE[n] \qquad (2.8)$$

and F is the number of frames in the video sequence. The later definition is formally correct, since it averages over the linear values. Averaging over logarithmic values results in a systematic error as a consequence of Jensen's inequality (MacKay 2006), which states that if $f(\cdot)$ is a convex function and X is a random variable, then

$$E\{f(X)\} \geq f(E\{X\})$$ (2.9)

where $E\{X\}$ denotes the expectation of X. A function $f(\cdot)$ is convex over an interval (a, b) if for all $x1, x2 \in (a, b)$ and $0 \leq \lambda \leq 1$ applies

$$f(\lambda.x1 + (1-\lambda) x2) \leq \lambda.f(x1) + (1-\lambda) f(x2)$$ (2.10)

that is, all points of $f(x)$ between the arbitrary chosen $x1, x2 \in (a, b)$ lay below or on the line connecting them. Since $\log10(1/x) = -\log10(x)$ is convex, PSNR will in general provide 'better' results (meaning higher quality) than PSNR. In practice and in literature, both waysof calculating PSNR can be found. For instance, JM outputs the PSNR value.The objective is to keep its length b as small as possible. The average bit rate Rb is the average number of bits used per unit of time torepresent a continuous medium such as audio or video. It is quantified in bits per second (bit/s)

$$R_b = \frac{b}{T}[bits / s]$$ (2.11)

where T is the time needed for the transmission of b from sender to receiver.[39]

The rate increase $\_R$ will be used to quantify the change in rate caused by a new method resulting in the rate $Rnew$ compared to a reference rate $Rref$

$$\Delta R = \frac{R_{new} - R_{ref}}{R_{ref}} .100 = \frac{b_{new} - b_{ref}}{b_{ref}} .100[\%]$$ (2.12)

under the assumption that T has to be the same for the reference bitstream and the bitstream after the application of the new method. However, for some applications as in resource allocation the average bit rate is not as important as the peak bit rate.

3

CODING PRINCIPLES

3.1 Coding of Images and Video

The purpose to transform coding is quantization and encode decorrelated transform coefficients relatively than the original pels of the images. The DCT is applied in standards as a block based approach usually on size 8 8 pels blocks. The DWT contrast is implemented in JPEG 2000 and MPEG-4 as frame based approach: block partitions are also possible. The block based DCT transform approach, input images are split into disjoint blocks of pels (e.g., of size 8 8 pels) as indicated in Figure 3.1.

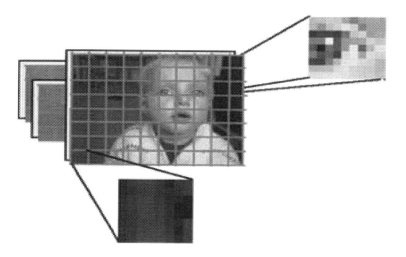

Figure 3.1: Decomposition of images into adjacent, nonoverlapping

In general, a linear, separable, and unitary forward 2-D-transformation strategy is represented as matrix operation on each blocks of N × N pels for transform coding (i.e., with the JPEG lossy coding standard). Color information in images is separated into RGB or YUV color images; UV components often subsampled and coded separately.

block matrix $\underline{I}$ using a N×N transform matrix $\underline{A}$ to obtain the N×N transform coefficients

$$\underline{C} = \underline{A}I\underline{A}^{T} \tag{3.1}$$

Most higher coefficients are small or zero later quantization, and small or zero appreciated coefficientstend to be clustered together. Thus, only a small number of quantized DCT coefficient needs to be transmitted to receiver is to obtain good approximated reconstruction of image blocks on the basis images as in Figure 3.2.

At very low bit rates, only few coefficients will be coded and the well-known DCT block artifacts will be visible (i.e., in low-quality JPEG or MPEG images andvideo).

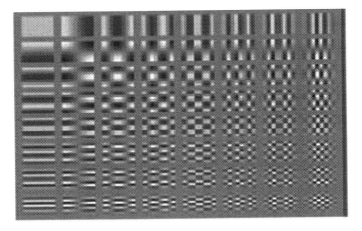

Figure 3.2: The 64 basis images B(k; l) of the 2-D 8×8 DCT.

Reconstruction of the stored or transmitted image blocks as a weighted superposition of these basis image is done by Block based DCT decoder such as JPEG, each weighted with the associated decoded DCT coefficient C (k; l).

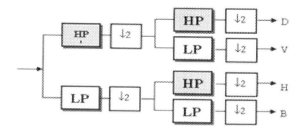

Figure 3.3: One stage of 1-D DWT decomposition

Figure 3.3 shows One stage of 1-D DWT decomposition, composedof low-pass (LP) and high-pass (HP) filters with subsequent subsampling.

3.2 First generation coding techniques

In order to better understand the new concepts introduced in second generation video coding schemes, it is important to review very basically the principles in which the coding techniques of the first generation are established. We present in this section a very brief summary of the concepts of first generation schemes that provide insight in the second generation. The basic schemes that are mainly considered first generation are pulse code modulation, predictive coding, transform coding, vector quantization and the myriad of schemes including combinations or particular cases of those such us subband and wavelets.

First generation image and video coding techniques achieve compression by reducing the statistical redundancy and the irrelevancy of the image data. To that end, the image is considered as a set of pixels that have to be uncorrelated.

One of the main achievements coming from the firrst generation is the hybrid scheme formed by combining motion compensated prediction in the temporal domain and a decorrelation technique in the spatial domain.

This scheme is used in current video standards and may serve as a starting point to introduce some of the basic concepts of the second generation approach. In this scheme the input image is divided into square blocks of usually 8x8 or 16x16 pixels. Three main problems arise when considering this structure:1)The blind division, without taking into account the semantic content of the image, results in block effect when high compression ratios are desired. 2)Motion models are applied to square blocks of pixels that may have little resemblance to the true motion of the ob jects that form the image.3)The properties of the human visual system are not taken into account. The main conclusions of the actual video coding schemes of the first generation in the context of very low bit-rate video coding can be stated as follows: The image deteriorates at high compression ratios, mainly due to the block effect appearance in the decoded image. The achievable bit rates range from 8 to 36 kbits/s depending on the difficulty of the video sequence and the desired quality. 8 kbits/s is only achievable for very steady head and shoulders sequences while it seems that bit rates around 24 kbits/s may be reached for more complicated sequences.

4

STANDARD VIDEO CODECS

4.1 H.261

H.261 is a ITU-Tvideo coding standard, ratified in Nov 88. It is the first member of H.26x family of video coding values in the domain of the ITU-T Video Coding Experts Group (VCEG), and was the first video codec that was valuable in practical terms.H.261 was originally designed for transmission over ISDN lines on which the data rates are multiples of 64 kbps. The coding algorithm was intended to be operated at video bit rates between 40 kbps and 2 Mbps. The standard supports 2 video frame sizes: CIF (176x144 chroma with 352x288 luma) and QCIF (88x72 chroma with 176x144) using a 4:2:0 sampling scheme. It also has a backward compatible trick for sending still picture visuals with 704x576 luma resolution and 352x288 chroma resolution (which was added in a later revision in 1993).

H.261 was the first truly practical digital video coding standard (in terms of product support).

In fact, all following international video coding standards (MPEG-1 Part 2, H.263, MPEG-4 Part 2, H.262/MPEG-2 Part 2and H.264/MPEG-4 Part 10) have been based thoroughly on the H.261 design. H.261 is a hybrid DPCM/ DCT video codec and the coding kemel comprises the motion estimation, the motion compensation and the discrete Cosine Transform Module. Due to the rigorous computation involved, current H.261 related products are almost all developed with the specific designed hardware or high end workstation based.The coding algorithm uses a hybrid of spatial transform coding with scalar quantization and motion compensated inter picture prediction, zig zag scanning and entropy encoding.

Basic Overview of the H.261 Recommendation

H.261 specifies a set of protocols that every compressed-video bitstream must follow and a set of operations that every standard, compatible decoder must be able to perform. The actual hardware codec implementation and the encoder structure can vary greatly from one design to another. The data structure of the encoder/decoder and the requirements of the video bitstream also are described. The video bitstream contains the picture layer, group-of-blocks layer, macroblock layer, and the block layer (with the highest layer having its own header, followed by a number of lower layers).Picture size: The only two picture formats that are allowed by the H.261 at the present time are the common-intermediate format (CIF) and quarter-common-intermediate format (QCIF) which is given in Table 4.1. The CIF picture size is 352 pixels (pels) per line by 288 lines while the QCIF is 176 pels per line by 144 lines. The QCIF picture size is half as wide and half as tall as the CIF picture.

This is because H.261 is designed for video telephony and video conferencing, in which typical source material is composed of scenes of talking persons, so-called head and shoulder sequences, rather than general TV programs that contain a lot of motion and scene changes.

Table 4.1: Picture Formats Supported by H.261 and H.263

Parameters	Sub-QCIF	QCIF	CIF	4CIF	16CIF
No. of Pixels per Line	128	176	352	704	1408
No. of Lines	96	144	288	576	1152
Uncompressed Bit Rate	4.4Mbs	9.1 Mb/s	37 Mb/s	146 Mb/s	584 Mb/s

Color-space: The 4:1:1 format is used. The picture color is made of three components: the luminance signal Y and the color-difference information signals CR and CB. The CR signal and the CB signal are each subsampled at half the rate of the Y-signal in both the horizontal and vertical direction. For every $2 \times \times 2 = 4$ Y samples, there is one sample of each for CR and CB. The bit size of each Y, CR, and CB sample is 8.

Picture Hierarchy: Picture frames are partitioned into 8 line by 8 pel image blocks square. Macroblocks (MB) are made of four Y blocks, one CR block, and one CB block at the same location as shown in Figure 4.3. A group of blocks (GOB) is made of 33 MBs. Figure 4.4 shows these relationships while Figure 4.5 shows how the video bitstream is separated into different layers.

Picture layer: Data for each picture consists of a picture header followed by data for a GOB. The data stream is a compressed videostream which contains:

* Picture start code (PSC), which is a fixed 20-bit pattern
* Temporal reference (TR), which is a 5-bit input-frame number, which can have 32 possible values that indicate the number of dropped frames.
* Type information, (PTYPE) which is a 6-bit field described as:

  - bit 1 – Split-screen indicator, defined as 0 for off, 1 for on
  - bit 2 – Document-camera indicator, defined as 0 for off, 1 for on
  - bit 3 – Freeze-picture release, defined as 0 for off, 1 for on
  - bit 4 – Source format, defined as 0 for QCIF, 1 for CIF
  - bit 5 – Optional still-image mode HI_RES, defined as 0 for on,1 for off
  - bit 6 – Spare
  - Optional spare field (PEI). If set to 1 indicates that a 9-bit valueappears in the PSPARE field, if set to 0, no data follows in the PSPARE field.

4.1.1 Real-time software encoder

To see real time limits of the audio pictorial communication, the utmostsignificant task is to build a realtime performance of an H.26 1 encoder:

(i) Motion Estimation (ME),
(ii) bit rate control,
(iii) forward discrete cosinetransform (FDCT). We will discuss them in the following.

i) Fast Motion Estimation (ME)

ME is one of the upmost vital issues in video encoding. So, there have been numerous fast algorithms developed for ME. Afterwards exhaustively experimenting, we create a trade-off betweencomputation load and the quality degradation and choose the conjugate direction search (CDS) algorithm to be motion estimator of our software H.261 encoder.In H.261, ME is achieved on the 16x16 luminance block.

If the minimum absolute error (MAE) is implemented to be distortion quantity, we need 256 subtractions, 255 branches and 255 additions to do each block corresponding. But it is usually needless to compute allerrors between two blocks if distortion portion of candidate block outdoes the current minimum. Figure 1 displays the rapportsamongst the cumulative error and the current minimum. In another words, we can eliminate the unqualified candidate block when the accumulation of whole errors beat the current minimum. Wecall this an Early Jump OutMotion Estimation (EJOME). On the basis of the EJOME, we speed up motion estimation by applying the new advanced EJO approach. Because of the jump out index occurs only when collective error curve exceeds the current minimum line which is ahorizontal one, we may jump out former is the current minimum is also the monotone increasing curve which is lower than the horizontal line.Figure 2.22 reveals this idea evidently and we obtain an EJO index that will eliminate disqualified blocks earlier than original E30 approach. The advanced EJO curve can be obtained by the linear interpolating the cumulative error curve and the current minimum line.

ii) Bit rate control

The bit rate controller plays an vital role in the software H.261 encoder. It monitors completeness of the network buffer to adjust the output bitrate and takes the responsibility of pictures qualitieskeeping. The controller is divided into the following three layers:

    (i).   Picture bit allocator (layer- l),
    (ii).   GOB enhancement layer(layer-2),
    (iii). Macroblock bit allocator(layer-3),

(i). Picture bit allocator

This bit allocator considers the fullness of network buffer as well as the total coded bit of the current picture so as to allocate the target bit rate for the next picture. According to the target bit rate, the bit allocator will select one appropriate "quantization-list" (Qlist) which is composed ofdifferent quantizers with different scales. This Q-list will be used for encoding the next picture. There are many Q-lists in our software H.261 encoder. Since the Q-lists are obtained during the developing phase through a training process with a lot of training video sequences, there is very little overheads for this allocation process.

(ii). GOB enhancement layer

For the video-phone or videoconference applications, the scene of the video sequence are oftencomposed of head and shoulder pictures so that there is only one moving head with some facial expressions and one still background. Furthermore, people usually focus their attention to the facial expression,s. We try to allocate more bits to the GOBs where the head often located onand less bits to the GOBs where the still background belongs to. GOBs are enhanced for the two different picture sizes defined in H.261. To allocate more bits to the target GOBs, we reduce the corresponding quantization scales in the Q-list which is defined bythe picture layer bit allocator. On the coqtrary, the scales in the Q-list for the background GOBs are increased.

(iii).Macroblock bit allocator

The macroblock bit allocator receives the Q-list coming from the GOB enhancemerit layer. First, it determines which coding mode is used to code this macroblock. If the distortion between the current block and the correspoding prediction block is larger than some predefined threshold, theINTRA coding mode is performed. Otherwise, the INTER coding mode is adopted. For the INTER coding mode, the bit allocator will select a proper quantizer from the Q-list according to the magnitude of the distortion. We classified the distortion into several classes.

By classfying the macroblock into one of the distortion classes, we can choose a quantizer from the Q-list to quantize the macroblock DCT coefficients. Finally, the information of the total coded bits of the current picture will then feedback to the picture bit allocator for encoding the next picture.

4.1.2 The Compression Algorithm

Compression of video data typically is based on two principles: the reduction of spatial redundancy and the reduction of temporal redundancy. H.261 uses discrete cosine transform to remove spatial redundancy, and motion compensation to remove temporal redundancy. Figure 4.1 shows the block diagram of a video encoder and Figure 4.2 shows the block diagram of a video decoder. At the encoder, the input picture is compared with the previously decoded frame with motion compensation. The difference signal is DCT transformed and quantized, and then entropy coded and transmitted. At the decoder, the decoded DCT coefficients are inverse DCT transformed and then added to the previously decoded picture with motion compensation.

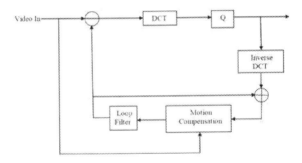

Figure 4.1: Block diagram of a video encoder

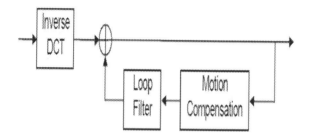

Figure 4.2: Block diagram of a video decoder

Since the prediction of the current frame is composed of blocks at various locations in the reference frame, the prediction itself (or simply called the predicted frame) may contain coding noise and blocking artifacts. These artifacts may cause a higher prediction error. It is possible to reduce the prediction error by passing the predicted frame through a lowpass filter before it is used as the prediction for the current frame. This filter is referred a loop filter, because it operates inside the motion compensation loop.

4.2 H.262/MPEG-2

MPEG-2 Video is similar to MPEG-1, but also offers support for interlaced video (the format used by analog broadcast TV systems). MPEG-2 video is not optimized for lesser bit-rates (less than 1 Mbit/s), but beats MPEG-1 at 3 Mbit/s and above. All standards conforming MPEG-2 Video decoders are completely capable of playing back MPEG-1 Video streams. The ISO/IEC endorsementprocedure was completed in Nov 1994.The first edition was accepted in July 1995and published by ITU-T and ISO/IEC in 1996.

In 1996 it was stretched by two amendments by preetham to contain the Registration of Copyright Identifiers and the 4:2:2 Profile. ITU-T published these amendments in 1996 and ISO in 1997. Recent growth in digital technology has thru the widespread usage of compressed digital video signals practical. Standardization has been very significant in the development of mutual compression methods to be used in the new services and products that are possible now. This lets the new services to interoperate with each oneanother and encourages the investment wanted in integrated circuits to make the technology economy. The most common MPEG-2 compression is main level ("CCIR 601") at 720 pixels x 480 lines, 30 frames/ second. The sweet points for MPEG-2 support the bandwidth bit rates of 2-6 Mbps, scaling up to 40 Mbps for very high-level HDTV applications. The MPEG-2 encoding standard builds on, and is backward compatible with, the statistical redundancy compression of MPEG-1. The most important difference between MPEG-1 and MPEG-2 is the encoding of interlaced frames for broadcast TV. MPEG-1 supports only progressive frame encoding, while MPEG-2 provides both progressive frame and interlaced frame encoding. Video movies, originally in a film format, are a progressive frame format.

MPEG-2 aims to be*general* video coding system assistant a diverse range of applications. Distinct algorithmic 'tools', developed for several applications, have been integrated into the full standard. To implement completely the features of the standard in entire decoders is gratuitously complex and a discarded of bandwidth, so a small figure of subsets of the filled standard, known as *profiles* and *levels*, have been cleared. A profile is subset of algorithmic tools and a level finds a set of restraints on parameter rates (such as picture size and bit rate). A decoder which keeps a particular profile and level is only essential to support the corresponding subset of the filled standard and set of parameter constraints.

Compression Skills Of Mpeg-2:-

MPEG 2 offers a way to compress this digital video signal to manageable bit rate. The compression capability of MPEG-2 video compression is made known in the table-1 followed. Therefore the greater the picture quality for a given Table Summary of compression capabilities Because the MPEG-2 standard offers good compression by standard algorithms, it has developed the standard for digital TV. It has the following features:

- Complete screen interlaced and/or progressive videotape (for TV and Computer displays)
- Enhanced audio coding (great quality, mono, stereo, and other audio skins)

- Transport multiplexing (combining diverse MPEG streams in a only transmission stream)
- Added services (GUI, interaction, encryption, data transmission, etc)

The list of systems which currently (or will soon) use MPEG-2 is extensive and continuously growing: digital TV(cable, satellite and terrestrial broadcast), Video on Demand, Digital Versatile Disc (DVD), individual computing, card payment, test and quantity, etc. The MPEG-2 video compression algorithm achieves very high quantities of firmness by exploiting theredundancy in video information. MPEG-2 eliminates both the temporal redundancy and spatial redundancy which are currently in motion video.

MPEG-2 in normal life:

i)DBS (Direct Broadcast Satellite)

The Hughes/USSB service will use MPEG-2 video and audio. Thomson has special rights to manufacture the decoding boxes for first 18 months of operation. No doubt Thomson's STi-3500 MPEG-2 video decoder chip will be introduced. Hughes/USSB DBS already initiated service in North America in 1994. Two satellites at 101 degrees West share the power supplies of 120 Watts per 27 MHz transponder. Multi-source channel rate regulate methods is hired to optimally allocate bits among several programs on one data carrier. An mediocre of 150 channels are planned.

ii)CATV (Cable Television)

Despite contradictoryoptions, the cableproduction has additional or less settled on MPEG-2 video. Audio is less than settled. For example, General Instruments (the largest U.S. consumer cable set-top box manufacturer) have declared the planned use of Dolby AC-3 audio algorithm.

iii)DigiCipher

The General Instruments DigiCipher I video sentence structure is alike to MPEG-2 sentence structure but uses smaller macroblock guesses and no B-frames. The DigiCipher II specification contains modes to support mutually the GI and full MPEG-2 Video Main Profile sentence structure. Services such as HBO will upgrade to DigiCipher II in 1994.At European IBC broadcast[78] technology resolution, in September 1994,GI demonstrated a sample DCII encoder which handles both digital encoding values. Fully configured the encoder will be capable to process 16 analogue video inputs, plus 32 stereo audio channels and 32 data channels into only high speed DataStream which can be passed on cable, satellite, microwave or ATM systems.

The technology of DCCI has now been licensed to Scientific Atlanta and Hewlett Packard (both set-top manufacturers) and to chip manufacturers Motorola, LSI Logic and C-Cube.All these manufacturers already support MPEG2 and plan to incorporate it with DCII into dual mode digital video decoder chips for the set-top terminal market.

For example, the block may be 'forward predicted' from a previous: picture, 'backward predicted' from a future picture, or 'bidirectionally predicted' by averaging a forward and backward prediction. The method used to predict the block may change from one block to the next. Additionally, the two fields within a block might be predicted separately with their own motion vector, or together using a common motion vector.

Another option is to make a zero-value prediction, such that the blocking of source image is preferred to the prediction error block is DCT coded. For each block to be coded, the coder chooses between these prediction modes, trying to maximize the decoded picture quality is within the constraints of the bit rate. The choice of prediction mode is transmitted to the decoder, with the prediction error, so that it may regenerate the correct prediction.

Picture types

In MPEG-2, three 'picture types' are defined. The picture type defines which prediction modes may be used to code each block.'Intra' pictures (I-pictures) are coded without reference to other pictures. Compression is achieved moderately by reducing spatial redundancy, but not temporal redundancy. They can be used periodically to provide access points in the bitstream where decoding can begin.

'Predictive' pictures (P-pictures) can make use the previous I- or P-picture for motion compensation and may be used as a reference for further prediction. Each block in a P-picture can either be predicted or intra-coded.

By reducing spatial and temporal redundancy, P-pictures offer increased compression compared to I-pictures.'Bidirectionally-predictive' pictures (B-pictures) can use the previous and next I- or P-pictures for motion-compensation, and offer the highest degree of compression. Each block in a B-picture can be forward, backward or bidirectionally predicted or intra-coded. To enable backward prediction from a future frame, the coder reorders the pictures from natural 'display' order to 'bitstream' order so that the B-picture is transmitted after the previous and next pictures it references. This introduces a reordering delay dependent on the number of consecutive B-pictures.

The different picture types typically occur in a repeating sequence, termed a 'Group of Pictures' or GOP. A typical GOP in display order is:

$$B_1 \ B_2 \ I_3 \ B_4 \ B_5 \ P_6 \ B_7 \ B_8 \ P_9 \ B_{10} \ B_{11} \ P_{12}$$

The corresponding bitstream order is:

$$I_3 \ B_1 \ B_2 \ P_6 \ B_4 \ B_5 \ P_9 \ B_7 \ B_8 \ P_{12} \ B_{10} \ B_{11}$$

A regular GOP structure can be described with two parameters: N, which is the number of pictures in the GOP, and M, which is the spacing of P-pictures. The GOP given here is described as $N=12$ and $M=3$. MPEG-2 does not insist on a regular GOP structure.

A decoder which supports a particular profile and level is only required to support the corresponding subset of algorithmic tools and set of parameter constraints.

Details of non-scalable profiles:

Two non-scalable profiles are defined by the MPEG-2 specification. The simple profile uses no B-frames, and hence no backward or interpolated prediction. Consequently, no picture reordering is required (picture reordering would add about 120 ms to the coding delay). With a small coder buffer, this profile is suitable for low-delay applications such as video conferencing where the overall delay is around 100 ms. Coding is performed on a 4:2:0 video signal. The *main profile* adds support for B-pictures and is the most widely used profile. Using B-pictures increases the picture quality, but adds about

120 ms to the coding delay to allow for the picture reordering. Main profile decoders will also decode MPEG-1 video. Currently, most MPEG-2 video decoder chip-sets support the main profile at main level.

Details of levels: MPEG-2 defines four levels of coding parameter constraints. Table 4.2 gives the constraints on picture size, frame rate, bit rate and buffer size for each of the defined levels. Note that the constraints are upper limits and that the codecs may be operated below these limits (e.g. a high-1440 decoder will decode a 720 pixels by 576 lines picture).

Table 4.2: MPEG-2 levels: Picture size,
frame-rate and bit rate constraints.

Level	Max. frame, width, pixels	Max. frame, height, lines	Max. frame, rate, HZ	Max.bit rate Mbit/s	Buffer size,bits
Low	352	288	30	4	475136
Main	720	576	30	15	1835008
High-1440	1440	1152	60	60	7340032
High	1920	1152	60	80	9781248

In broadcasting terms, standard-definition TV requires main level and high-definition TV requires high-1440 level. The bit rate required to achieve a particular level of picture quality approximately scales with resolution.

4.2.1 Levels and Profiles

Typical Main Level bit rates for common applications

MPEG-2 video at the appropriate storage medium can easily adjusted to the quality of many of the current video distribution formats.The Table 4.3 gives MPEG-2 bit rates compared to common video distribution formats.Even at a low bit rate it still maintains a perfect quality. The following table provides an overview about bit rates compared to current distribution formats. The MPEG-2 video is coded ML@MP with IPB frames.

Table 4.3: MPEG-2 bit rates compared to
common video distribution formats

Coded rate (IBP)	Application
2 Mbit/s	Equivalent to VHS
4 Mbit/s	PAL Broadcast Quality
10 Mbit/s	DVD Quality
15 Mbit/s	Equivalent to DV Quality

Profiles limit syntax (compression tools, i.e. algorithms)

Levels limit encoding parameters (sample rates, frame dimensions, coded bitrates, buffer size etc.)

Variable bit rate for video encoding

In any given video section, certain parts contain more movement than others or more fine detail.For example a clear blue sky is simpler to encode than a picture of a tree. As a result the number of bits needed to faithfully encode without artefacts varies with the video material. In order to encode in the best possible way, it is advantageous to save bits from the simple sections and use them to encode complex ones. This is, in a simple way, what variable bit rate encoding does, however the process by which the bit rates are calculated is complex. Variable bit rate encoding can be carried out in one or two passes of the video data.

For fixed size storage applications such as DVD12, the amount of encoded video information must be known in advance, therefore two passes of the video information are required. This ensures that the amount of data is not too small (quality compromised) or too large (not enough storage space). The first pass is used to analyse and store encoding information about the video data, the second pass uses the information to perform the actual encoding.Where the amount of encoded data produced is not so critical, encoding can be carried out in one pass of the input video.

Fixed bit rate encoding

For some applications, it is necessary to transmit the encoded video information with a fixed bitrate. For example, in broadcast mediums (satellite, cable, terrestrial etc.), practical limitations mean that current transmission is restricted to using a fixed bit rate. This is why fixed bit rate MPEG-2 encoders are available. It is true that a fixed bit rate encoder is not as efficient as the variable bit rate system, however the MPEG-2 system still provides very high quality video for both encoding methods.

Very importantly, fixed bit rate encoding can also be carried out in real time, i.e. one pass of the video information. For live broadcasts, and satellite linkups etc. the real time encoding capability is essential.

Advantages of using a variable bit rate

The advantage of using a variable bit rate is mainly the gain it gives in encoding efficiency. For fixed storage mediums (e.g. DVD) the variable bit rate is ideal. By reducing the amount of spaceneeded to store the video (whilst retaining very high quality), it leaves more space on the medium for inclusion of other features e.g. multiple language soundtracks, extra subtitle channels, interactivity, etc. The other important feature of the variable bit rate system is that it gives constant video quality for all complexities of program material. A constant bit rate encoder provides variable quality.

Summary

Variable bit rate = constant quality
Constant bit rate = variable quality[97,98]

4.3 H.263

The coding algorithm of H.263 is similar to that used by H.261, however with some improvements and changes to improve performance and error recovery. Half pixeprecision is used for motion compensation whereas H.261 used fulpixeprecision and a loop filter. The support of 4CIF and 16CIF means the codec could then compete with other higher bitrate video coding standards such as the MPEG standards.

VIDEO SIGNAL COMPRESSION AND STANDARDS

Sampling frequency

Pictures are sampled at an integer multiple of the video line rate. This sampling clock and the digital network clock are asynchronous.

Source coding algorithm

A hybrid of inter-picture prediction to utilize temporal redundancy and transform coding of the remaining signal to reduce spatial redundancy is adopted.[102,105]The decoder has motion compensation capability, allowing optional incorporation of this technique in the coder. Half pixel precision is used for the motion compensation, as opposed to Recommendation H.261 where full pixel precision and a loopfilter are used. Variable length coding is used for the symbols to be transmitted. In addition to the core H.263 coding algorithm, four negotiable coding options are included that will be described in the subsequent subclauses. All these options can be used together or separately.

Unrestricted Motion Vector mode

In this optional mode motion vectors are allowed to point outside the picture. The edge pixels are used as prediction for the not existing pixels. With this mode a significant gain is achieved if there is movement across the edges of the picture, especially for the smaller picture formats. Additionally, this mode includes an extension of the motion vector range so that larger motion vectors can be used. This is especially useful in case of camera movement.

Syntax-based Arithmetic Coding mode

In this optional mode arithmetic coding is used instead of variable length coding. The SNR and reconstructed pictures will be the same, but significantly fewer bits will be produced.

Advanced Prediction mode

In this optional mode Overlapped Block Motion Compensation (OBMC) is used for the luminance part of P-pictures (see also Annex F). Four 8××8 vectors instead of one 16××16 vector are used for some of the macroblocks in the picture. The encoder has to decide which type of vectors to use.

Four vectors use more bits, but give better prediction. The use of this mode generally gives a considerable improvement. Especially a subjective gain is achieved because OBMC results in less blocking artifacts.

PB-frames mode

A PB-frame consists of two pictures being coded as one unit. The name PB comes from the name of picture types in Recommendation H.262 where there are P-pictures and B-pictures. Thus a PB-frame consists of one P-picture which is predicted from the previous decoded P-picture and one B-picture which is predicted from both the previous decoded P-picture and the P-picture currently being decoded. The name B-picture was chosen because parts of B-pictures may be bidirectionally predicted from the past and future pictures. With this coding option, the picture rate can be increased considerably without increasing the bit rate much.

Bit rate

The transmission clock is provided externally. The video bit rate may be variable. In this Recommendation no constraints on the video bit rate are given; constraints will be given by the terminal or the network.

Buffering

The encoder shall control its output bit stream to comply with the requirements of the hypothetical reference decoder defined in Annex B. Video data shall be provided on every valid clock cycle. This can be ensured by MCBPC stuffing or, when forward error correction is used, also by forward error correction stuffing frames.

The number of bits created by coding any single picture shall not exceed a maximum value specified by the parameter BPPmaxKb which is measured in units of 1024 bits.

The minimum allowable value of the BPPmaxKb parameter depends on the largest source picture format that has been negotiated for use in the bit stream. An encoder may use a larger value for BPPmaxKb than as specified in Table 4.4, provided the larger value is first negotiated by external means, for example Recommendation H.245.

Table 4.4:BPPmaxKb for each of the source picture formats

Source format	BPPmaxKb
Sub-QCIF	64
QCIF	64
CIF	256
4CIF	512
16CIF	1024

Symmetry of transmission

The codec may be used for bidirectional or unidirectional visual communication.

Error handling

Error handling should be provided by external means (for example Recommendation H.223). If it is not provided by external means (for example in Recommendation H.221) the optional error correction code and framing as described in Annex H can be used. A decoder can send a command to encode one or more GOBs of its next picture in INTRA mode with coding parameters such as to avoid buffer overflow. A decoder can also send a command to transmit only non-empty GOB headers. The transmission method for these signals is by external means (for example Recommendation H.245).

Multipoint operation

Features necessary to support switched multipoint operation are included in Annexure.

Source coder
Source format

The source coder operates on non-interlaced pictures occurring 30 000/1001 (approximately 29.97) times per second.The tolerance on picture frequency is +/-50 ppm. Pictures are coded as luminance and two colour difference components (Y, CB and CR). The Positioning of luminance and chrominance samplesis shown in figure 4.14.These components and the codes representing their sampled values are as defined in ITU-R Recommendation 601.

* Black = 16;
* White = 235;
* Zero colour difference = 128;
* Peak colour difference = 16 and 240.

These values are nominal ones and the coding algorithm functions with input values of 1 through to 254.H.263 supports five resolutions. In addition to QCIF and CIF that were supported by H.261 there is SQCIF, 4CIF, and 16CIF. SQCIF is approximately half the resolution of QCIF. 4CIF and 16CIF are 4 and 16 times the resolution of CIF respectively. The Table 4.5 gives the Number of pixels per line and number of lines for each of the H.263 picture formats.The support of 4CIF and 16CIF means the codec could then compete with other higher bitrate video coding standards such as the MPEG standards.For each of these picture formats, the luminance sampling structure is dx pixels per line, dy lines per picture in an orthogonal arrangement. Sampling of each of the two colour difference components is at dx/2 pixels per line, dy/2 lines per picture, orthogonal.

The values of dx, dy, dx/2 and dy/2 are given for each of the picture formats. For each of the picture formats, colour difference samples are sited such that their block boundaries coincide with luminance block boundaries as shown in Figure 4.3.

The pixel aspect ratio is the same for each of these picture formats and is the same as defined for QCIF and CIF in Recommendation H.261: (4/3) * (288/352). The picture area covered by all picture formats except the sub-QCIF picture format has an aspect ratio of 4:3.

TABLE 4.5:Number of pixels per line and number of lines for each of the H.263 picture formats

Picture Formats Supported								
Picture format	Luminance pixels	Luminance lines	H.261 support	H.263 Support	Uncompressed bitrate (Mbit/s)			
					10 frames/s		30 frames/s	
					Grey	Colour	Grey	Colour
SQCIF	128	96		Yes	1.0	1.5	3.0	4.4
QCIF	176	144	Yes	Yes	2.0	3.0	6.1	9.1
CIF	352	288	Optional	Optional	8.1	12.2	24.3	36.5
4CIF	704	576		Optional	32.4	48.7	97.3	146.0
16CIF	1408	1152		Optional	129.8	194.6	389.3	583.9

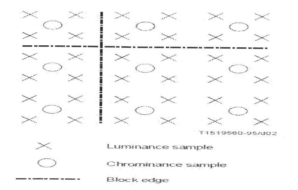

T1519560-95/d02

×   Luminance sample

○   Chrominance sample

–·–·–·–   Block edge

Figure 4.3: Positioning of luminance and chrominance samples

All decoders shall be able to operate using sub-QCIF. All decoders shall also be able to operate using QCIF. Some decoders may also operate with CIF, 4CIF or 16CIF. Encoders shall be able to operate with one of the formats sub-QCIF and QCIF. The encoders determine which of these two formats are used, and are not obliged to be able to operate with both. Some encoders can also operate with CIF, 4CIF or 16CIF. Which formats can be handled by the decoder is signalled by external means, for example Recommendation H.245. For a complete overview of possible picture formats and video coding algorithms, refer to the terminal description, for example Recommendation H.324. NOTE – For CIF, the number of pixels per line is compatible with sampling the active portions of the luminance and colour difference signals from 525- or 625-line sources at 6.75 and 3.375 MHz respectively. These frequencies have a simple relationship to those in ITU-R Recommendation 601. Means shall be provided to restrict the maximum picture rate of encoders by having a minimum number of non-transmitted pictures between transmitted ones.Selection of this minimum number shall be by external means (for example, Recommendation H.245). For the calculation of the minimum number of non-transmitted pictures in PBframes mode, the P-picture and the B-picture of a PB-frames unit are taken as two separate pictures.

Applications

Despite the fact that now H.264 is more extended, H.263 is still widely employed by internet applications such as Flash Video content (as used on sites such as YouTube, Google Video, MySpace, etc.), desktop video conferencing, video telephony, surveillance and monitoring, 3GPP files for playback on mobile phones. It is also required for IP Multimedia Subsystem (IMS) and Multimedia Messaging Service (MMS).

4.4 H.264/MPEG-4 PART 10/AVC:

Video coding is a principal technology for applications such as digital television, digital video authoring, video telephony, DVD and Blu-Ray disks, mobile TV, videoconferencing and internet video streaming. Compared to MPEG-2 and H.263, the H.264 is an advanced video coding method to provide maximum compression of video signals with low and high bit rates from 3G to HD. It was developed by ITU-T Video Coding Experts Group (VCEG) and the ISO/IEC Moving Pictures Experts Group (MPEG). It is also called as MPEG-4 part 10.The H.264 has Video Coding Layer (VCL) and Network Abstraction Layer (NAL) to represent video encoding process and handles the VCL data. The H.264 gives remarkable reduction in bit rates hence cost of bandwidth and storage is reduced. The key features of H.264 are enhanced motion compensation, transform and entropy coding and improved deblocking filter. It has seven profiles each strive to specific areas of applications. This paper provides the overview of video coding using H.264 including the history, profiles, levels, coding tools, Error resilience tools, features and complexity.

VIDEO SIGNAL COMPRESSION AND STANDARDS

Introduction

THE H.264 is the latest video coding standard which outperforms previous video coding standards (MPEG-2, H.263 or MPEG-4 part 2).The H.264 is capable of providing good video quality at lower bit rates. This standard is also called as Advanced Video Coding(AVC). The application range from digital television broadcasting to video over 3G wireless, Blu-Ray disc and HDTV etc., The H.264 design provides current balance between implementation complexity, coding efficiency and cost. A new amendment was added to this standard is called Fidelity Range Extension (FRExt).It introduces four additional profiles to improve the coding efficiency further and to enable higher quality video. Three basic feature set called profiles were established to address these application domains: the Baseline, Main and Extended profiles.

The additional goal of H.264 was to provide enough flexibility to allow the standard to be applied to a wide variety of applications and to make design work effectively on a wide variety of networks and systems. However, those algorithms also require more processing power to encode and decode the video content. The H.264 gives improved efficiency with increased algorithmic complexity. This chapter gives the overview of modules, Profiles and performance. In section 2 of this paper presents the history and features of H.264/AVC. Section 3 explains the coding tools including Intra prediction, Inter-frame prediction, Transform and quantization, In-loop deblocking filter, CAVLC and CABAC.

4.4.1 History and Features

History

The H.261 recommendationwas the first standard developed by VCEG for video conferencing applications in late 1980's.The Motion Picture Experts Group (MPEG) introduced MPEG-1 standardin early 1990s for storage of video on CD-ROMs. The MPEG-2 (H.262) standardwas a joint project of ISO/IEC (MPEG) and ITU-T (VCEG) for digital TV and HDTV with commensurate video quality. Later on the two groups separately published two new advanced standards namely H.263and MPEG-4for coding video at low bit rates like Interactive TV, Internet video.MPEG-4 part 2 were achieved in the capability of video objects with improved efficiency.In early

1998, the VCEG issued a call for proposals on a project called H.26L, with the target to double the coding efficiency in comparison to any other video coding standards for a broad variety of applications.The evolution of video coding standards as shown in Figure 4.4.

The first draft design for that new standard was adopted in October of 1999. In December 2001,VCEG and MPEG formed a Joint Video Team(JVT),with the charter to finalize the draft new video coding standard for the formal approval submission as H.264[1]in march 2003 and approved by ITU-T in may 2003.It is also called as MPEG-4 part 10,AVC.It promises significantly higher compression than earlier standards.

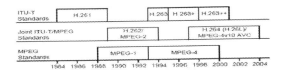

Figure 4.4: Evolution of video coding standards ITU-T and MPEG

Features

The H.264/AVC is an attractive candidate for many applications due to the following features.

1. Error robustness so that transmission errors over various networks are tolerated.
2. Straightforward syntax specification that simplifies implementation.
3. Variable block size motion compensation with block sizes range from 16*16 to 4*4.
4. Multiple reference picture motion compensation which uses previously encoded pictures as references up to 16 reference frames.
5. Implementations that deliver an average bit rate reduction of 50%, given a fixed video quality with any other standard.
6. It supports sample bit-depth precision ranging from 8 to 14 bits per sample.
7. Data partitioning is used to separate more important and less important coded information of each region.
8. Switching slices called SP&SI, allowing an encoder to direct with decoder with an ongoing video stream.

9. It supports monochrome 4:2:0, 4:2:2 format 4:4:4 colour sampling structures.
10. In-loop debocking filter can be used in inter-picture prediction.
11. Context-adaptive coding, Redundant slices (RS), Frame numbering, Picture order count, etc.,

H.264 delivers excellent quality across a wide operating range, from 3G to HD and everything in between. Whether creating video for mobile phones, iChat AV,the Internet, broadcast, or satellite delivery, H.264 provides exceptional video quality at impressively low data rates.It is shown in Figure 4.5.

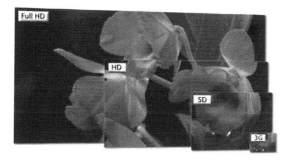

Figure 4.5: H.264: Exceptional quality at any size

4.4.2 Coding Tools

Coding of video is performed picture by picture. A given picture is divided into a number of slices. A slice consists of sequence of macro blocks. Each Macro block consists of three components Y,Cb,Cr. The Luminance component Y of the picture sampled at these frame resolutions, while the chrominance component, Cb and Cr, are down sampled by two in the horizontal and vertical directions.This H.264 standard consists of large number of coding tools designed to address efficient coding over a wide variety of video material.

A coded video sequence in H.264 consists of a sequence of coded pictures. A coded picture represents either an entire frame or a single _eld, as was also the case in MPEG-2 video. H.264 uses 4:2:0 sampling format in which chroma (Cb and Cr) samples are aligned horizontally with every second luma sample and are located vertically between two luma samples. A picture is partitioned into _xed-size macroblocks that each cover a rectangular picture area of 16*16 samples of the luma component and 8*8 samples ofeach of the chroma components. A picture maybe split into one or several slices. In H.264 slices consist of macroblocks processed in raster scan order when not using flexible macroblock ordering (FMO). Using FMO, a picture can be split into many macroblock scanning patterns such as interleaved slices, dispersed macroblock allocation, one or more \foreground" slice groups and a \leftover" slice group, or a checker-board type of mapping. The H.264/ MPEG-4 design shown in Figure 4.6 covers a Video Coding Layer (VCL), which efficiently represents the video content, and a Network Abstraction Layer (NAL), which formats the VCL representation of the video and provides header information in a manner appropriate for conveyance by particular transport layers (such as Real Time Transport Protocol) or storage media. All data are contained in NAL units, each of which contains an integer number of bytes. A NAL unit specifies a generic format for use in both packet-oriented and bitstream systems. The format of NAL units for both packet-oriented transport and bitstream delivery is identical - except that each NAL unit can be preceded by a start code prefix in a bitstream-oriented transport layer.

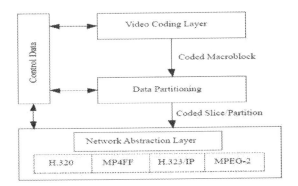

Figure 4.6: Structure of H.264/AVC video encoder [123].

Figure 4.7 illustrates the structure of the H.264 encoders. The slices which are valuble for resynchronization should some data to be lost.These macro blocks are coded in Intra or Inter mode. In the Inter mode, a macro block is predicted using motion compensation. For motion compensated prediction displacement vector is estimated and transmitted for each block (Motion Data) that refers to the corresponding position of its image signal in an already transmitted reference image stored in memory. In Intra mode, former standards sets the prediction signal to zero such that the image can be coded without reference to previously sent information. All the luma and chroma samples are either spatially or temporally predicted, and the prediction residual is encoded using the integer transform and the transform co-efficients are quantized using transform and quantization block.The deblocking filter is used to reduce the blockiness of the picture. Filtered pictures are used to predict the motion for other pictures. Depending upon the subset of coding tools used, a slice can be of I(Intra),P(Predicted),B(Bi-Predicted),SP(Switching P),SI(Switching I)type.The reference pictures can be used as references for inter-frame prediction whereas non-reference pictures cannot.

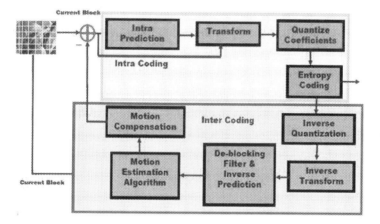

Figure 4.7: Structure of H.264 encoder

I-slices

In I-slices (and in intra macroblocks of non-I slices) pixel values are first spatially predicted from their neighboring pixel values. After spatial prediction, the residual information is transformed using a 4x4 transform or an 8x8 transform (FRExt-only) and then quantized. In FRExt, the quantization process supports encoder-specified perceptual-based quantization scaling matrices to optimize the quantization process according to the visibility of the specific frequency associated with each transform coefficient.

P-slices

In P-slices (predictively-coded, or "inter" slices), temporal (rather than spatial) prediction is used, by estimating motion between pictures. Innovatively, motion can be estimated at the 16x16 macroblock level or by partitioning the macroblock into smaller regions of luma size 16x8, 8x16, 8x8, 8x4, 4x8, or 4x4. A distinction is made between a *macroblock partition*, which corresponds to a luma region of size 16x16, 16x8, 8x16, or 8x8, and *submacroblock partition*, which is a region of size 8x8, 8x4, 4x8, or 4x4. When (and only when) the macroblock partition size is 8x8, each macroblock partition can be divided into sub-macroblock partitions

B-Slices

In B-slices, two motion vectors, representing two estimates of the motion per macroblock partition or sub-macroblock partition are allowed for temporal prediction. They can be from any reference picture in future or past in display order. Again, a constraint on the number of reference pictures that can be used for motion estimation is specified in the Levels definition. A weighted average of the pixel values in the reference pictures is then used as the predictor for each sample.

SP and SI Slices

Switching P (SP) and Switching I (SI) slices are close cousins of the usual P and I slices, utilizing either temporal or spatial prediction as before; however, their main virtue is that they can allow reconstruction of specific exact sample values, even when using different reference pictures or a different number of reference pictures in the prediction process.

The main usefulness of this property (which naturally comes at some cost in coding efficiency when compared to the usual P and I slices) is to allow bitstream switching, as well provide additional functionalities such as random access, fast forward, reverse, and stream splicing. These tools are only available in the Extended Profile.

Intra prediction

The H.264 uses spatial domain intra prediction to predict the pixels in an Intra-MB from the neighbouring pixels in adjacent blocks. The prediction residual along with prediction modes is coded rather than actual pixels in the block. Intra prediction and coding based on Motion Estimation (ME)and Motion Compensation (MC) to take the advantages of temporal redundancies that exist between successive frames, hence proving very efficient coding of video sequences.There are nine advanced prediction modes for luminance when the MB is partitioned into 4*4 blocks. Only four prediction modes used for intra 16*16 blocks. The intra prediction for chrominance is similar to intra 16*16 type for luminance signal.Both chroma blocks, Cb and Cr, use the same prediction modes shown in Figure 4.8.

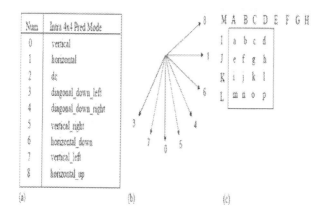

Figure 4.8:(a) Intra 4*4 prediction modes, (b) prediction directions, (c) block prediction process

Table 4.13: Intra 16*16 prediction modes

The modes are Mode1(Horizontal prediction),Mode2 (DCPrediction),Mode3 (Diagonal-down-left prediction),Mode4 (Diagonal-down-right prediction),Mode 5(Vertical right Prediction), Mode 6(Horizontal-down prediction), Mode 7(Vertical-left prediction) and Mode 8(Horizontal-up prediction).The modes used for Intra 16*16 mode are Mode 0,Mode 1,Mode 2 and Plane prediction as shown in Table 4.13. The plane prediction uses linear function between the neighbouring samples to the left and to the top in order to predict the current samples.

Inter-frame prediction

It includes ME, Mode selection and MC. The residual data of original predicted blocks are transforming coded. The H.264 standard is more flexible in the selection of Motion Compensation block sizes and shapes than all previous standards, with a minimum luma MC block size as small as 4*4[11].For 16*16 MB, the partitioning choice of a MB into 16*16,8*16,16*8or 8*8 blocks is determined by mb-type shown in Figure 4.17.In 8*8 mode,each of the block is further divided independently into 8*8,8*4,4*8 or 4*4 sub partitions by sub-mb type. The Fig 4.9 shows the Different modes of dividing a macro block.

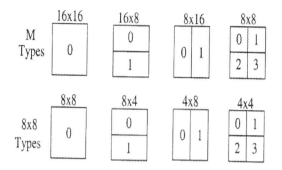

Figure 4.9: Partitioning of a macroblock and a
submacroblock for motion compensated prediction

Transform and Quantization

Another uniqueness of H.264 is that the conventional DCT transform is
replaced by a DCT-like integer transform. The transform can be implemented
with additions and shifts only (therefore, so-called 'multiplication-free'),
which is believed to have a significant computational advantage compared
with DCT transforms. Moreover, the precise integer transform eliminates
any mismatch between the encoder and the decoder.The task of Transform
is to reduce the spatial redundancy of the prediction error signal. The H.264
employs a 4*4 integer transform compared to 8*8 floating point DCT used
in other standard codec's.The transform matrix is given as

$$T_{4x4} = \begin{bmatrix} 1 & 1 & 1 & 1 \\ 2 & 1 & -1 & -2 \\ 1 & -1 & -1 & 1 \\ 1 & -2 & 2 & -1 \end{bmatrix} \tag{4.1}$$

$$H_{2x2} = \begin{bmatrix} 1 & 1 \\ 1 & -1 \end{bmatrix}, H_{4x4} = \begin{bmatrix} 1 & 1 & 1 & 1 \\ 1 & 1 & -1 & -1 \\ 1 & -1 & -1 & 1 \\ 1 & -1 & 1 & -1 \end{bmatrix} \qquad (4.2)$$

The first type is applied to all the blocks. The second one is hadamard transform for the luma 4*4 arrays which transforms 16 Dc co-efficient which is already transformed blocks of luma signal in the format 4:4:4. The third is also Hadamard transform which transforms 4 DC co-efficients of chrominance component in the format 4:2:0.For 4:2:2 chromas need both the matrices.After the transformation the co-efficients are quantized using a quantization parameter. This quantization is also called as scaling. The quantization takes 52 different values. The step size doubles with each increment of 6 of QP. These values are arranged hence an increase of QP by 1.It denotes the increase of quantization step size approximately by 12%. Rather than constant increment, the step size increases at compounding rate. The rate-control algorithm in the encoder controls the value of Quantization Parameter (QP).

Inverse Transformation and Dequantization

The use of transform coding in H.264 improves the compression efficiency as data correlations in the video frames can be efficiently exploited in the spatial domain. H.264 uses a DCT like integer transform as opposed to the usual floating point 8x8 DCT which is used in MPEG2 and MPEG4 Simple and Advanced Simple Profile. The integer transform can be computed exactly in terms of integer arithmetic with transform coefficients falling in the range from –2 to 2. In a hardware implementation this is highly advantageous as the transform and inverse transform can be implemented using only shift, add and subtract operators which can be efficientlyimplemented in a minimal number of gates. Within the H.264 transform algorithm smaller block sizes are also employed and this combined with the integer nature of the transform serves to reduce blocking and ringing artifacts. Simple scalar quantization is used within H.264 following the integer transformation. During encoding the output samples from the transform stage are quantized to reduce their overall precision and to eliminate high frequency components. The quantizer is also used for constant bit rate applications where the quantization coefficient is varied to control the output bit rate. All coefficients are quantized by scalar quantization with a variable quantization step size which changes for each user defined adjustment in quantization parameters. This variation in step size allows a wide range of quality levels to be effected.

For low levels of data quantization fine quantization control is viable whilst at high levels it is possible to more coarsely control the output Within the H.264 hardware decoder core the inverse transformation and dequantization blocks are contained within the Byte Stream Decoder. In terms of hardware implementation both these units are of significantly lower complexity than the equivalent operations which have been defined in prior standards.

In-loop Deblocking filter

It operates on the horizontal and vertical block edges within the prediction loop in order to remove the artifacts caused by block prediction error. Loop filtering operates on the edges of both MB and 4*4 sub-blocks. The strength of filtering is adaptively controlled by the coded information such as QP and the block texture. It adjusts its strength depending upon the compression mode of a macro block (Intra or Inter), QP, MV, frame or field coding decision and the pixel values.

Figure 4.10 illustrates the principle of deblocking filter using two neighbouring 4*4 blocks as with the actual boundary between p0 and q0.The sample p0 and q0 are filtered, if the absolute difference falls below the threshold α. The absolute difference between edges on each side is (|p1-p0| and |q1-q0|) have to fall below another threshold β. The β is considerably smaller than α.

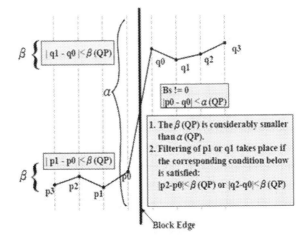

Figure 4.10: Principle of deblocking filter

To enable filtering for p1 and q1, the threshold value has to be smaller than α and the absolute difference (|p2-p0|and|q2-q0|) falls below β. For smaller quantizer values, the thresholds both become zero, and the filtering is effectively turned off.

Entropy coding

Before transmission, generated data of all types are entropy coded. In H.264, two methods of entropy coding are supported. The first one is CAVLC and the second method is called as CABAC.Entropy coding based on single codeword table instead of using different VLC tables for each syntax element.

CAVLC

The basic coding tool consists of single VLC of structured Ex-Golomb codes, which by means of individually customized mapping is applied to all the syntax elements except those related to quantized transform co-efficients. The number of non-zero quantized co-efficients and the actual size and position are coded separately. The Zigzag scanned quantized co-efficients of a residual block are coded using context-adapting VLC tables.

The already coded information of the neighbouring blocks and the coding status of the current block determine the context.

CAVLC is signed to take advantage of several characteristics of quantized 4x4 blocks:

- After prediction, transformation and quantization, blocks are typically sparse (containing mostly zeros).
- The highest non-zero coefficients after zigzag scan are often sequences of +/- 1. CAVLC signals the number of high-frequency +/- 1 coefficient in a compact way.
- The number of non-zero coefficients in neighboring blocks is correlated. The number of coefficients is encoded using a look-up table; the choice of look-up table depends on the number of non-zero coefficients in neighboring blocks.
- The level (magnitude) of non-zero coefficients tends to be higher at the start of the reordered array (near the DC coefficient) and lower towards the higher frequencies. CAVLC takes advantage of this by adapting the choice of VLC look-up table for the "level" parameter depending on recently-coded level magnitudes.

The important parameters to be encoded.

1. Number of nonzero coefficients (numCoef) and Trailing Ones (T1)
2. The pattern of Trailing Ones (T1)
3. The nonzero coefficients (Levels)
4. Number of zeros embedded in the nonzero coefficients (Total_zeros)
5. The location of those embedded zeros (run_before)

CABAC

The CABAC one of the entropy coding methods for gaining additional performance relative to CAVLC coding. In this mode, the generated data including headers and residual data are coded using Binary Arithmetic Coding Engine(BACE).To increase the coding efficiency of arithmetic coding, the underlying probability model is adapted to the changing statistics within a video frame through a process called context modeling.Figure 4.11 shows CABAC engine.

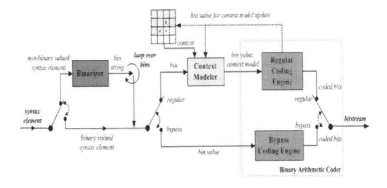

Figure 4.11: CABAC engine

The CABAC based on the key elements: Binarization, Context model selection, Arithmetic encoding and Probability update. The Binarization is used for unique mapping of non-binary syntax elements to a sequence of bits, a so called bin string i.e. A non- binary –valued symbol is converted into a binary code prior to arithmetic coding. For each element of the bin string a context model is defined based on the neighboring information and the coder status. The BACE codes the bins using probability estimates which depend on specific context. After encoding of each bin, the probability tables are updated to adjust upward the probability estimate for the bin value that was encoded.

The binary arithmetic codingengine consists of two sub-engines: regular and bypass, as shown in Figure 4.11. The regular coding engine utilizes adaptive probability models, but the bypass coding engine assumes a uniform probability model to speed up the encoding process. To encode a bin, the regular coding engine requires the probability model (pStateIdx, MPS) and the corresponding interval range (width) R and base (lower bound) L of the current code interval. The interval is then divided into two subintervals according to the probability estimate (ρLPS) of the least probable symbol (LPS).

Figure 4.12 shows the flow diagram of AC encoding for a given bin value, *binVal*, in the Decision mode. AC is consisted of three parts, (1) Interval Maintainer, (2) Probability Updating and (3) Renormalization.

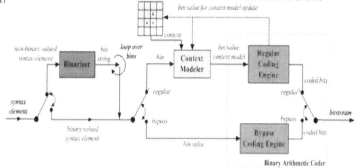

Fig: 4.12: Flow diagram of arithmetic coding

Data compression is reached applying principles of arithmetic coding, and it depends on an accurate estimation of symbol occurrence probabilities. There are 460 context indexes specified in the H.264/ AVC Standard for videos in the *main* or *high* profile.

Huffman

Huffman coding is based on the frequency of occurrence of a data item (pixel in images). The principle is to use a lower number of bits to encode the data that occurs more frequently. Codes are stored in a Code Book which may be constructed for each image or a set of images. In all cases the code book plus encoded data must be transmitted to enable decoding.

The technique works by creating a binary tree of nodes. These can be stored in a regular array, the size of which depends on the number of symbols(N). A node can be either a leaf node or an internal node. Initially, all nodes are leaf nodes, which contain the symbol itself, the weight (frequency of appearance) of the symbol and optionally, a link to a parent node which makes it easy to read the code (in reverse) starting from a leaf node. Internal nodes contain symbol weight, links to two child nodes and the optional link to a parent node. As a common convention, bit '0' represents following the left child and bit '1' represents following the right child. A finished tree has N leaf nodes and N−1 internal nodes. A linear-time method to create a Huffman tree is to (along with pointers to the associated leaves), and combined weights (along with pointers to the trees) being put in the back of the second queue. This assures that the lowest weight is always kept at the front of one of the two queues.

The encoding method of a set of symbols may be determined as follows:

1. Arrange the source symbols in descending order of probability.
2. Create a new source with one less symbol by combining (adding) the two lowestprobability symbols.
3. Repeat steps 1 and 2 until a single-symbol source is achieved.
4. Associate a one and a zero with each pair of probabilities so combined.
5. Encode each original source symbol into the binary sequence generated by thevarious combinations, with the first combination as the least significant digit in the sequence.

Huffman's algorithm is an example of a greedyalgorithm. In general, greedy algorithmsuse small-grained, or local minimal/maximal choices in attempt to result in a globalminimum/maximum. At each step, the algorithm makes the near choice that appears tolead toward the goal in the long-term.

4.3 ADVANTAGES

- Algorithm is easy to implement
- Produce a lossless compression of images

4.4 DISADVANTAGES

- Efficiency depends on the accuracy of the statistical model used and type of image.
- Algorithm varies with different formats, but few get any better than 8:1 compression.
- Compression of image files that contain long runs of identical pixels by Huffman is not as efficient when compared to RLE.

4.4.3 Profiles And Levels

The H.264/AVC was introduced to address large range of applications, resolutions, bit rates, services and qualities. All the coding tools are not required for an application. Thus a number of subsets has been defined in coding tools called as profiles. So in an application an encoder can select any one subset (Profile) of the coding tools. Level places all the constraints on some key parameters of the bit stream.The H.264 consists of seven profiles, each of which targets a specific class of applications which is as given in Table 4.6 & 4.7.The Extended Profile (XP), Main Profile (MP) and Baseline Profile (BP) are defined directly in the original standard. FRExt Amendment defines the remaining four high profiles.

Table 4.6: Profiles & features

S.No	Coding tools	Base	Extended	Main	High	High10	High 4:2:2	High 4:4:4
1	I & P slices	√	√	√	√	√	√	√
2	B slices	X	√	√	√	√	√	√
3	CAVLC	√	√	√	√	√	√	√
4	CABAC	X	X	√	√	√	√	√
5	Multiple reference frames	√	√	√	√	√	√	√
6	In-loop deblocking filter	√	√	√	√	√	√	√
7	SI and SP slices	X	√	X	X	X	X	√
8	Enhanced error resilience (FMO,ASO,RS)	√	√	X	X	X	X	√
9	Data Partitioning	X	√	X	X	X	X	√
10	Monochrome video format	X	X	X	√	√	√	√
11	4:2:0 chroma format	√	√	√	√	√	√	√
12	4:2:2 chroma format	X	X	X	X	X	√	√
13	4:4:4 chroma format	X	X	X	X	X	X	√

Table 4.7: Profiles and Applications

S NO	Profile Name	Applications
1	Baseline	Networkcameras,Video encoders,Telephone,Some Videoconferencing and Mobile applications
2	Main	General AV applications, standard definition digital TV broadcast,entertainment
3	Extended	Streaming applications, wireless or wired environments
4	High	HDTV, Blu ray Disc
5	High 10	Industrial use
6	High 4:2:2	Professional use, broadcast and DVD
7	High 4:4:4	Professional use , Camcorders

The H.264 defines 16 different levels which is given in the Table 4.8.Each level specifies upper limits for the picture size ranging from QCIF to above 4K*2K,decoder processing rate from 250K pixels/s to 250M pixels/s,size of the memory for multipicture buffers, video bit rate ranging from 64Kbps to 240Mbps, and video buffer size.The higher the resolution, the higher the level required.

Table 4.8: Different levels in H.264

Motion compensation:

Using motion compensation, a video stream will cover some full (reference) frames; then theinformation needed to transform the previous frame into the next frame will alone be stored in it.Equivalent to prediction, there is also two kinds of compensation, intra compensation for I-type frame and inter compensation for P-type and B-type frame. Intra Compensation – According to the encoding process, intra compensation regenerates the current block pixels by one of 13 modes (9 for Intra4x4 and 4 for Intra16x16) for luminance component and one of 4 modes for chrominance components. Inter Compensation (Motion Compensation) – Inter compensation is used in a decoding path to generate the inter-frame motion predicted (estimated) pixels by using motion vectors, reference index and reference pixel from inter prediction. In H.264, inter compensation also allows variable block-size, multiple reference frames and quarter-pixel accurate motion vector. Its luminance interpolation uses a 6-tap filter for half-pixel and a 2-tap filter for quarter pixel while the chrominance one uses neighboring four integer pixels to predict pixels up to accuracy of 1/8 pixel. It can refer to forward frames for P macroblocks and both forward and backward frames for B macroblocks. It allows arbitrary weighting factors for bidirectional weighted prediction.

In block motion compensation (BMC), the frames are separated in blocks of pixels (e.g. macroblocks of 16×16 pixels in MPEG). Each of this block is predicted from a block in the reference frameof equal size. The transformation done in this block is just the shifting of the position of the predicted block and no other change is done. This shift is denoted by a motion vector. To exploit the redundancy among neighboring block vectors, it is common to encode just the difference between the current and previous motion vector in the bit-stream.

Error Robustness and Network Friendliness

The NAL defines the link between the outside world and the video codec itself. It operates on NAL *units* which supports the packet-based method of most prevailing networks.Furthermore to the NAL concept, the VCL itself contains several features giving error robustness and network friendliness being necessaryparticularly for real-time services such as conferencing,streaming, and multicasting applications due to onlinedecoding and transmission. These techniques are supported in H.264/ AVC by numerousways, specifically frame dropping of non-reference frames resulting in popular temporal scalability, the multiple reference frame perceptionin grouping with generalized B-pictures allowing a enormous flexibility on frame dependencies to be exploited for temporal scalability and rate shaping of the video that is encoded and the opportunity of changingover between unlike bit streams which are encoded at unlike bit rates, this method is called version switching.

Switching pictures can also be functional for error resilience purposes as well as additional features,While for relaxed-delay applications such as broadcast/multicast, streaming, and download- and-play residual errors can typically be avoided by using powerful retransmission protocols and forward error correction, the low delay necessities for conversational applications impose additional challenges as transmission errors due to link-layer imperfectness and congestions can usually not be avoided. Hence, these video applications neederror resilience features. H.264/AVC standardization process recognized thisby adopting a set of common test circumstances for IP based transmission.

Total bit rate which reults including a 40 byte IP/UDP/RTP header equals exactly 64 kbit/s. As performance measure the average luminance peak signal to noise ratio (PSNR) is picked and adequate statistics are attained by transmitting at least 10000 data packets for each experiment along with applying Internet error patterns1 and a simple packet loss simulator.

COMPLEXITY

The Complexity mostly depends on the features of platform on which it is mapped(e.g. DSP processor, FPGA, ASIC),space (or storage) complexity and time complexity. Time complexity is measured by the approximate number of operations essential to perform a particular implementation of an algorithm.

FURTHER TECHNICAL DEVELOPMENTS

A set of extensions for scalable video coding (SVC) is currently being designed in the JVT, aimed at the reconstruction of video signals with lower spatio temporal resolution or lower quality from subsets of the coded video representation (i.e., from partial bitstreams.) Moreover, as an important side condition, SVC is additionally aimed at achieving a coding efficiency with the remaining partial bitstream that is comparable to that of "single-layer" H.264/AVC coding. In other words, the quality produced by decoding a subset of an SVC bitstream should be comparable to the quality produced by decoding an H.264/AVC bitstream that was encoded at the same bit rate in a nonscalable fashion.

HEVC, the High Efficiency Video Coding standard, is the most recent joint video project of the ITU-T VCEG and ISO/IEC MPEG standardization organizations, working together in a partnership known as the Joint Collaborative Team on Video Coding (JCT-VC). HEVC / H.265 reduces bit-rate requirement by 50% compared to H.264/AVC High Profile with same picture quality. HEVC / H.265 standard increases the computational complexity of HEVC decoder (1.6x) and HEVC Encoder compared to the H.264 standard. HEVC has been designed to address essentially all existing applications of H.264/MPEG-4 AVC and to particularly focus on two key issues: increased video resolution and increased use of parallel processing architectures.

CONCLUSION

H264 offersworthy quality and with improved compression rates. Next significant fact is that this H.264 is a open standard and public. The H.264/AVC denotesa good deal of improvements in standard video coding technology, in terms of both flexibility and coding efficiency for effective use in almost all diversity of network kinds and application areas. H.264 model has some additional features: packet segmentation and Si/Sp frame support. The packet segmentation provisionpermits the model to be used abovenumerous underlying protocols.Improvement of the encoder conforming to the standard is still believed to be a challenging problem, particularly for real-time applications such as video-conferencing.

ACKNOWLEDGEMENTS

I would like to thank Dr.Gray Sullivan,Mr.Ajay Luthra,D.Marpe,John Osterman and Iain E Richardson for providing useful information to develop review of H.264 without whom the publication of this book is not possible.I also thank the experts of ISO/IEC MPEG, ITU-T VCEG, and ITU-T/ISO/IEC Joint Video Team for their suggestions for improvement.

4.4.4 Software Used

H.264 Reference Software

The H.264 joint-reference model (JM) was utilized for the creation of H.264 video streams. The version used for these experiments was JM v7.5b (the latest version at the time of writing this thesis was v9.0). Many features in the JM reference software are unstable. Generally, the encoding parameters were chosen to maximize encoding quality at the expense of increased encoding complexity. Error-resilient tools were disabled.More details on encoding techniques employed in the JM reference software is described in the website.

Widespread Industry Adoption of H.264

Standards bodies and industry consortia supporting H.264 include the following.

Moving Picture Experts Group (MPEG). As stated earlier, H.264 has previously beenapproved by the MPEG committee as part of the MPEG-4 standard, precisely calledMPEG-4 Part 10 or Advanced Video Coding (AVC).

International Telecommunication Union (ITU). The cocreator of H.264, ITU, hasapproved H.264 as its succeeding video conferencing standard.

DVD Forum. H.264 has been designated by the DVD Forum as obligatory for itsHD DVD requirement, which describes one of two formats for next-generation,High definition DVDs.

Blu-ray Disc Association. H.264 has also been selected by the Blu-ray Disc Associationas mandatory for its Blu-ray Disc specification, which describes the other of the twoformats for next-generation, high-definition DVDs.

Digital Video Broadcasting (DVB). This European-born consortium for producing digitaltelevision standards has selected H.264 as part of its specification for broadcast of bothHDTV and SDTV.

T-DMB. Terrestrial Digital Multimedia Broadcasting is an ETSI standard stated toinclude H.264 for video. T-DMB has been accepted in South Korea and Germany. Numerousother European countries are presently in trials.

3rd Generation Partnership Project (3GPP). This group produces standards for mobilemultimedia on GSM-type mobile networks. It has chosen H.264 as the main videocodec in its Release 6 specification.

Internet Streaming Media Alliance (ISMA). H.264 has been accepted by the ISMA,which was designed to quicken the deployment and adoption of open standards forstreaming rich media content over Internet protocols.

MPEG Industry Forum (MPEGIF). This group was formed to further the adoptionof MPEG standards, together with H.264, through promotion, certification programs,interoperability testing, and other activities.

4.5 MPEG-1

Huffman Coding is a very widely held method of entropy coding, and used in MPEG-1 video to shrink the data size. The data is examined to discoversequences that repeat frequently. Those sequences are then placed into a special table, with the most regularly repeating data allocated the shortest code. This retains the data as small as possible with this form of compression. Once the table is built, those sequences in the data are substituted with their (much smaller) codes, which reference the applicablerecord in the table. The decoder merely reverses this procedure to produce the original data.

This is the last step in the video encoding method, so the result of Huffman coding is known as the MPEG-1 video "bitstream."

GOP configurations for specific applications

I-frames store whole frame informationcontained by the frame and is consequently suited for random access. P-frames offer compression by means of motion vectors relative to the preceding frame (I or P). B-frames offer maximum compression nevertheless requires the preceding as well as succeeding frame for computation. Hence, processing of B-frames need more buffer on the decoded side. A configuration of the Group of Pictures (GOP) should be designated based on these factors. I-frame only orders gives smallest compression, but is beneficial for random access,editability and FF/FR. I and P frame orders give reasonable compression but add a confident degree of random access, FF/FR functionality. I,P & B frame orders give very high compression but also growths the coding/decoding delay meaningfully. Such configurations are consequently not suitable for video-conferencing or video-telephony applications.The characteristic data rate of an I-frame is 1 bit per pixel while that of a P-frame is 0.1 bit per pixel and for a B-frame, 0.015 bit per pixel.

4.5.1 The Mpeg-1 Video Coding Model

This unit briefly defines the MPEG-1 video coding model. Additionalwholeexplanations are given in the standard [ISO/IEC 1993]. Video data can be denoted as a set of images, $I1, I2, \ldots, IN$, that are displayed successively. Each image is denoted as a two dimensional array of *RGB triplets*, where an RGB triplet is a set of three values that give the red, blue and green levels of a pixel in the image. The Figure 4.13 shows a sample video sequence.

Figure 4.13: A sample video sequence.

MPEG-1 video coding uses three methods to compress video data. The technique first we see is *transform coding*, is very alike to JPEG image compression. Transform coding deeds two facts: (1) the human eye is comparativelyunresponsive to high frequency visual data and (2) definite mathematical transforms focus the energy of a photo, which permits the photo to be denoted by smaller amountof values. The discrete cosine transform (DCT) is one such convertion. The DCT also decays the photo into the frequency domain, creating it upfront to take benefit of (1). In MPEG-1 transform coding, each RGB triplet in an photo is converted into a YCrCb triplet. The Y value indicates the *luminance* (black and white) level and the Cb and Cr values signify*chrominance* (color information). Since the human eye is less sensitive to chrominance than luminance, the Cb and Cr planes are *subsampled*.

In other words, the heightwidth of the Cb and Cr planes are split fifty-fifty (i.e., 4:2:0 sampling).Processing continues by dividing the photo into *macroblocks*. Each macroblock corresponds to a 16 by 16 pixel area of the original image. A macroblock is composed of a set of six 8 by 8 pixel *blocks*, four from the Y plane and one consistent block from each of the (subsampled)Cb andCr planes. Each of these blocks is then treated in the same manner as JPEG: the blocks are transformed using the DCT and the resultant coefficients are quantized, then they are run length encoded to remove all zeros, and later it is entropy coded. The particulars can be found in the standard, but the significantrealities for this paper are: (1) the frame is organized as a set of macroblocks, (2) each of the block in the macroblock is treated using the DCT, and (3) each block, after the quantization, holds a large number of zeros.

The next it is, the second technique of MPEG-1 uses to compress video, known as *motion compensation*, feats the fact that a frame Ix is expected to be alike to its precursor $Ix-1$, and so can be closelybuilt from it. For example, think through the order of frames in Figure 4.14, which might be taken by a camera in a car which is driving on a city road.1 Numerous of the macroblocks in frame $I2$ can be approximated by fragments of $I1$, which is called the *reference frame*. By *fragments*we mean any 16 by 16 pixel area in the reference frame. Likewise, numerous macroblocks in $I3$ can be approximated by fragments of either $I1$ or $I2$. The vector representing the suitablepart of the reference frame necessitates fewer bits to encode than the original pixels. This encoding results in essential data compression. Note, though, that the right edge of $I2$ (and $I3$) cant be achieved from a previous frame. Nor can the portion of the background congested by the tree in $I1$ since these areas enclose new data not present in the reference frame.

When such kind of macroblocks are found, they are encoded without motion compensation, with the help of transform coding technique. Additionally compression can be achieved if, at the time $I2$ is coded, both $I3$ and $I1$ are obtainable as reference frames. This strategy necessitates buffering the frames and presents a very small time delay in both decoding and encoding. $I2$ can then be constructed using both $I3$ and $I1$. When a greater pool of reference frames is accessible, motion compensation can be used to build more of the frame being encoded, thereby dropping the number of bits required to encode the frame.[170]

In summary, MPEG-1 uses three techniques (i.e., motion compensation, transform coding, and entropy coding) for compressing a video data. The standard describes three types of frames, called I-, P-, and B-frames. These frames use zero, one, or two reference frames for motion compensation, correspondingly. Frames are signified as an array of macroblocks, and both transform coding functionand motion compensation on macroblocks.

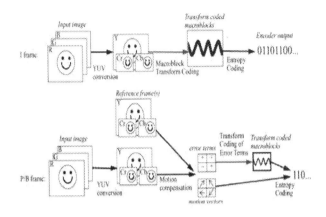

Figure 4.14: The MPEG-1 encoding process.

A frame constructed from one reference frame is known as a *P-frame* (predicted), and a frame constructed from both a previous frame and a succeeding frame is called a *frameB* (bi-directional).

4.6 MPEG-4

In addition, MPEG-4 provides a synchronized text tract for courseware improvement and a synchronized metadata path for indexing and admission at the frame level.

MPEG-4 builds on the proven success of three fields:

- Digital television;
- Interactive graphics applications (synthetic content);
- Interactive multimedia (World Wide Web, distribution of and access to content)

MPEG-4 offers the standardized technicalfeaturespermitting the combination of the manufacture, delivery and content access paradigms of the three fields. MPEG-4 is being roughly and gradually adopted, across traditional industry barricades. It is already the established standard for low bandwidth multimedia on 3G mobile terminals. MPEG-4 is at present being conversed in some of the most active groups within DVB, the world's foremost digital television standards recruiting body.

Numerous streaming suppliers have accepted MPEG-4 together with Apple, who adopted MPEG-4 Simple Visual Profile and Advanced Audio Coding for its QuickTime platform, RealNetworks, who supports decoding of the MPEG-4 content, and the popular DivX codec is also a MPEG-4 compliant. In actual fact, to maximum – if not all - of the major streaming players provision, either through plug-ins or natively, the MPEG-4 standard in their presentlyorganizedproducts and infrastructure. RealNetworks supports MPEG-4 on its Helix servers, which makes it fairly easy to make use of MPEG-4 currently. Apple supports MPEG-4 natively in their Darwin Streaming Servers, which are accessible for free of cost, and in its new QuickTime 6.At the time of introducing, QuickTime 6 has been downloaded 25 million times since its introduction in summer 2002.

Finallythe last but not the least, a number of MPEG-4 sellersproposal plug-ins for Microsoft's Windows Media Player that empowerconsumers to watch MPEG-4 content in this player. In terms of hardware seller support, Sony is sending its newer DVCams and PDAs with MPEG-4. Numerous commercially available digital still cameras permit the capture of MPEG-4 onto flash memory media storage. Snell & Wilcox's Ingest Station structures a browsing system based on MPEG-4. Both this browser and the company's SmartFile Transcoder were industrialized in combination with codec seller Dicas.

The MPEG-4 standard (ISO/IEC 14496) is prearranged to comprise of the following basic parts. Other parts may be added when the essential is acknowledged.

    _ ISO/IEC 14496-1: Systems.
    _ ISO/IEC 14496-2: Visual (Natural and Synthetic Video).
    _ ISO/IEC 14496-3: Audio (Natural and Synthetic Audio).
    _ ISO/IEC 14496-4: Conformance.
    _ ISO/IEC 14496-5: Software.
    _ ISO/IEC 14496-6: DMIF.

The Figure 4.15 depicts the basic concept for coding an MPEG-4 video sequence using a sprite panorama image. It is assumed that the foreground object (tennis player, image top right) can be partitioned from the background and that the sprite panorama image can be extracted from the sequence prior to coding. (A sprite panorama is a image that describes as a static image the content of the background over all frames in the sequence). The large panorama sprite image is transmitted to the receiver only once as a first frame of the sequence to describe the background – the sprite remains is stored in the sprite buffer.

In each consecutive frame only the camera parameters related to the background are transmitted to the receiver. This permits the receiver to reconstruct the background image for each frame in the sequence based on the sprite. The moving foreground object is transmitted as an arbitrary-shape video object. The receiver composes both the foreground and background images to reconstruct each frame. For low delay applications, it is possible to transmit the sprite in multiple pieces over consecutive frames or to build up the sprite at the decoder progressively.

This Subjective evaluation tests within MPEG have shown that the combination of these techniques can result in a bitstream saving of up to 50% compared with the version 1, depending on content type and datarate.

Figure 4.15: Sprite Coding of Video Sequence

Two dimensional animated meshes

MPEG4 takes only triangular meshes where the patches are triangles. A 2-D dynamic mesh also called 2-D mesh geometry and motion information of all mesh node points within a temporal segment of interest. Triangular meshes have long been used for 3-D object shape (geometry) modeling and rendering in computer graphics. 2-D mesh modeling considered as projection of such 3-D triangular meshes onto the image plane.

4.6.1 Tools

Stream management: the object description framework

The object description framework provides the glue between the scene description and the streaming resources} the elementary streams} of an MPEG-4 presentation, as indicated in Fig. 1. Unique identifiers are used in the scene description to point to the *object descriptor*, the core element of the object description framework. The object descriptor is a container structure that encapsulates all of the setup and association information for a set of elementary streams. A set of sub-descriptors, contained in the object descriptor, describe the individual elementary streams, including the configuration information for the stream decoder as well as the flexible sync layer syntax for this stream. Each object descriptor, in turn, groups a set of streams that are seen as a single entity from the perspective of the scene description. Object descriptors are transported in dedicated elementary streams, called object descriptor streams, that make it possible to associate timing information to a set of object descriptors.

Furthermore, textual descriptors about content items, called *object content information* (OCI), and descriptors for the intellectual property rights management and protection (IPMP) have been defined. The latter allow conditional access or other content control mechanisms to be associated to a particular content item. These mechanisms may be different on a stream-by-stream basis and possibly even a multiplicity of such mechanisms could co-exist. A single MPEG-4 presentation, or program, may consist of a large number of elementary streams with a multiplicity of data types. The object description framework has been separated from the scene description to account for this fact and the related consequence that service providers may possibly wish to relocate streams in a simple way.

Advantages:

View-dependent scalability

The view-dependent scalability enables to stream texture maps, which are utilized in realistic virtual environments. It consists in taking into account the viewing position in the 3-D virtual world in order to send only the most visible information.

Only a fraction of the information is sent, depending on object geometry and viewpoint displacement. This fraction is computed both sides(encoder and decoder. This approach allows to rminimize large amount of transmitted information between a remote database and a user, given that a back-channel is available. This scalability can be implemented both with DCT and Wavelet based encoders. It is easily achieved in DCT encoders, in which each 8x8 texture block is DCT transformed and encoded separately.

Saves money, makes money

MPEG-4 saves money for content businesses by eliminating the need for costly duplicate production in a number of different multimedia formats. MPEG-4 makes money for content businesses by offering multiple new broadband and narrowband platforms for the distribution of their content, such as wireless networks, digital television and the Internet.While it is not possible with MPEG-2 to create interactive content and then deploy it on both DVDs and interactive broadcast networks, this is easy with MPEG-4, and a feature which is attractive to major movie studios.MPEG-4 consists of closely interrelated but distinct individual Parts, that can be individually implemented (e.g., MPEG-4 Audio can stand alone) or combined with other parts.

Issues addressed by MPEG-4 Systems:

- A standard file format encourage the exchange and authoring of MPEG-4 content Interactivity, including: client and server-based interaction; a general event model for triggering events or routing user actions; general event handling and routing between objects in the scene, upon user or scene triggered events.

- Java (MPEG-J) is used to be able to query to terminal and its environment support. There is also a Java application engine to code 'MPEGlets' and A tool for interleaving of multiple streams into a single stream, including timing information (FlexMux tool).
- A tool for storing MPEG-4 data in a file (the MPEG-4 File Format, 'MP4')
- Interfaces to different aspects of the terminal and networks, in the form of Java API's (MPEG?J)
- Transport layer independence. Mappings to related transport protocol stacks, like (RTP)/UDP/IP or MPEG-2 transport stream can be or are being defined jointly with the responsible standardization bodies. Text representation includes with international language support, font and font style selection, timing and synchronization.
- The initialization and continuous management of the receiving terminal's buffers.
- Timing identification, synchronization and recovery mechanisms.
- Datasets covering identification of Intellectual Property Rights relating to media objects

5

OPEN VIDEO CODECS

5.1 Real video

The official player for RealVideo is RealNetworks RealPlayer SP, currently at version 15, and is available for various platforms including Windows, Macintosh, and Linux.Several other players exist, including MPlayer and Real Alternative.Many of these rely on the dynamically linked libraries (DLLs) from the official RealPlayer to play the video, and thus require RealPlayer to be installed (or at least its DLLs, if not the actual player).

However, the open source ffmpeg library (and its DirectShow counterpart ffdshow) can play RealVideo and does not require RealPlayer or any parts thereof. The latest version of RealPlayer that can run on Windows 9x is RealPlayer 8; but this version can be easily modified to play RealPlayer 9 and 10 files, by the manual addition of just three .dll files (codecs and plugins), from Microsoft's free distribution of RealPlayer 10, that aren't included in RealPlayer 8 Basic.RealNetworks has also developed the open source Helix player, however support for RealVideo in the Helix Project is limited because RealNetworks is still keeping the codecs proprietary. RealPlayer does not record RealVideo streams, and RealNetworks has advertised this feature to content owners such as broadcasters, film studios, and music labels, as a means of discouraging users from copying video. However, other software exists which can save the streams to files for later viewing. Such copying, known as time-shifting, is legal in most countries.

VIDEO SIGNAL COMPRESSION AND STANDARDS

Video compression formats and codecs

RealVideo files are compressed using several different video compression formats.Each video compression format is identified by a four character code. Below is a list of the video compression formats and the version in which each was introduced:

- rv10, rv13: RealVideo 1.0, based on H.263 (included with RealPlayer 5)
- rv20: RealVideo G2 and RealVideo G2+SVT, also based on h.263 (included with RealPlayer 6)
- rv30: RealVideo 8, suspected to based largely on an early draft of H.264 (included with RealPlayer 8)
- rv40: RealVideo 9, suspected to be based on H.264 (included with RealPlayer 9)
- rv40: RealVideo 10, aka RV9 EHQ (included with RealPlayer 10). This refers to an improved encoder for the RV9 format that is fully backwards compatible with RV9 players – the format and decoder did not change, only the encoder did. As a result it uses the same FourCC.

The newest version of RealPlayer can play any RealVideo file, as can programs using FFmpeg. Other programs may not support all video compression formats.The pros and cons of Real video codec are given in Table 5.1.Table 5.2 explaining the specification of Real video(standard) and Table 5.3 explaining Real video(Fractal).

Table 5.1: Real Video Codecs

Codec (Primary Use)	Pros	Cons	Availability
RealVideo (Standard) WWW video below 3KBps	Encodes quickly, better at lower data rates & higher action	Requires high-end PowerMac or Pentium for proper playback	Included with RealVideo Encoder
RealVideo (Fractal) WWW video above 3KBps	Plays better than RealVideo (Standard) on lower-end systems; higher quality for scenes with less action.	Still requires mid-range to fast PowerMac or Pentium for proper playback, no live encoding.	Available from Iterated Systems

Note:The Progressive's free RealVideo encoder includes a demo version of the Fractal codec,which is a version of Iterated's ClearVideo. If you wish to use the Fractal codec for data rates above 5 kbps with RealVideo, you must purchase Iterated's ClearVideo codec; the demo version will watermark movies at data rates higher than 5 kbps.

Table 5.2: Specification of Real video(standard)

Ideal source material	Low-motion video, below 3KBps
Supported bit depths	32-bit color
Compression time	Asymmetrical
Temporal compression?	Yes
Special features	-
Encoder requirements	PowerMac, Pentium
Decoder requirements	PowerMac, Pentium
Encoder availability	Part of RealVideo Encoder kit (included with Media Cleaner Pro)
Decoder availability	Built into RealPlayer installer
Manufacturer	Progressive Networks

Table 5.3: Specification of Real video(Fractal)

Ideal source material	Video with relatively low motion, around 3-30KBytes/s
Supported bit depths	32-bit color
Compression time	About 4x as slow as Cinepak
Temporal compression?	Yes
Special features	-
Encoder requirements	PowerMac, Pentium
Decoder requirements	PowerMac, Pentium
Encoder availability	No longer sold individually
Decoder availability	RealMedia: built-in QT: Freely available from Iterated
Algorithm	Fractal
Manufacturer	Iterated Systems, Inc.

The RealMedia architecture was developed by Progressive Networks, makers of RealAudio. It was designed specifically to support live and on-demand video and audio across the WWW.The first version of RealMedia is focused on video and audio, and is referred to as RealVideo. Later releases of

RealMedia will including MIDI, text, images, vector graphics, animations, and presentations.The specification of Real video(Fractal) are enumerated in Table 5.3.

A Netscape plug-in is also available.The main disadvantage to RealMedia is that it currently requires a PowerMac or Pentium computer to view. As such, RealMedia movies aren't available to the full range of potential users.The latest free downloads and more information, are available at Real Network's site. The Real Audio Codecs are depicted in Table 5.4.

Table 5.4: Real Audio Codecs

Codec (Primary Use)	Pros	Cons	Availability
Voice	Extremely low data rates allow use over 14.4 modem, or leave more bandwith for video	Don't accurately reproduce music or sound effects	Included in RealVideo Encoder
8, 12KBps Music	Acceptable reproduction of music, especially instrumental-only	Mono only; not as good on vocals	Included in RealVideo Encoder
High bitrate Music	Very good reproduction of wide range of music	Requires faster connection	Included in RealVideo Encoder

One of the Real Video(TM) video streams listed below. Source for the codec names are from Karl Lillevold on Doom9. The CodecPrivate element contains a "real_video_props_t" structure in Big Endian byte order as found in librmff. The Table 5.5 gives the different Versions of Real video.

Table 5.5: Versions of Real video

VERSIONS	TYPE	FUNCTION
V_REAL/RV10	RealVideo 1.0 aka RealVideo 5	Individual slices from the Real container are combined into a single frame.
V_REAL/RV20	RealVideo G2 and RealVideo G2+SVT	Individual slices from the Real container are combined into a single frame.
V_REAL/RV30	RealVideo 8	Individual slices from the Real container are combined into a single frame.
V_REAL/RV40	rv40 : RealVideo 9	Individual slices from the Real container are combined into a single frame.

5.1.1 RealVideo 10 Compression

Whether used for download or streaming, RealNetworks' RealVideo 10 codec delivers unparalleled quality from narrowband to HDTV. By providing dramatically enhanced compression over previous generation technologies, RealVideo 10 reduces bandwidth costs while enabling high-quality, rich media experiences — at any bit rate and on any device. The Figure 5.1 shows the RealVideo 10 Decoder.

Algorithm

RealNetworks' engineers have spent several years developing the technology that goes into RealVideo 10 and have leveraged the insight and know-how gained while developing past RealVideo codecs. RealVideo 10 is a motion equalised hybrid coder that employs RealNetworks patented, and patent pending, technology including:

- Highly accurate motion modeling
- Proprietary spatial pixel prediction methods
- Multi-resolution residual analysis/synthesis stage
- Context adaptive entropy coding
- Psycho-visually tuned segmentation and filtering schemes
- Rate-Distortion optimized encoding algorithms
- Two-Pass encoding

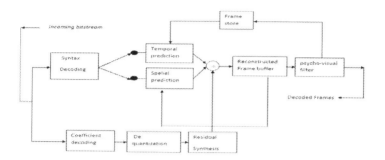

Figure 5.1: The RealVideo 10 Decoder

Many video codecs employ "block-based" algorithms to do both compression and decompression of video. These algorithms process many pixels of video together in blocks. As the compression ratios increase, these block-based algorithms tend to denotes individual blocks as simply as possible. A single block may be represented as a single color (e.g. the entire block is all "light-blue"). Carefully studying competing video codecs, one can see this visual effect (so-called visual "artifacts")easil). When using this block-based algorithms strong discontinuities, so-called block edges, can become very pronounced. RealVideo 10 avoids blockiness by employing sophisticated algorithms that are able to most perfectly compress the video. New proprietary analysis and synthesis algorithms (transforms), more comfortable motion analysis, content adaptive filtering technology, and other compression schemes built inside RealVideo 10 allow it to gives a higher fidelity reproduction of the video and maintain a more natural look and feel. RealVideo 10 does no post-processing in the decoder.The core RV10 algorithms are a significant improvement over existing video codecs. Excellent video quality is achieved without it.

Realvideo 10 encoder

RealVideo 10 supports a wide range of video applications from real-time streaming to download and play to storage and archive. To accommodate these applications the RV10 encoder supports the following encoding modes:

- Constant Bitrate
- Variable Bitrate (with a possible maximum constrained bitrate)
- Quality-Based Encoding (with a possible maximum constrained bitrate)

In Constant Bitrate mode, the encoder maintains the target bitrate throughout the duration of the content; with a small allowed buffer for slight deviations in bit usage. The size of this buffer discovers the pre-buffering time and is settable in the Helix Producer Plus using the maximum startup latency setting. This mode should be used for real-time streaming applications to maximize visual quality over a constant bitrate connection. Using the Variable Bitrate mode, the encoder attempts to meet the target bitrate over the length of the content, but makes no effort to maintain a constant rate throughout. Variable Bitrate encoding should be used when theoverall bitrate or file size needs to be constrained, but there are no instantaneous bitrate requirements, such as for downloaded content.

RealVideo 10 Quality

RealVideo 10 achieves a superior visual quality over competing technologies. The figure below compare the bitrates required to achieve the same level of fidelity (a.k.a. Peak Signal-to-Noise Ratio, or PSNR) using RealVideo 10 and other popular video formats. However, the objective measures used below, like PSNR, d'not always correctly represent perceived visual quality, and RealVideo 10 provides a good example of that. While PSNR results tells roughly 15-20% reduction in bitrate, Figure 5.2 demonstrates that RealVideo 10 provides the same, or even better, *visual* quality using a 30% lower bitrate.

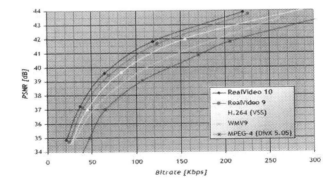

Figure 5.2: PSNR results for low action (talking head) content

For this comparison, the Highest Quality, "Slowest" and "Slow" encoding settings were used for Windows Media 9 Series, DivX 5.05 and VSS H.264, respectively. To remove the effects of bitrate-control, quality-based encoding was used, and all pre- and post-processing options (smoothing, color correction) were turned off. The PSNR was calculated for the Y component of each decoded YV12 frame, and the average PSNR over all frames is reported.

RealVideo 10 Error Resiliency

Error resiliency is a major component of our media delivery platform. Error resiliency features implemented in our platform include:

- The ability to dynamically set FEC packet insertion rates at nearly every stage of the delivery network, from Producer to Server, Server to Server, Server to Proxies, Proxies to Clients, etc.
- Automatic retransmission requests allow clients to resend data packets that are lost.
- The ability to enable error resiliency modes in our RealVideo family of codecs.

This mode, settable at encode time, adds layered error correction and error mitigation information to the RealVideo bitstream that intelligently protect more important video data.

RealVideo 10 Decoder Performance

Since RealVideo 10 is developed for use on a wide variety of clients with very different performance capabilities, RealVideo 10 has built-in CPU scalability in both the encoder and decoder that allows the higher processing of video if needed.

CPU usage

The encoder/decoder complexity is asymmetric with the difference in complexity between the encoder and decoder near a factor of 3-5 times under normal (default) encoder and decoder operation. The following systems are recommended for high quality playback of RealVideo10 on PCs.

- CIF or QCIF for dial-up connections – For playback of typical content for dial-up speeds (176 x 132), a 200 MHz Pentium II (or better) is recommended.
- Full Screen – For playback of 640 x 480 video at full 24 fps (for film) or 30 fps (for video), a 750 MHz Pentium III (or better) is recommended.
- HDTV – For playback of HD-resolution content (e.g. 720p), a 2.6 GHz Pentium 4 (or better) is recommended. Tables 1 - 3 show the CPU performance of RealVideo 10 running on popular device processors. In Tables 2 and 3, the performance is measured on actual devices running the RealVideo 10 decoder optimized for that platform.

5.2 DivX

DivX is a brand name of products developed by DivX, Inc. (formerly DivXNetworks, Inc., later purchased by Sonic Solutions and currently part of the Rovi Corporation formerly known as Macrovision), including the DivX Codec which was well known because of its ability to compress lengthy video segments into small sizes while maintaining relatively high visual quality. DivX® is the name of a famous new video compression technology developed by DivX, Inc. The format was designed to enable users to play and create best-quality videos in a fast and convenient way, while still maintaining the best quality possible. The DivX® codec is presently the most popular MPEG-4 based codec due to its quality, speed and efficiency as well as the wide range of DVD players that support the DivX® format. There are two different DivX codecs; the regular MPEG-4 Part 2 DivX codec and the H.264/MPEG-4 AVC DivX Plus HD codec. It is one of several codecs generally associated with ripping, whereby audio and video multimedia are transferred to a hard disk and transcoded.

History

The "DivX" brand is different from "DIVX" that was a former video rental system created by Circuit City Stores which required special discs and players to function. The winking emoticon in the previous DivX codec name was a tongue-in-cheek reference to the DIVX system. Although not developed by them, the DivX company adopted the name of the popular DivX codec.The video codec, which was exactly not MPEG-4 compliant, was extracted around 1998 by French hacker Jerome Rota (also known as Gej) at Montpellier. The Microsoft codec actually required that the reduced output be put in an ASF file. It was modified to allow other containers such as Audio Video Interleave (AVI). Rota hacked the Microsoft codec since newer versions of the Windows Media Player wouldn't play his video portfolio and résumé that were encoded with it. In case of re-encoding his portfolio, Rota and German hacker Max Morice determined to reverse engineer the codec, which took about a week. The Table 5.6 shows different file formats and the respective algorithms.

Table 5.6:File formats and Algorithms

File formats		Video compression algorithm	Audio compression algorithm
— Native support —			
Advanced Systems Format	wmv, asf	H.264	Advanced Audio Coding
Audio Video Interleave	avi	MPEG-4 ASP	MPEG-1 Audio Layer 3
DivX Format	divx	Windows Media Video	Windows Media Audio
Matroska	mkv		Vorbis

OpenDivX was used as an open-source project on the Project Mayo web site hosted at projectmayo.com (the name comes from "mayonnaise", because, according to Rota, DivX and mayonnaise are both French and very hard to make. The company's internal developers and some external developers worked jointly on OpenDivX for the next several months, but the project eventually slowed down. The Table 5.7 gives Identification and description and Table 5.8 depicts Sustainability factors. The Quality and functionality factors are explained in Table 5.9.

Table 5.7: Identification and description

Full name	AVI (Audio Video Interleaved), DivX Video Codec
Description	File format that wraps a DivX video bitstream with other data chunks, e.g., audio
Production phase	Generally a middle-state format (often used as the video source when producing lower-resolution streaming versions). Note: DivX version 6 codecs were released beginning in late 2005; at this writing (2011), the compiler of this page has not yet investigated whether AVI may also wrap DivX 6.x.
Relationship to other formats	
Subtype of	AVI,
May contain	DivX_5,
May contain	WAVE,
May contain	MP3_CBR,

Table 5.8: Sustainability factors

Adoption	AVI is widely adopted for video production and filemaking; the Ligos Corporation FAQ (viewed in March 2012, FAQ dated 2007) for the competing Indeo codec includes this statement: Many video files being distributed over the Internet use the DivX AVI format. In early 2006, Google began to offer downloadable videos, including gvi files in the AVI_DivX format (said to be DivX4 with MP3 audio).

Table 5.9:Quality and functionality factors

	Moving Image
Normal rendering	Good support.
Clarity (high image resolution)	Moderate to good, given that this is a format typically used for compression and does not support interlaced video. Outcome will depend on the type and extent of compression, and the encoder used. High resolution work is limited in the Windows environment due to file size limits (2 GB with FAT 16 technology; theoretical 8 GB with later technologies)

5.2.1 PLAYERS

Windows Media Player v11.0

Windows Media Player (WMP) is actually the most generally used player for DivX videos, mainly because the player comes pre-installed with Windows and is eligible of playing all video formats as long as you have the required video and audio codecs installed. This player must be available on your system, if you want to upgrade to the latest version you can download it here.

Media Player Classic v6.4.9.0 (Windows XP/2000)

Media Player Classic (MPC) for Windows XP/2000 is a famous media player replacement that looks and feels just like Windows Media Player, but without the unwanted extras. However, don't be cheated by its looks, it offers all of the features you would expect from a modern media player and has been updated to support all well known video formats. We suggest this excellent media player for everyone.

Media Player Classic v6.4.9.0 (Windows ME/98)

Media Player Classic (MPC) for Windows ME/98 is a famous media player alternate that reminds us of previous versions of Windows Media Player before it got so bulky. However, don't be confused by its appearance, it has been upgraded to support all video formats and offers all of the features you would expect from a modern media player. We suggest this great media player for everyone.

BSPlayer v1.37

BSPlayer is another video player with support for most media files (AVI, MPG, WMV, ASF, MP3, WAV) and subtitle formats (SubRip, Subviewer and MicroDVD). The player also characterizes custom subtitle options for fonts, colors, positions and transparency. The player holds skins and can be easily customized to look the way you want. At last, this player offers very efficient memory and CPU usage, so if you're having problems with cutting while watching movies then you should give this player a try.

DVD refers to Digital Versatile/Video Disc, DVDR stands for DVD Recordable and DVDRW for DVD ReWriteable. If you're comfortable with regular audio/music CDs or regular DVD-Video discs, then you will know what a recordable DVD looks like. A recordable DVD saves up to 2 hours of very high quality DVD-Video, including various audio tracks in formats like stereo, Dolby Digital or DTS and also progressed menu systems, subtitles and still pictures that can be played by many standalone DVD Players and most computer DVD-ROMs.

If you choose to reduce the video quality it is possible to store several hours video on a recordable DVD using low bitrates and low resolution with video quality more like VHS, SVHS, SVCD, CVD or VCD. It is also capable to have up to 4.37* GB ordinary data or mix DVD-Video and data on a recordable DVD that can be played by all computer DVD-ROMs.

Hardware and Software requirements

To have a smile on your face when you finish reading this tutorial, you will need:

- A computer (really?) with at least 128MB RAM, a large amount of defragmented hard disc space (=>2GB), a CPU with at least 800MHz clock rate and a stable Windows 98SE/ME/2000/XP installation.
- A TerraTV+/TerraTValue/Cinergy card with the official TerraTec WDM software
- A soundcard (i.e. Aureon/DMX6fire/EWS)
- The DivX codec (available for free under http://www.divx.com)
- The Fraunhofer MP3 codec (should have been bundled with your Windows, otherwise it can easily be downloaded) or an alternative MP3 codec (like Lame).

Of course your TV card must be properly installed, and the same applies for the soundcard as well as the rest of the system.

5.3 WINDOWS MEDIA VIDEO

The Simple and Main profile levels in WMV 9 are compliant with the same profile levels in the VC-1 specification. The Advanced Profile in VC-1 is enforced in a new WMV codec called Windows Media Video 9

Advanced Profile. It improves compressions efficiency for interlaced content and is made transport-independent, making it able to be encapsulated in an MPEG transport stream or RTP packet format. The codec is not compatible with former WMV 9 codecs, however.WMV is a mandatory video codec for PlaysForSure-certified online stores and devices, as well as Portable Media Center devices. The Microsoft Zune, Xbox 360, Windows Mobile-powered devices with Windows Media Player, as well as many uncertified devices, support the codec.WMV HD mandates the use of WMV 9 for its certification program, at quality levels designated by Microsoft. WMV used to be the only affirmed video codec for the Microsoft Silverlight platform, but H.264 codec is at present also affirmed starting with versiol.

Windows Media Video Screen

Windows Media Video Screen (WMV Screen) is a screencast codec. It can captivate live screen content, or convert video from third-party screen-capture programs into WMV 9 Screen files. It functions best when the source material is chiefly static and contains a small color palette. Depending on the complexity of the source material, the codec may switch between lossy and lossless encoding to increase compression efficiency. One of the uses for the codec is computer step-by-step presentation videos. The first version of the codec was WMV 7 Screen. The second and current version, WMV 9 Screen, supports VBR encoding in addition to CBR.

Video quality

While Windows Media Video 7 and 8 codecs were comparable to MPEG-4 ASP in terms of visual quality, Windows Media Video 9 (especially the later SMPTE-compliant VC-1 implementations) is corresponding to H.264 Main and High Profile. While WMV9/VC-1 does have certain rewards over H.264 such as affirm for non-square integer transforms, H.264 is more systematically able to yield better picture quality since it supports multiple reference frames, reference B-frames, context-adaptive binary arithmetic coding (CABAC) and firmer in-loop filtering. H.264's quality advantage is typically more evident at less bitrates.

Players

Software that can play WMV files include Windows Media Player, RealPlayer, MPlayer, The KMPlayer, Media Player Classic and VLC Media Player. The Microsoft Zune media management software supports the WMV codec, but uses a Zune-specific variation of Windows Media DRM which is used by PlaysForSure. Many third-party players exist for several platforms such as Linux that use the FFmpeg implementation of the WMV codecs.On the Macintosh platform, Microsoft released a PowerPC version of Windows Media Player for Mac OS X in 2003, but further development of the software has ceased. Microsoft presently endorses the 3rd party Flip4Mac WMV, a QuickTime Component which allows Macintosh users to play WMV files in any player that uses the QuickTime framework, free of charge to view files but indictable to convert formats. The WMV installer is clustered with Microsoft Silverlight by default, installation without Silverlight can be accomplished with a "Custom" install. According to the Flip4Mac website, WMV files with DRM encryption are not compatible with the component.

Decoders / Transcoders

Linux users can trust on FFmpeg based software like MPlayer, MEncoder. For Mac or Windows users who want to convert non-DRM WMV to MP4, HandBrake is Free Software that will do the job.

Encoders

Software that exports video in WMV format include Avid (PC Version), Windows Movie Maker, Windows Media Encoder, Microsoft Expression Encoder, Sorenson Squeeze,Sony Vegas Pro,Adobe Premiere Pro, Adobe After Effects, Telestream Episode, Total video converter and Telestream FlipFactory. Programs that convert using the WMV Image codec accept Windows Media Encoder and Photo Story.

Versions

The versions of WMV and their descriptions are given in Table 5.10.

Table 5.10: Versions of WMV

Public Name	FourCC	Description
Windows Media Video 7	WMV1	DMO-based codec.
Windows Media Screen 7	MSS1	DMO-based codec. Optimized for low-bitrate sequential screen captures or screencasts. Deprecated in favor of Windows Media 9 Screen codec.
Windows Media Video 8	WMV2	DMO-based codec.
Windows Media Video 9	WMV3	DMO-based codec. Video for Windows (VfW/VCM) version also available. [2]
Windows Media Video 9 Screen	MSS2	DMO-based codec. Optimized for low-bitrate sequential screen captures or screencasts.
Windows Media Video 9.1 Image	WMVP	DMO-based codec. Optimized for encoding video from sequential bitmap images. Used, for instance, by Photo Story.
Windows Media Video 9.1 Image V2	WVP2	DMO-based codec. Optimized for encoding video from sequential bitmap images. Used, for instance, by Photo Story.
Windows Media Video 9 Advanced Profile	WMVA	DMO-based codec. Deprecated as non-VC-1-compliant.
Windows Media Video 9 Advanced Profile	WVC1	DMO-based codec. VC-1 compliant format.

Windows Media Components for QuickTime, also known as Flip4Mac WMV Player by Telestream, Inc. is one of the few commercial products that admit playback of Microsoft's proprietary audio and video codecs interior QuickTime for Mac OS X.

It allows playback of:

- Windows Media Video 7, 8, 9, SD and HD
- Windows Media Audio 7, 8, 9, Professional and Lossless

It also admits a web browser plug-in to allow playback of embedded Windows Media files in web pages.

5.3.1 Detailed information for file extension WMV:

Primary association: Windows Media File
Company: Microsoft Corporation
Mime type: video/x-ms-wmv
Identifying characters Hex: 30 26 B2 75 8E 66 CF 11 A6 D9 00 AA 00 62 CE 6C, ASCII: 0& u f b l
Program ID: ASFFile, IrfanView.WMV, SlowView AVI, Winamp.File, Winamp3.File, Windows Media Video, WMVFile, and more

Related links: Media Player Formats, Xbox, Media Player for the Macintosh, Play Windows Media Files in Quicktime, FILExt CODEC and Video Player FAQ

Windows Media 9 Series is the most recent generation of digital media technologies originated by Microsoft. Although the origins of Windows Media concentrated on streaming compressed audio and video over the Internet to personal computers, the vision moving forward is to enable good delivery of digital media through any network to any device. Figure 5.3 illustrates a variety of examples of how Windows Media technology is being used today. In addition to Internet-based applications (e.g., subscription services, video on demand over IP, web broadcast, etc.), content compacted with Windows Media codecs is being used up by a wide range of wired and wireless consumer electronic devices.

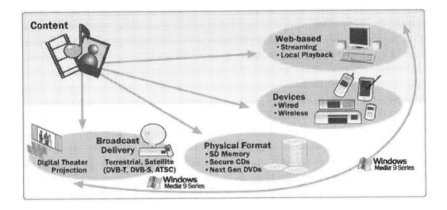

Figure 5.3: Examples of current Windows Media technology applications.

When streaming or transmitting a media clip, the server adapts its throughput and transmit again lost packets intelligently, using feedback from the network quality metrics. For on-demand streaming, the latest server takes advantage of the additional bandwidth usable (above the average bit rate of the clip) to cut down the start-up delay.

In addition, such server reduces the likelihood of losing the connection (which manifests as playback glitches and re-buffering to the viewer) by sending more data to the playback device, so that the device can continue playing even when there is network collision. A robust and scalable server is essential for Internet delivery, but evidently having a solid network connection is also critical. The latter is addressed by content delivery networks (CDNs) such as Akamai, Digital Fountain, and SMC. The combination of robust servers and networks result in TV-like receives that are unmistakably superior to those of internet swarming in the recent past. As mentioned earlier, one can also deliver Windows Media content through other means as in DVB-based transmittance systems, or using physical formats such as CD or DVD.

5.3.2 Windows Media Video 9: overview

Windows Media 9 Series admits a variety of audio and video codecs, which are key constituents for authoring and playback of digital media. The Windows Media Video 9 (WMV-9) codec is the most recent video codec in this suite and is based on technology that can attain state-of-the-art compressed video quality from very small bit rates (such as 172_120 at 10 Kbps for modem applications) through very large bit rates (1280_720/ 1920_1080 at 4–8 Mbps for high-definition video, and even higher bit rates for mastering). This section depicts in detail the overall structure of the WMV-9 codec, and covers the key innovations critical for its better performance.

Structure of the codec

The internal color format for WMV-9 is 8-bit 4:2:0. The codec uses a block-based motion compensation and spatial transform scheme which, at a high level, is similar to all famous video compression standards since MPEG-1 and H.261. Broadly speaking, these standards—as well as WMV-9—perform block-by-block motion compensation from the former reconstructed frame using a two-dimensional quantity called the motion vector (MV) to signal spatial displacement. A foretelling of the stream block is formed by looking up a same-sized block in the former reconstructed frame that is moved from the current position by the motion vector. Afterwards, the displaced frame difference, or residual error, is computed as the difference between the actual block and its motion-compensated prediction. This residual error is transformed using a linear energy-compacting transform then quantized and entropy coded. On the decoder side, quantized transform coefficients are entropy decoded, dequantized and inverse transformed to produce an approximation of the residual error, which is then added to the motion-compensated prediction to generate the reconstruction. The high level description provides a high level overview and does not discuss implementation details. The remainder of this section describes, in depth, the innovations in WMV-9 that distinguish it from other competing video coding solutions such as the MPEG standards.

WMV-9 has intra (I), predicted (P) and bidirectionally predicted (B) frames. Intra frames are those which are coded independently and have no dependence on other frames. Predicted frames are frames that depend on one frame in the past.[220,221]Decoding of a predicted frame can occur only after all reference frames prior to the current frame starting from the most-recent I frame have been decoded. B frames are frames that have two references—one in the temporal past and one in the temporal future. B frames are transmitted later to their references, which means that B frames are sent out of order to ensure that their references are available at the time of decoding. B frames in WMV-9 are not used as a reference for later frames. This places B frames outside of the decoding loop, allowing shortcuts to be taken during the decoding of B frames without drift or long-term visual artifacts. The above definition of I, P and B frames holds for both liberal and interlaced sequences.

Innovations

WMV-9 addresses R–D quality and visual performance using a variety of techniques. The important ones that distinguish WMV-9 from MPEG standards are:

1. Adaptive block size transform & Limited precision transform set,
2. Motion compensation,
3. Quantization and dequantization,
4. Advanced entropy coding,
5. Loop filtering,
6. Advanced B frame coding,
7. Interlace coding & Low-rate tools
8. Overlap smoothing & Fading compensation

5.4 THEORA

Theora is an open video codec based on On2's VP3 codec, open sourced in 2001.It's being formulated by the Xiph.org foundation of Ogg and Vorbis fame. If you want to be sure there are no legal effects with your software, Theora is a good choice, altough it's technically not as advanced as MPEG-4 or WMV9.

Version 1.0 of the codec has been discharged in 2008 Novembver, in 2009 Septemer version 1.1 came out, improving the encoding quality while preserving full compatibility. The video format is frozen (has been since 2004, but there are buggy videos developed by old encoders around and not playing well) so it's safe to produce Theora files for future use. Theora uses the Ogg container format and is usually combined with Vorbis audio. Theora files can be swarmed using the Icecast 2 streaming server, usable for most recent Linux distributions. VideoLAN ships Theora support. There are also builtin support or plugins for other media players such as Xine, MPlayer, Helix Player and Windows Media Player.Theora is a variable-bitrate, DCT-based video compression scheme. Like most usual video codecs, Theora also uses chroma subsampling, block-based motion compensation and an 8-by-8 DCT block. Pixels are sorted into various structures, namely super blocks, blocks and macroblocks. Theora supports intra-coded figures and forward-predictive frames, but not bi-predictive frames which are found in H.264 and VC-1. Theora also does not support interlinking, or bit-depths greater than 8 bits per component.[2]The Theora video-compression format is essentially compatible with the VP3 video-compression format, comprising of a backward-compatible superset.[10][11] Theora is a superset of VP3, and VP3 streams (with some minor syntactic modifications) can be converted into Theora streams without recompression (but not vice versa).[11] VP3 video compressing can be decoded using Theora implementations, but Theora video compression usually cannot be decoded using old VP3 implementations.

5.4.1 Technology Overview

Also this codec can be classified as belonging to the family of block-based hybrid video codecs. As with international standards, the specification details the decoder operation and data field order in the byte stream. As a concatenation of data packets, this stream can easily be encapsulated in any suitabletransport container format. The standard allows progressive video material with 8bpp accuracy and arbitrary dimensions, ranging from below QCIF to significantly more than 4K. The sequence may have a YUV color space with 4:2:0, 4:2:2, and 4:4:4 chroma subsampling.A compliant decoder comprises five main components. The byte stream data are first entropy decodedemploying Huffman codes.The decoded transform coefficients are then passed to the inverse quantization process and, subsequently, to an inverse 8×8 DCT, producing a frame difference signal, or frame delta. The frame delta pixels are then added to the predicted frame to form the reconstructed frame which is processed by a deblocking filter before picture display and storage in the frame buffer. The filter has hence an in-loop position, and it is applied to block edges.The block-based MC process utilizes forward prediction (P-frames) based on a single reference frame, as well as simple block copying, but no bi-predictive (B-) frames. The accuracy is either full pel or half pel. Otherwise it is of interest that that most algorithms make use of new data scanning orders in order not to infringe any patents. Arbitrarily accessing I-frames in the code stream is possible under the constraint that the byte stream header must have been transmitted and processed for decoder initialization previously. Other than that, it is worth mentioning that Theora does not provide the possibility for scalable picture decoding, and it lacks further the option of later lossless data migration from data stored in Theora format to another format, as it does not provide any means for lossless coding.

Coded Video Structure

Theora's encoding and decoding process is based on 8×8 blocks of pixels. This sections describes how a video frame is laid out, divided into blocks, and how those blocks are organized.

Frame Layout

A video frame in Theora is a two-dimensional array of pixels. Theora, like VP3, uses a right-handed coordinate system, with the origin in the lower-left corner of the frame. This is contrary to many video formats which use a left-handed coordinate system with the origin in the upper-left corner of the frame. Theora divides the pixel array up into three separate color planes, one for each of the Y 0, Cb, and Cr components of the pixel. The Y 0 plane is also called the luma plane, and the Cb and Cr planes are also called the chroma planes. Each plane is assigned a numerical value, as shown in Table 5.12.

Table 5.12: Color Plane Indices

Index	Color Plane
0	Y0
1	Cb
2	Cr

In some pixel formats, the chroma planes are subsampled by a factor of two in one or both directions. This means that the width or height of the chroma planes may be half that of the total frame width and height. The luma plane is never subsampled.

Picture Region

An encoded video frame in Theora is required to have a width and height that are multiples of sixteen, making an integral number of blocks even when the chroma planes are subsampled. However, inside a frame a smaller picture region may be defined to present material whose dimensions are not a multiple of sixteen pixels, as shown in Figure 5.4. The picture region can be offset from the lower- left corner of the frame by up to 255 pixels in each direction, and may have an arbitrary width and height, provided that it is contained entirely within the coded frame.It is this picture region that contains the actual video data. The portions of the frame which lie outside the picture region may contain arbitrary image data, so the frame must be cropped to the picture region before display. The picture region plays no other role in the decode process, which operates on the entire video frame.

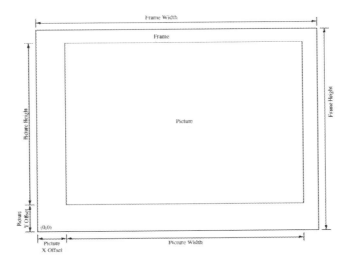

Figure 5.4: Location of frame and picture regions

Blocks and Super Blocks

Each color plane is subdivided into blocks of 8×8 pixels. Blocks are grouped into 4×4 arrays called super blocks as shown in Figure 5.5. Each color plane has its own set of blocks and super blocks. If the chroma planes are subsampled, they are still divided into 8×8 blocks of pixels; there are just fewer blocks than in the luma plane.

The boundaries of blocks and super blocks in the luma plane do not necessarily coincide with those of the chroma planes, if the chroma planes have been subsampled.

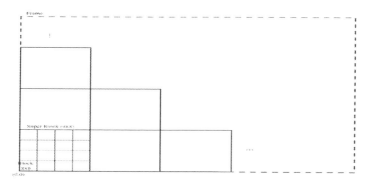

Figure 5.5: Subdivision of a frame into blocks and super blocks

Blocks are accessed in two different orders in the various decoder processes. The first is raster order, illustrated in Table 5.11. This accesses each block in row-major order, starting in the lower left of the frame and continuing along the bottom row of the entire frame, followed by the next row up, starting on the left edge of the frame, etc. The second is coded order. In coded order, blocks are accessed by super block. Within each frame, super blocks are traversed in raster order, similar to raster order for blocks.

Table 5.11: Raster ordering of n ×m blocks

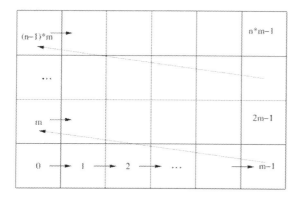

Within each super block, however, blocks are accessed in a Hilbert curve pattern, illustrated in Table 5.12. If a color plane does not contain a complete super block on the top or right sides, the same ordering is still used, simply with any blocks outside the frame boundary ommitted. To illustrate this ordering, consider a frame that is 240 pixels wide and 48 pixels high. Each row of the luma plane has 30 blocks and 8 super blocks, and there are 6 rows of blocks and two rows of super blocks. When accessed in coded order, each block in the luma plane is assigned the following indices:Here the index values specify the order in which the blocks would be accessed. The indices of the blocks are numbered continuously from one color plane to the next. They do not reset to zero at the start of each plane. Instead, the numbering increases continuously from the Y plane to the Cb plane to the Cr plane.

Table 5.12: Hilbert curve ordering of blocks within a super block

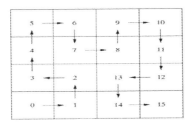

The implication is that the blocks from all planes are treated as a unit during the various processing steps. Although blocks are sometimes accessed in raster order, in this document the index associated with a block is always its index in coded order.

Macro Blocks

A macro block contains a 2×2 array of blocks in the luma plane and the co-located blocks in the chroma planes, as shown in Figure 5.6. Thus macro blocks can represent anywhere from six to twelve blocks, depending on how the chroma planes are subsampled. This is in contrast to super blocks, which only contain blocks from a single color plane. Macro blocks contain information about coding mode and motion vectors for the corresponding blocks in all color planes.

Macro blocks are also accessed in a coded order. This coded order proceeds by examining each super block in the luma plane in raster order, and traversing the four macro blocks inside using a smaller Hilbert curve, as shown in Table 5.13. If the luma plane does not contain a complete super block on the top or right sides, the same ordering is still used, with any macro blocks outside the frame boundary simply omitted. Because the frame size is constrained to be a multiple of 16, there are never any partial macro blocks. Unlike blocks, macro blocks need never be accessed in a pure raster order.

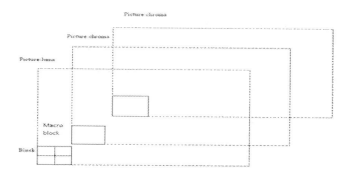

Figure 5.6: Subdivision of a frame into macro blocks

Table 5.13: Hilbert curve ordering of macro blocks within a super block

Using the same frame size as the example above, there are 15 macro blocks in each row and 3 rows of macro blocks. The macro blocks are assigned the following indices: The Table 5.14 shows the Macroblocks arrangement.

Table 5.14: Macroblocks

30	31	32	33	...	42	43	44
1	2	5	6	...	25	26	29
0	3	4	7	...	24	27	28

5.4.2 Coding Modes and Prediction

Each block is coded using one of a small, fixed set of coding modes that define how the block is predicted from previous frames. A block is predicted using one of two reference frames, selected according to the coding mode. A reference frame is the fully decoded version of a previous frame in the stream. The first available reference frame is the previous intra frame, called the golden frame doubles the number of customers that can receive a media clip at the same time. A server can either streamthe clip (transmit it with as little delay as possible) or download it (transmit and store it) over the internet into a user's playback device. The transmission of the clip can be performed live (for news, sports, concerts, or similar events) or on demand (for music videos, movies on demand, and so on).

The second available reference frame is the previous frame, whether it was an intra-frame or an inter frame. If the previous frame was an intra-frame, then both reference frames are the same.Two coding modes in particular are worth mentioning here. The INTRA mode is used for blocks that are not predicted from either reference frame. This is the only coding mode allowed in intra frames. The INTER NOMV coding mode uses the co-located contents of the block in the previous frame as the predictor. This is the default coding mode.

High-Level Decode Process

Decoder Setup

Before decoding can begin, a decoder MUST be initialized using the bitstream headers corresponding to the stream to be decodeduses three header packets; all are required, in order, by this specification. Once set up, decodemay begin at anyintra-frame packet|or even inter-frame packets, provided the appropriate decoded reference frames have already been decoded and cached belonging to the Theora stream. In Theora I, all packets are intra-frame or inter-frame packetsafter the three initial headers. The header packets are ordered as the identification header, the comment header, and the setup header.

Comment Header

The comment header includes user text comments (`tags`) andproduced the streamby a vendor string for the application/library. The format of the comment header is the same as that used in the Vorbis I and Speex codecs, with slight modifications due to the use of a different bit packing mechanism. A complete description of how the comment header is coded appears in Section 6.3, along with a suggested set of tags.

Setup Header

The setup header includes extensive codec setup information, including the com- plete set of quantization matrices and Huffman codebooks needed to decode the DCT coefficients. A complete description of the setup header appears in Section 6.4.

Decode Procedure

The decoding and synthesis procedure for all video packets is fundamentally the same, with some steps omitted for intra frames.

- Decode packet type ag.
- Decode frame header.
- Decode coded block information (inter frames only).
- Decode macro block mode information (inter frames only).

- Decode motion vectors (inter frames only).
- Decode block-level qi information.
- Decode DC coe_cient for each coded block.
- Decode 1st AC coe_cient for each coded block.
- Decode 2nd AC coe_cient for each coded block.
. : : :
- Decode 63rd AC coefficient for each coded block.
- Perform DC coe_cient prediction.
- Reconstruct coded blocks.
- Copy uncoded bocks.
- Perform loop filtering.

Theora makes equivalence easy to check by defining all decoding operations in terms of exact integer operations. No oating-point math is required, and in particular, the implementation of the iDCT transform MUST be followed precisely. This prevents the decoder mismatch problem commonly associated with codecs that provide a less rigorous transform specification. Such a mismatch problem would be devastating to Theora, since a single rounding error in one frame could propagate throughout the entire succeeding frame due to DC prediction.

5.5 AVS CHINA

Video coding Standard (AVS) was developed by the Working Group of China in the same name and approved by the Chinese Science and Technology Department of Ministry of Information Industry in June 2002. Compared with other standards, AVS has been designed to provide near optimum performance and a considerable reduction in complexity.

The decoder shown in Figure 5.7 accepts the constant rate signal from the storage or transmission and stores it temporarily in a rate buffer. The data is read out at a rate demanded by the decoding of each macroblock and picture.

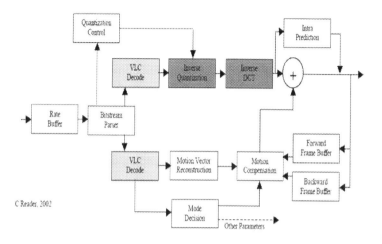

Figure 5.7: Block diagram of AVS decoder.

The signal is parsed to separate the quantization parameter, motion vectors and other side information from the coded data signal.The signal is parsed to separate the quantization parameter, motion vectors and other side information from the coded data signal. The motion vectors are decoded, reconstructed and used by the motion compensation unit to produce a prediction for the current picture. This is added to the reconstructed prediction error to produce the output signal. In the case of intra-coded macroblocks, the data passes from the DCT through the intra prediction process.The Table 5.15 gives list the development of AVS china.Table 5.16 and Table 5.17 gives AVS video profiles, coding tools and applications.

Table 5.15: Standardization of AVS China

Parts of AVS	Contents	Stage
Part 1	System for broadcasting	Final committee draft
Part 2	SD/HD Video	National Standard
Part 3	Audio	Final draft
Part 4	Conformance test	Final committee draft
Part 5	Reference software	Final committee draft
Part 6	Digital right management	Final committee draft
Part 7	Mobility video	Final draft
Part 8	System over IP	Final draft
Part 9	File format	Final draft

Table 5.16:AVS video profiles and applications

Profiles	Key application
Jizhun Profile	Television Broadcasting,HDTV
Jiben Profile	Mobility applications
Shenzhan Profile	Video Surveillance
Jiaqiang Profile	Multimedia entertainment

Table 5.17: Summary of profiles

Profiles	Jizhun	Jiben	Shenzhan	Jiaqiang
Available color formats	4:2:0, 4:2:2	4:2:0	4:0:0 4:2:0	4:2:0 4:2:2
Minimum block unit and transform size	8×8	4×4	8×8	8×8
Intra Prediction	8×8	4×4	8×8	8×8
Inter Prediction	Both P-prediction And B-prediction	Only P-prediction Non-reference P	Both P-prediction And B-prediction, Background reference frames,Non-reference P	Both P-prediction And B-prediction
Interpolation	Two steps four taps interpolation	Two steps four taps interpolation	Two steps four taps interpolation	Two steps four taps interpolation
Maximum number of reference frames	2	2	2	2
Quantization	Fixed quantization	Fixed quantization	Fixed quantization, Weighted quantization,scene-adaptive Weighted quantization	Fixed quantization Weighted quantization, scene-adaptive Weighted quantization
Entropy coding	8×8 2D-VLC	4×4 2D-VLC	8×8 2D-VLC	$8 \times 8$2D-VLC, 8×8 EAC
Interlaced support	Frame coding (or) Field coding	Frame coding only	Frame coding (or) Field coding	Frame coding, Field coding or PAFF
Error resilience	-	Scene signalling in SEI	Core picture,flexible picture header,flexible slice set, constrained DC intra-prediction	-

5.5.1 Coding tools in AVS China

The major coding tools of AVS China part-2 are listed below:

1. 8 X 8 spatial prediction

Spatial prediction is used in intra coding in AVS Part 2 to exploit spatial correlation of picture. The intra prediction is based on 8x8 block. It uses decoded information in the current frame as the reference of prediction, exploiting statistical spatial dependencies between pixels within a picture. If MBPAFF is applied, intra-frame prediction can only take the MBs within the same stage as reference. There are five luminance intra prediction modes, and four chrominance intra prediction modes. Each of the four 8x8 luminance blocks can be predicted using one of the five intra-prediction modes.A head of prediction of DC mode (Mode2), diagonal down left (Mode3) mode and diagonal downright mode(Mode 4), a three-tap low-pass filter (1,2,1) is applied on the samples that will be used as references of prediction. It needs to be pointed out that in DC mode each pixel of current block is predicted by an average of the vertically and horizontally corresponding reference pixels.Hence, the prediction values of different pixels in a block might be different. This results in a fine prediction for a large block. Prediction of the most probable mode is according to the intra-prediction modes of neighboring blocks. This will help to reduce average bits needed to describe the intra-prediction mode in video bitstream. The reconstructed pixels of neighboring blocks before deblocking filtered is used as reference pixels for the current block is shown in Figure 5.8.

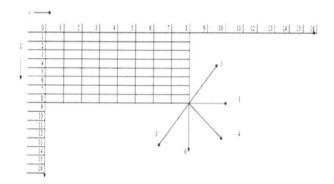

Figure 5.8: Neighbor pixels in luminance intra prediction

Inter prediction

P-picture and B-picture are specified in AVS Part 2. There are four macroblock partition types for inter prediction, 16x16, 16x8, 8x16 and 8x8. Figure 5.9 shows different types of macroblock and sub-macroblock partitions.

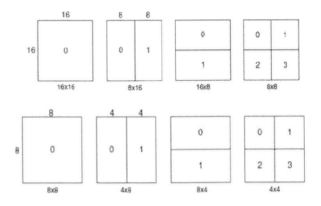

Figure 5.9: Macroblock and sub-macroblock partitions.

P-Prediction

In P-picture, there are 5 inter prediction modes, PSkip (16x16), P_16x16, P_16x8, P_8x16, and P_8x8. For the latter 4 modes in P-frame, each partition of macroblock is predicted from one of the two candidate reference frames, which are latest decoded I- or P-frame. For the latter 4 modes in P-field, each partition of macroblock is predicted from one of the four latest decoded reference fields.

Bi-prediction

There are two kinds of bi-predictions in AVS Part 2, symmetric-prediction and direct-prediction. In symmetric-prediction, only one forward motion vector is transmitted for each partition. The backward motion vector is derived from the forward one by a symmetric rule (as shown in Figure 5.10). In direct-prediction, forward and backward motion vectors are all derived from the motion vector of the collocated block in the backward reference picture.

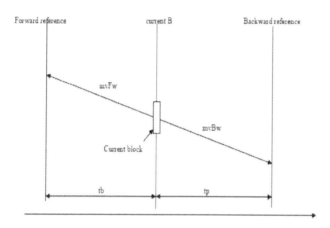

Figure 5.10: Symmetric mode of AVS Part 2

Interpolation

A 1/4-pixel interpolation method named as Two Steps Four Taps interpolation
(TSFT) is adopted in AVS Part 2.1/2-pixel samples are interpolated in step 1
and 1/4-pixel samples in step 2. 1/2-pixel interpolation filter is a 4-tap filter
Hi (-1/8, 5/8, 5/8, -1/8).

For ordinary 1/4-pixel samples, a, c, d, f, I, k, n and q in Figure6, a 4-tap
filter H2 (1/16, 7/16, 7/16, 1/16) is applied, and four special 1/4-pixel samples,
e, g, p and r, are filtered by 2-tap bi-linear filter H3(1/2, 1/2)"

Reference frames

Maximum of two reference pictures is allowed in inter-frame prediction
of AVS-video. In particular, two reference frames are maximum when
the current frame is coded with frame coding, while the reference index
is no more than three (beginning from zero) when applying field coding.
References are the nearest coded frames/fields of the current frame/field,
except that the second field in B picture cannot take the first field of the same
picture as its reference, as shown in Figure 5.11. Especially, reference can
only be taken from the previous stages of the current macroblock pair in

P-prediction when MBPAFF is applied. For video surveillance, normally the scene is not changed or changed slightly, background reference frames can replace one of the above two reference pictures and provide better coding efficiency.

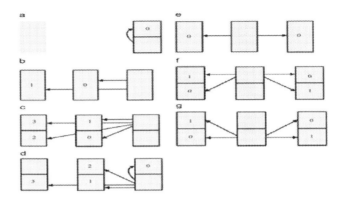

Figure 5.11: Maximum of two reference pictures in AVS-video:

(a) reference of current (the second) field in field-coded I picture,
(b) references of current frame in frame-coded P picture,
(c) references of current (the first) field in field-coded P picture, 21
(d) references of current (the second) field in field-coded P picture,
(e) references of current frame in frame-coded B picture
(f) references of current (the first) field in field-coded B picture and
(g) references of current (the second) field in field-coded B picture

Transform and Quantization

In a typical block based compression scheme like AVS, the residual block is transformed using a 8x8 integer transform. These integer transforms are a variation of discrete cosine transform (DCT). The transform outputs a set of coefficients, each of which is a weighting value for a standard basis pattern.The Figure 5.12 shows the Quantization of the transform coefficients of the image block.

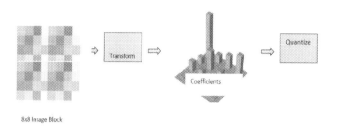

Figure 5.12: Quantization of the transform coefficients of the image block

The output of the transform, a block of transform coefficients, is quantized, i.e. each coefficient is divided by an integer value. Quantization reduces the precision of the transform coefficients according to a quantization parameter (QP).

Typically, the result is a block in which most or all of the coefficients are zero, with a few non-zero coefficients. Setting QP to a high value means that more coefficients are set to zero; resulting in high compression at the expense of poor decoded image quality.Setting QP to a low value means that more non-zero coefficients remain after quantization, resulting in better decoded image quality but lower compression.

In-loop deblocking filter

uses the de-blocking filter in motion compensation loop. In-loop deblocking filter is applied in AVS Part 2, to reduce the blocking artifacts and enhance both subjective and objective performance. The de-blocking process directly acts on the reconstructed reference first across vertical edges and then across horizontal edges.Obviously, different image regions and different bit rates need different smoothes. Therefore, the de-blocking filter is automatically adjusted in AVS depending on activities of blocks and QPs.

2D VLC (Variable Length Coding)

In AVS Part 2, an efficient context-based 2D-VLC entropy coder is designed for coding 8x8 block-size transform coefficients. 2D-VLC refers to a pair of Run-Level is regarded as one event and jointly coded. Context-based is a technique, which utilizes the coefficient information to switch among different VLC tables. High performance can be achieved with the cost relatively low complexity.

5.5.2 Results for AVS China

AVS China results for sequence foreman_cif.yuv file

- File used foreman_cif.yuv
- Resolution: 358X 288
- Frame rate: 25 fps
- Original file size: 44550 Kilobytes
- Number of frames used: 100

Table 5.18 shows PSNR, MSE, SSIM and compression ratios for different bitrates. Figure 5.13 shows decoded images at different bitrates for AVS China. Figure 5.14, 5.15 and 5.16 gives the curve between Bitrate and PSNR, MSE ans SSIM values.

Table 5.18 MSE, PSNR and SSIM for
foreman_cif.yuv file for AVS China[240]

QP	Compressed file size(KB)	Bit rate (Kbit/s)	Bits/Pixel	Y-PSNR (dB)	Y-MSE	Y-SSIM	Compression ratio
0	20734	17100	6.75	60.54	0.0573	0.9997	2.15:1
15	6213	5123.57	2.02	45.8679	1.6837	0.9942	7.17:1
31	1045	860.94	0.34	37.6255	11.234	0.9737	42.63:1
45	206	169.21	0.07	31.2507	48.7547	0.9186	216.26:1
63	34	27.67	0.01	23.8649	267.0482	0.7114	1310.29:1

Figure 5.13: Foreman_cif.yuv sequence compressed
AVS China files at different bitrates.

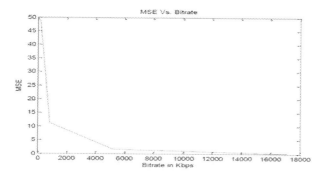

Figure 5.14: PSNR Vs. Bitrate for foreman_cif.yuv sequence for AVS China

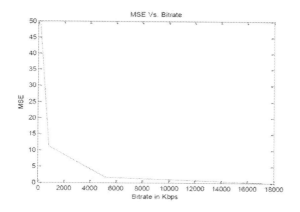

Figure 5.15: MSE Vs. Bitrate for foreman_cif.yuv sequence for AVS china

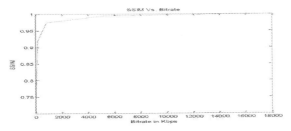

Figure 5.16: SSIM Vs. Bitrate for foreman_cif.yuv sequence for AVS China

5.6 VP 8

VP8 uses three reference frames for inter prediction, but the scheme is somewhat different from the multiple reference motion compensation scheme seen in other formats. VP8's design is used to limit the buffer size requirement into three reference frame buffers and yet achieving effective de-correlation in motion compensation.VP8 makes extensive uses of intra and inter prediction.streaming support in modern video codecs is both an important component of codec design and relatively rare in real world implementations. Few transport layers will pass 51 malformed packets, instead opting to drop them in their entirety.Thus, codecs have to deal less with bit errors, and more with missing frames, headers, context tables, and metadata.

VP8 Streaming Support

VP8 offers relatively few streaming features. Like H.264, many of VP8's encoding features, such as the arithmetic coder, are context adaptive. If an incremental update to such an adaptive table is lost, all data until the table is fully defined again (usually at an I frame) will be corrupt. VP8 can optionally fully define all adaptive context tables at all golden frames, allowing the stream to recover quickly.

To analyze VP8 effectively, tests were designed to measure how each vital feature of VP8 compares to a similar feature in H.264, as well as how each performs overall and in several use case scenarios.A recommendation is made for improving VP8's implementation, and recommends which codec to use for which purposes if legal and TCO implications are not a factor. Not every use case or feature is possible to test, and there is room for further analysis and recommendations. For the purpose of this thesis, H.264 indicates H.264/AVC. H.264/SVC was not analyzed in detail, although some discussion of some of its features and how they compare to VP8 are mentioned. Work on comparing VP8 to H.264/SVC has been studied by Seelinget. al[1], and is not duplicated here.The general method for comparing VP8 and H.264 is to analyze the components that define the codecs, design methodology to compare these individual features, and run tests on a varied set of source videos to gain an accurate understanding of how each component compares to its counterpart in the other codec.

By analyzing the codec by parts, rather than by the whole, emphasis can be placed on where optimization should take place. This also gives a more detailed view on the codecs, and can ignore implementationspecific bugs and shortcomings. VP8, the video codec in theWebM media container released by Google Inc., in May 2010, is a modern video codec with many advanced features designed to have a high visual quality at a low bitrate. This chapter covers VP8 in detail, explaining its encoding process, quantization, transformation, entropy coding, prediction, and filtering. Adirect comparison with H.264 is made, discussing inter-prediction differences, adaptive behavior – including segmentation and slices, quantization, transformations, and entropy coding, and network streaming support. HEVC, the next video standard being developed by the Joint Collaborative Team on Video Coding (JCT-VC), is introduced and compared with VP8. The ease of implementation of VP8 in hardware is discussed, and the reference hardware implementation is compared with implementations of H.264 in hardware.

5.6.1 VP8 Internals

The encoding process of VP8 follows five steps in order. First, the macroblock to be encoded gets a predictor. The predictor, is subtracted from the macroblock. Next, the macroblock is transformed, using either the DCT or the WHT, depending on the prediction mode. After transformation, the quantization step takes the outputs of the transformation process, and restricts them to a certain output range. Figure 5.17 shows the encoding process. The output from the Prediction block is the predictor, and is subtracted from the macroblock by value. The Prediction block uses spatial information (pixel values surrounding the sub-block), and temporal information (motion vectors from other frames).

The Transform block uses the prediction mode to decide whether or not to use the WHT or the DCT. The predicted, transformed, and quantized macroblock is then run through the loop filter, discussed in Section 2.1.7, and finally entropy encoded, as discussed in Section 1.3.3.

Quantization

Quantization is an signal processing technique where a continuous or large set of input ranges are mapped to a discrete or smaller set of ranges. VP8, like many other video codecs, uses quantization as a method for discarding superfluous data to enhance the compression efficiency.

To quantize the residue, each coefficient is divided by one of six quantization factors, the selection of which depends upon the plane being encoded. In VP8, a plane is a set of two-dimensional data with metadata describing the type of that data. There are four types of planes in VP8: Y2, the virtual plane from the WHT, Y, the luminance plane, U, the chroma red plane, and V, the chroma blue plane.

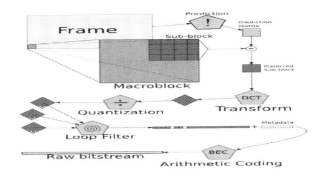

Figure 5.17: A Flowchart of the Encoding Process tizer lookup table.

The quantization step also depends upon the coefficient position, either DC – coefficient 0, or AC – coefficients 1 through 15. These values are specified in one of two ways, via an index into a look-up table, or as an offset to an index.The baseline quantization factor, Yac, is specified as a 7-bit lookup into the AC quan- tizer lookup table.

Yac is added to each of the other quantization factors, which are specified as 4-bit positive or negative offsets from the index of Yac. Yac is added to each of the other quantization factors, which are specified as 4-bit positive or negative offsets from the index of Yac. Each other factor is specified as a four bit offset from the Yac index, and include a sign bit. This means that if Yac = 16, then a value of Y1 = 3 would be 19, and a value of Y2 = -10 would be 6. This allows an index range of +/-15 from the index of Yac. In the VP8 itstream, the five factors other than Yac are optional, and only included if a flag is true. If they are omitted, they are set to zero, which indicates that the same quantization factor as Yac should be used for them. To dequantize the residue before inverting the transform during decoding, each coefficient is multiplied by one of six dequantization factors.

Transforms

The quantized DCT coefficients are coded for each macroblock, and they make up what is known as the residue signal. The residue is added to the prediction blocks to form the final reconstructed macroblock. Unlike H.264, VP8 uses only 4×4 DCT and WHT for its transformations. The DCT is used for the 16 Y sub-blocks of a macroblock, the 4 U sub-blocks, and the 4 V sub-blocks.The WHT is used to construct a 4×4 array of the average intensities of the 16 Y sub-blocks. This is a stand-in for the 0th DCT coefficients of the Y sub-blocks. This is known as Y2, and is considered a virtual subblock, contrasted to the 24 other, real, sub-blocks. The subblock Y2 is conditional, based upon the prediction mode. The 4× 4 DCT in H.264 and VP8 can be computed with integer arithmetic only.

This enables it to operate quickly and with low complexity, as it avoids floating point operations. Further, only 16-bit arithmetic is required for both the H.264 DCT and the VP8 DCT, allowing it to function well on lower end microprocessors. The H.264 DCT transform is less precise than VP8's DCT transform.

Inverse DCT and WHT

Before dequantizing the DCT andWHTfactors, the inverse transform must be performed. If the Y2 block exists (if a prediction mode other than B PRED for intra- and SPLITMV for inter-prediction is used), then it is inverted via the WHT. The WHT is defined in Eq. 2.26, and is the inverse WHT is implemented in Alg. 1 on page 24, where input and output are arrays of signed 16-bit integers. This is an O (n log n) implementation of the FastWalsh-Hadamard Transform, which uses an architecture similar to the Cooley-Tukey algorithm for Fast Fourier Transforms[19]. There is also an optimization if there is only one non-zero DC value in the input array. For the inverse DCT, two passes of a 1D inverse DCT is used. Alg. 2 on page 41 is used to compute the inverse DCT. The two constants f1 and f2 are typically expressed as 16-bit fixed-point fractions, and are given in the bitstream reference as

$$f_1.2^{16}=20091 \text{ and } f_2.2^{16}=34568 \tag{5.1}$$

Boolean Entropy Encoder

The VP8 data stream is compressed via a boolean entropy encoder, which is a type of arithmetic coder. For this type of arithmetic coding, there are only two symbols, true or false. The goal of VP8's other steps, such as the DCT coefficient coding and prediction is to insert more false values than true values, so that the probability of a false value is higher, thus increasing the efficiency of the boolean entropy encoder. The equation for determining the smallest datarate per value is in Eq. 2.27, where R is measured in bits/value.

$$R= -p\log_2(p)-(1-p)\log_2(1-p) \tag{5.2}$$

At the value $p = 1\ 2$, $R = 1$ bits=value, which is the worst case of the boolean entropy encoder. However, at $p = 1\ 1175$, $R = 0{:}01$ bits=value, which is substantially better than encoding every single boolean.

Bit Representation of the Entropy Encoder

The probabilities that the boolean entropy encoder works with in VP8 are unsigned 8-bit integers, p0. To get the actual probability $p\ 2\ [0;\ 1]$, the 8-bit integer is divided by 256. The state of the encoder is maintained with five values, the current bit position n, the bit string already written, w, the bottom value, an 8-bit integer ibot, and the range, another 8-bit integer, irng. The range is clamped to within a specified boundary, so that the probabilities remain accurate, irng 2.

The value v is the next value of w, and the final value of v is the end condition, where $v = x$. v must satisfy the inequality in Eq. 5.3. The scale of the bit position 8-bits ahead is generated as, $s = 2 \times n \times 8$. Another value, split, is calculated as follows, split $= 1 + p'(irng-1)/256$, and is constrained, split 2 [1; irng - 1].

$$W+(s\; i_{bot}) \leq v < W+(s\; (i_{bot} + i_{rng}))$$ (5.3)

The boolean value to be encoded, b, has a zero probability of p0 256, where p0 2 [1; 255]. The process for encoding one boolean value b into the output w is shown in Alg. 3. This algorithm is repeated for each boolean value that must be encoded. This is parallelized in the VP8 encoder to process 8-bits at one time. To decode a boolean encoded by Alg 3, the decoding process described in Alg. 4 on page 42 is used.

Intraframe Prediction

VP8 uses two types of prediction vectors to achieve high compression performance. The simpler type is intra-prediction, where the frame is predicted from other components of the already constructed frame. As macroblock prediction is resolved in raster-scan order, intra-prediction generally works from the top left, to the bottom right.

Chroma Intraframe Prediction

Chroma intra-prediction works on the 8-by-8 blocks of both U and V chroma. The components of intra-prediction are M, which is the 8-by-8 matrix of either U or V, as shown in Figure 5.18. A is the bottom row of the macroblock above the current macroblock M, and is 1-by- 8. If M is currently in the topmost position, then the values of A are all 127. L is the rightmost right of the macroblock to the left of the current macroblock M, and is 8-by-1. If M is currently in the leftmost position, then the values of A are all 129.

P is a scalar, the bottom-rightmost chroma value from the macroblock above and to the left of the current macroblock M. If M is currently in the topmost and leftmost position, then the value of P is 129.

Vertical Prediction:

Vertical prediction, known as V PRED in the libvpx source code, fills every 8 chroma column of M with copies of L. See Figure 5.19 for a graphical representation of vertical prediction.

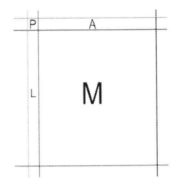

Figure 5.18: The area around a macroblock that will be intra-compressed

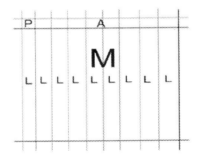

Figure 5.19: An intra-predicted macroblock using vertical prediction

Horizontal Prediction:

Horizontal prediction, known as H PRED in the libvpx source code, fills every 8 chroma row of M with A. See Figure 2.5 for a graphical representation of horizontal prediction.

DC Prediction:

In DC prediction mode, known as DC PRED in the libvpx source code, every chroma in M is filled with the same value. This is shown in Figure 5.20.The DC value is shown in Eq. 2.79.

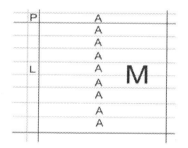

Figure 5.20: An intra-predicted macroblock using horizontal prediction

$$\forall_i \forall_j \ M_{i,j} = (1/16)\sum_{k=1}^{8} A_k + (1/16)\sum_{k=1}^{8} L_i \qquad (5.4)$$

Interframe prediction:

Interframe prediction is accomplished with a reference frame and offsets relative to the reference frame, known as motion vectors. Motion vectors are vectors through three dimensions: two-dimensions in space, to show movement from one position in a frame to another, and a third in time, to allow the motion to occur. Each macroblock for the current frame is predicted using the 16 luma sub-blocks and the 8 chroma red and 8 chroma blue sub-blocks.Macroblocks in interframes can be intra-coded. This can be used to provide intrarefreshes between long key frames, where, at specific intervals, each interframe codes one column of intra-coded macroblocks. These columns sweep from left to right, refreshing the image as a fully coded key frame would.

Adaptive loop filtering:

Loop filtering is a process of removing blocking artifacts by quantization of the DCT coefficients from block transforms. VP8 brings several loop-filtering innovations that speed up decoding by not applying any loop filter at all in some situations. VP8 also supports a method of implicit segmentation where different loop filter strengths can be applied for different parts of the image, according to the prediction modes or reference frames used to encode each macroblock. It would be possible to apply stronger filtering to intra-coded blocks and at the same time specify that inter coded blocks that use the Golden Frame as a reference and are coded using a (0,0) motion vector should use a weaker filter. The choice of loop filter strengths in a variety of situations is fully adjustable on a frame-by-frame basis, so the encoder can adapt the filtering strategy in order to get the best possible results. In addition, similar to the region-based adaptive quantization in section 3, VP8 supports the adjustment of loop filter strength for each segment.

Fig. 4 shows an example where the encoder can adapt the filtering strength based on content.VP8 seems to outperform H.264 Baseline (both x264 and JM) for these six videos in terms of PSNR. Videos with a large amount of detail, such as Mobile and Bridge Close, have the largest difference between VP8 and H.264 Baseline. Videos that have less temporal and spacial complexity, such as Akiyo and Students, have less of an obvious benefit. Videos that have an average amount of detail and camera movement, such as Coastguard and Foreman, VP8 outperforms H.264 Baseline, but not by such a large degree. In all cases, VP8 uses less bandwidth to achieve these benefits. The Figure 5.21 shows the PSNR Summary of Videos at CIF, 150 Kbps, H.264 Baseline and VP8 Good Deadline.

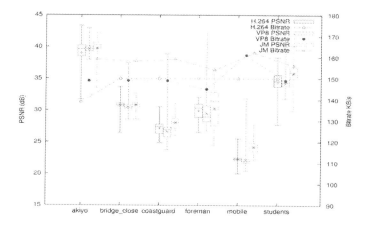

Figure 5.21: PSNR Summary of Videos at CIF, 150
Kbps, H.264 Baseline and VP8 Good Deadline

Rate Distortion Curve Results

In RD curve for the Foreman video, SSIM results, using the right Y-axis, is shown above the PSNR results, which uses the left Y-Axis. Table 5.19 shows the p-values for Foreman, computed using a Student's t-test if the variances were statistically equal or a Welch's t-test otherwise. No value met the threshold for significance of _ = 0:1, and thus the RD curves for Foreman are statistically significant. However, it's obvious that, on the average H.264 Baseline performs worse than VP8 and H.264 High profile. There doesn't seem to be a significant difference between the two VP8 encodings and H.264. The Figure 5.22 shows Parkrun at 720p, encoded at 1000 Kbps and Figure 5.23 shows the Foreman CIF Video RD Curve for H.264 and VP8.

Table 5.19: p-values for RD curve for Foreman

Encoder	PSNR p-value	SSIM p-value
Baseline/Good	0.45291	0.56182
High/Best	0.90875	0.79636

Figure 5.22: Parkrun at 720p, encoded at 1000 Kbps

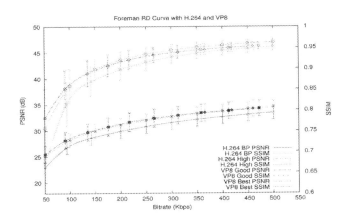

Figure 5.23: Foreman CIF Video RD Curve for H.264 and VP8

VP8's support and implementations are tenuous, due to its immaturity. Its quality alone does not warrant a switch to VP8: in fact, the opposite is true. VP8's encoded videos are, in general, lower quality than H.264's except in low resolution, low bitrate scenarios. Combined with the possibility for a low cost, high performance hardware implementation, VP8 seems well suited to the surveillance market. Because widespread adoption of a codec is not necessary for such video – only the encoder and decoder need match, which is simple in proprietary video systems – widespread acceptance is not necessary. Due to its open source implementation, there are no upfront fees, and Google provides a perpetual patent grant. As a result, there is great potential for innovations in future versions of VP8 encoder and decoder.

5.7 DIRAC

5.7.1 Dirac encoder&decoder

In the Dirac encoder (Figre 5.24)the entire compressed data is packaged in a simple byte stream. This has synchronization, giving access to any frame quickly and efficiently - making editing simple. The structure in which the entire byte stream can be packaged in many of the existing transport streams. This feature allows a wide range of coding options, easy access to all the other data transport systems required for production or broadcast metadata. Streaming video quality is partly dependent upon the video encoding process and the amount of bandwidth required for it to be viewed properly. While encoding a video, a high degree of compression is applied to both the video and audio tracks so that it will stream at this speed.

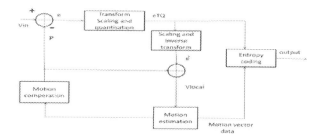

Figure 5.24: Dirac encoder architecture

Dirac decoder

The Dirac decoder (Figure 5.25) performs the inverse operations of the encoder. The decoding process is carried out in three stages as shown in Figure 5.29. At the first stage, the input encoded bit-stream is decoded by the entropy decoding technique. Next, scaling and inverse quantization is performed. In the final stage, inverse wavelet transform is applied on the data to produce the decoded, uncompressed video output. A trade off is made between video quality and motion vector bit rate.

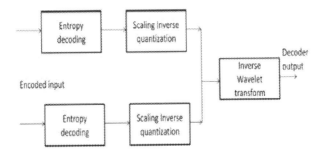

Figure 5.25: Stages of decoding in Dirac

The Dirac's decoder implementation is designed to provide fast decoding whilst remaining portable across various software platforms.

Stages of Encoding and Decoding in Dirac

Wavelet transform

The 2D discrete wavelet transform provides Dirac with the flexibility to operate at a range of resolutions. This is because wavelets operate on the entire picture at once, rather than focusing on small areas at a time. In Dirac, the discrete wavelet transform plays the same role as the DCT in MPEG-2 in de-correlating data in a roughly frequency-sensitive way, whilst having the advantage of preserving fine details better than block based transforms.

Synthesis filters can undo the aliasing introduced by critical sampling and perfectly reconstruct the input. The wavelet transform is constructed by repeated filtering of signals into low- and high-frequency parts. For two-dimensional signals, this filtering occurs both horizontally and vertically as shown in Figure 5.26. At each stage, the low horizontal / low vertical frequency sub-band is split further, resulting in logarithmic frequency decomposition into sub-bands.

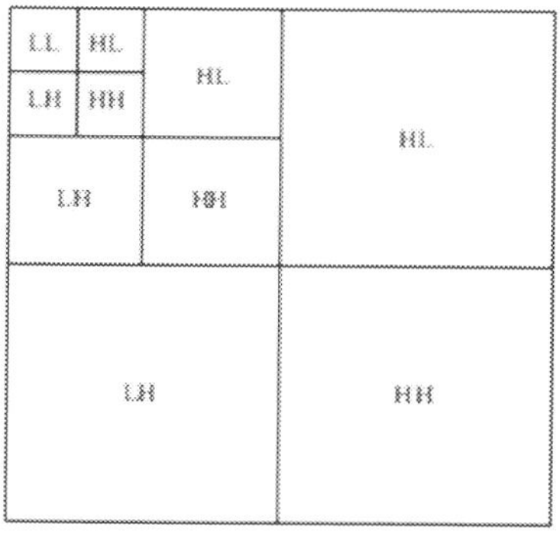

Figure 5.26: Wavelet transform frequency decomposition

Scaling and Quantization

Dirac uses a dead-zone quantization (Figure 5.27) which differs from orthodox quantization by making the first set of quantization steps twice as wide. This allows Dirac to perform coarser quantization on smaller values compared to codecs such as the MPEG-4.

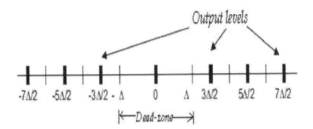

Figure 5.27: Dead-zone quantizer with quality factor (QF)

Entropy coding

Entropy coding is entered after wavelet transform to minimize the number of bits used. It consists of three stages: binarization, context modeling and arithmetic coding as shown in Figure 5.28. Arithmetic coding performs lossless compression and is both flexible and efficient.

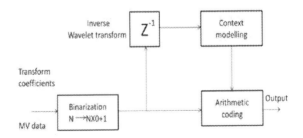

Figure 5.28: Dirac's entropy coding architecture

Motion estimation and motion compensation

Motion estimation exploits temporal redundancy in video streams by looking for similarities between adjacent frames. Dirac implements hierarchical motion estimation as shown in Figure 5.29.

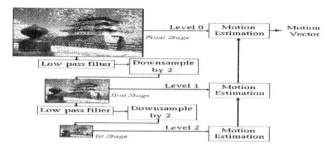

Figure 5.29: Hierarchical motion estimation

Motion compensation is used to predict the present frame. Dirac uses overlapped block-based motion compensation (OBMC) to achieve good compression and avoid block-edge artifacts which would be expensive to code using wavelets. OBMC allows interaction of neighboring blocks (Figure 5.30). Dirac provides sub-pixel motion compensation with motion vectors and thereby improves the prediction rate up to 1/8th pixel accuracy. Techniques used such as predicting a frame using only motion information and predicting a frame to be nearly identical to a previous frame at low bit rates are also supported. It involves uses the motion vectors to predict the current frame in such a way as to minimize the cost of encoding residual data.

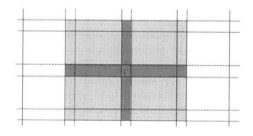

Figure 5.30: Overlapping blocks in OBMC

5.7.2 Implementation

Dirac can be fully implemented in C++ programming language which allows object oriented development on all common operating systems. The C++ code compiles to produce libraries for common functions, motion estimation, encoding and decoding, interface called as C. An application programmer's interface can be written in C for simplicity and integrated with various media players, video processing tools and streaming software.

Compression ratio test

By evaluating the magnitude of the *.drc and *.264 files, compression ratio results in comparison to the file size of the original sequence are produced from Dirac and H.264 respectively. Figure 5.31 shows a comparison of how Dirac and H.264 perform in compression for QCIF, CIF and SDTV sequences respectively. Dirac achieves higher compression ratios for lower bit rates than H.264 in case of QCIF sequences. At higher QCIF bit rates both Dirac and H.264 achieve similar compression. H.264 provides better compression at higher bit rates especially for CIF, SD and HD media.

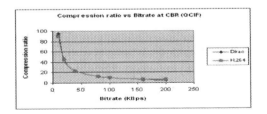

Figure 5.31: Compression ratio comparison of Dirac
and H.264 for "Miss-America" QCIF sequence

PSNR test

H.264 achieves higher PSNR than Dirac as seen in Figure 5.32. Since Dirac has not been designed to maximize PSNR, measurements of PSNR performance against other codecs are not meaningful.Objective tests are divided into three sections, namely (i) Compression, (ii) Structural similarity index (SSIM) [16], and (iii) Peak to peak signal to noise ratio (PSNR).

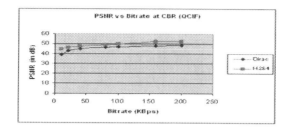

Figure 5.32: PSNR comparison of Dirac and H.264
for "Miss-America" QCIF sequence

The test sequences "Miss-America" QCIF (176x144) [23], "Stefan" CIF (352x288) [23] and "Susie" standard-definition (SD) (720x480) [24] are used for evaluation. Only few are presented in this chapter. Objective test methods attempt to quantify the error between a reference and an encoded bitstream. [5] To ensure the accuracy of the tests, each codec must be encoded using the same bit rate. [5]Since the latest version of Dirac does include a constant bit rate (CBR) mode, the comparison between Dirac and H.264's [11-14] performance was produced by encoding several test sequences at different bit rates. By utilizing the CBR mode within H.264, we can ensure that H.264 is being encoded at the same bit rate as that of Dirac.

Applications

Dirac suits a wide range of applications from 2 K formats used for E-Cinema through to QSIF found on hand-held devices. Dirac Pro offers high quality and low latency, with the high bandwidth operations found in production and post production, archiving and contribution links.Dirac offers high compression for narrow bandwidth environments such as broadcasting and internet downloads, podcasting, peer-to-peer distribution and access services. Whatever the application, it is possible to select parameters which offer the solution you need.

- Clip Distribution, Live Streaming Video, Pod Casting
- Creative Archive
- Peer to Peer transfers
- HDTV with SD Simulcast capability
- Higher density channel packing
- Desktop Production

- News links
- Archive Storage
- Digital Intermediate Film Out file storagePVRs
- Multilevel Mezzanine 3 GBit/s into1.5 GBit/s, 1.5 GBit/s into 270 MBit/s, etc

Conclusions

Overall Dirac is very promising. According to BBC R&D [1] [2], Dirac was developed with a view to optimize its performance with compression ratio and perceptual quality at the forefront. Dirac's simplistic nature provides robustness and fast compression which is very beneficial, therefore to a large extent Dirac has succeeded in its aim. [5]Expert viewing suggests that, amazing simple toolset, Dirac is very comparable to other state-of-the-art codecs such as H.264. [5] Dirac performs better than H.264 / MPEG-4 in terms of computation speed and efficiency. SSIM indicates that H.264 has slightly greater improvement in terms of quality. The choice of the codec will depend on the end users application which will decide if the enormous cost in royalty fees decides the additional increase in quality (as in the case of H.264/MPEG-4). Both Dirac and H.264 maintain a near constant quality at low bit rates, which is beneficial for applications such as video streaming.In conclusion, Dirac is an extremely simple yet robust codec, nearly equaling H.264 in performance sans the cost of royalty fees. SMPTE VC-2 is based on the intra-frame version of Dirac called DiracPro [45]. It is being standardized by SMPTE (SMPTE S2042). It is aimed at professional applications and not for end user distribution.

6

COMPARISON OF VIDEO CODING STANDARDS

Performance Comparison

- Bit Rate
- Quality
- PSNR (Peak Signal Noise Ratio)
- MSE (Mean Squared Error)
- SSIM (Measuring Codec Quality Metric)
- Compression Ratio

• Bit Rate

bit rate (bitrate or as a variable R) is the number of bits that are conveyed or processed per unit of time.

Data Rate After compression, the video sequence is indicated with a corresponding string of binary digits (bits) denoted by b. The objective is to keep its length b as small as possible. The average bit rateRb is the average number of bits used per unit of time torepresent a continuous medium such as audio or video. It is quantified in bits per second (bit/s)

$$R_b = \frac{b}{T}[bits/s] \tag{6.1}$$

where T is the time needed for the transmission of b from sender to receiver. The rate increase _R will be used to quantify the change in rate caused by a new method resulting in the rate Rnew compared to a reference rate Rref

$$\Delta R = \frac{R_{new} - R_{ref}}{R_{ref}} .100 = \frac{b_{new} - b_{ref}}{b_{ref}} .100[\%] \tag{6.2}$$

under the assumption that T has to be the same for the reference bitstream and the bitstream after the application of the new method. However, for some applications as in resource allocation the average bit rate is not as important as the peak bit rate. The frame rate determines the time of the picture rendering. The play-out buffer compensates partially for the variable bit rate.

Variable bit rate (VBR) is a strategy to maximize the visual video quality and minimize the bit rate. On fast moving scenario, a variable bit rate uses more bits than it does on slow motion scenes of similar duration yet achieves a consistent visual quality. For instance and non-buffered video streaming when the available bandwidth is fixed, e.g. in videoconferencing delivered on channels of fixed bandwidth, a constant bit rate (CBR) must be used.

- Full reference methods (FR), where the whole original video signal is available
- Reduced reference methods (RR), where only partial information of the original video is available
- No-reference methods (NR), where the original video is not available at all.

Some example NR metrics are:

- Blocking measure — measurement power of so called *blocking artefacts* (extremely noticeable without deblocking filter usage on low bitrates)
- Blurring measure — measurement of common video blurring (washout)

Subjective video quality

This is concerned with how video is perceived by a viewer and designates his or her opinion on a particular video sequence. Subjective video quality tests are quite expensive in terms of time (preparation and running) and human resources.There is an enormous number of ways of showing video sequences to experts and of recording their opinions. A few of them have been standardized. They are thoroughly described in ITU-R recommendation BT.500.

The reason for measuring subjective video quality is the same as for measuring the MeanOpinion Score for audio. Opinions of experts can be averaged; average mark is usually given with confidence interval. Additional procedures can be used for averaging, for example experts who give unstable results can be rejected (for instance, if their correlation with average opinion is small).In case of video codecs, this is a very common situation. When codecs with similar objective results show results with different subjective results, the main reasons can be:

- Pre- and postfilters are widely used in codecs. Commonly codecs use prefilters like video denoising, deflicking, deshacking, etc. Denoising and deflicking commonly maintain PSNR value, but increase visual quality (the best slow denoising filters also increase PSNR on middle and high bitrates). Deshacking seriously decreases PSNR, but increases visual quality. The same situation with postfilters — deblocking and deringing maintain PSNR, but increase quality. Graining (suggested in H.264) essentially increases video quality especially on big plasma screens, but decrease PSNR.
- Motion estimation (ME) search strategy can also cause different visual quality for the same PSNR. So called *true motion* search commonly will not reach minimum sum of absolute differences(SAD) values in codec ME, but may result in better visual quality. Also such methods require more compression time.
- Rate control strategy. VBR commonly cause better visual quality marks than CBR for the same average PSNR values for sequences.

It is difficult to use long sequences for subjective testing. Commonly, three or four ten-second sequences are used, compared with full movies used for objective metrics. Sequence selection is important — those sequences that are similar to the ones used by developers to tune their codecs are more competitive.

• PSNR (Peak Signal Noise Ratio)

The number of colour components corresponds to the cardinality $|C|$ of the set. Row index i and column index j address the individual elements of the colour component matrix. For image distortion, the MSE is most commonly quoted in terms of the equivalent reciprocal measured Peak Signal to Noise Ratio (PSNR) defined in (1.16) as:

$$PSNR[n]=10.\log_{10}((2^q-1)^2/MSE[n])[dB]$$

(OR)

$$PSNR=10.\log_{10}(MAX_1^2/MSE) \tag{6.3}$$
$$=20.\log_{10}(MAX_1/\sqrt{MSE}) \tag{6.4}$$
$$=20.\log_{10}(MAX_1)-10.\log_{10}(MSE) \tag{6.5}$$

where q represents the number of bits used to express the colour component values. In YUV colourspace the two chrominance parts are usually smoother than the luminance. PSNR measures the pixel error between an original and image that has been compressed and decompressed. PSNR studies must be accompanied by subjective viewing by experts and users. With that caveat in mind, we will present each example in terms of PSNR values with comments on perceived quality. Therefore, especially for the applications that handle all components in the same way, it may be more discriminative to compare the distortion of luminance only ($C = \{Y\}$) by means of Y-MSE[n] or Y-PSNR[n].

The average MSE defined by

$$\overline{MSE} = \frac{1}{F}\sum_{n=1}^{F} MSE[n] \tag{6.6}$$

and F is the number of frames in the video sequence.

The later definition is formally correct, since it averages over the linear values. Averaging over logarithmic values results in a systematic error as a consequence of Jensen's inequality (MacKay 2006), which states that if f $(\cdot)$ is a convex function and X is a random variable, then

$$E\{f(X)\} \geq f(E\{X\}) \tag{6.7}$$

where $E\{X\}$ denotes the expectation of X. A function $f(\cdot)$ is convex over an interval (a, b) if for all $x1, x2 \in (a, b)$ and $0 \leq \lambda \leq 1$ applies

$$f(\lambda.x1 + (1 - \lambda) x2) \leq \lambda.f(x1) + (1 - \lambda) f(x2). \tag{6.8}$$

that is, all points of $f(x)$ between the arbitrary chosen $x1, x2 \in (a, b)$ lay below or on the line connecting them. Since $\log 10(1/x) = -\log 10(x)$ is convex, PSNR will in general provide 'better' results (meaning higher quality) than PSNR. In practice and in literature, both ways of calculating PSNR can be found. For instance, JM outputs the PSNR value. Thus, in this book, the Y-PSNR values averaged per sequence correspond also to PSNR in order to ease the comparison with literature where the JM experiments are presented. Whereas PSNR estimates the user perceptual subjective quality well for packet-loss impairments, it does not necessarily reflect the user evaluation of compression impairments. Nevertheless, it is still the most used distortion metric and therefore also one that allows the results to be compared with other methods without having to implement them.

• MSE (Mean Squared Error)

The performance of error resilience methods can be evaluated by measuring the end-user distortion in the presence of transmission errors with given characteristics and by analyzing the cost determined by increasing the rate and/or complexity. In this section, metrics are presented that are used throughout this book for performance evaluation. Distortion To evaluate the distortion within the nth video frame Fn with respect to a reference (distortion-free) frame Rn, the mean square error (MSE) can be used:

$$MSE[n] = \frac{1}{M.N.|C|}\sum_{c \in C} \sum_{i=1}^{N} \sum_{j=1}^{M} \left[F_n^{(c)}(i,j) - R_n^{(c)}(i,j)\right]^2 \tag{6.9}$$

(OR)

$$MSE = \frac{1}{mn} \sum_{i=0}^{m-1} \sum_{j=0}^{n-1} [I(i,j) - K(i,j)]^2 \tag{6.10}$$

where $N \times M$ is the size of the frame and C is the set of colour components, for RGB colour space $C = \{R, G, B\}$.

• SSIM (Measuring Codec Quality Metric)

A new metric (suggested in 2004) which shows better results than PSNR at the cost of a reasonable increase in computational complexity.

$$SSIM(x,y) = \frac{(2\mu_x\mu_y + C_1)(2\sigma_{xy} + C_2)}{(\mu_x^2 + \mu_y^2 + C_1)(\sigma_x^2 + \sigma_y^2 + C_2)} \tag{6.11}$$

$$\sigma_{xy} = \frac{1}{N-1} \sum_{i=1}^{N} (x_i - \mu_x)(y_i - \mu_y) \tag{6.12}$$

• Compression Ratio

In order to evaluate the performance of a compression method, one of the two major criteria is bit-rate, which is expressed in terms of bit per pixel (bpp). It is dened as the average number of bits required by the compressed image for each pixel of the image(discussed in video compression section). Thus

$$b_{pp} = \frac{size\ of\ compreesed\ image\ in\ bits}{no\ of\ pixels\ in\ the\ image} = \frac{k}{MN} \tag{6.13}$$

Sometimes, the amount of compression is also de_ned as compression ratio (CR),Where

$$CR = \frac{size\ of\ original\ image}{size\ of\ compressed\ image} = \frac{MNb}{K} \tag{6.14}$$

Another criterion is the quality of the reconstructed image. The amount of compression, the quality and the computation time are closely interrelated and one of them may be more important than others depending on the speci_c application. A compression algorithm can be thought of as means to o_er the best trade o_ among these three. The measurement of visual quality of the reconstructed image or video is very important. There are two types of quality (visual) assessments: the subjective assessment, and the objective assessment. Each of these has its own merits and demerits.

6.1 Comparison of H.264 vs MPEG-2

MPEG-2 is the most common standard used for high quality video storage and transmission. We compare the coding performance of MPEG-2 and the emerging H.264 standard on first and second set of video sequences. We used an MPEG-2 encoder based on the codec developed in University of California at Berkeley, enhanced with rate-distortion optimized macroblock mode decision and motion estimation and an advanced rate control module to generate the MPEG-2 results. We used the public JM-4.2 test model encoder to generate the H.264 results.In the tests, we used same GOP structure, with two B-type pictures between each P-P or I-P pictures. The GOP size was selected as 15. The H.264 encoder was configured to have five frames for inter motion search, 1/4 -pel motionvector resolution, context-based adaptive binary coding (CABAC) for symbol coding, and rate-distortion optimized mode decision. Both encoders used full search motion estimation with same search range that is 16 £ 16 for both PandB-type pictures. In H.264 simulations, constant quantization parameter values of 26, 28, 31, 36, and 41 were used to cover a practical range of low to moderately high bit rates. For MPEG- 2, the bit rates were chosen such as the encoded video visual qualities (PSNR) are close to the corresponding H.264 video streams.

For each sequence, rate-quality curves are produced. Fig shows the rate-quality curves for CAROUSEL and FLOWER GARDEN sequences, respectively. For each sequence, the coding gain of H.264 over MPEG-2 is estimated by averaging the bit savings for each simulation point on the rate-quality curves. The coding gains of H.264 over MPEG-2 are summarized in table 1 and 2 for each of the sequences in set-1 (CCIR-601 format) and set-2 (CIF format), respectively. The H.264 encoder achieves an average of 49:3% coding gain over MPEG-2.

6.2 Comparison of H.264 and H.263 baseline encoders

H.263 is commonly used for low-delay and low to medium bit-rate applications such as video conferencing. We do not use B-type pictures in both the H.263 and the H.264 encoders to satisfy the low delay requirements. We used the public H.263 codec by Telenor to produce the baseline H.263 encoding results. For the H.263 baseline encoder, advanced prediction and syntax-based arithmetic coding options were turned on. For both encoders, the first picture was encoded as I-type, and the remaining frames are encoded as P-type.The H.264 encoder was configured to have five frames for inter motion search, 1 4 -pel motion vector resolution, context-based adaptive binary coding (CABAC) for symbol coding, and rate-distortion optimized mode decision. The sequences chosen for this comparison are from set two and three.

The average sequence bit rates and PSNR values of encoding for each sequence are collected using constant quantization parameter values of 21, 26, 31, and 41 for H.264 and 8, 15, 20, and 33 for H.263. These parameters correspond to a range of low to moderately high bit rates for low latency applications. Table 6.1 and 6.2 show the coding gains obtained by the H.264 encoder over the H.263 encoder for CIF and QCIF sequences, respectively. H.264 achieves an average of 49:2% gain for the selected five CIF sequences at 30 fps, and 45:6% gain for the selected 12 QCIF sequences at 15 fps. The Figure 6.1 and 6.2 shows Rate-PSNR curves of CIF PARIS & QCIF FOREMAN sequence encoded using H.264, H.263 Baseline and H.263 CHC encoders.

Table 6.1:Coding gain of H.264 over H.263 Baseline
Profile for various CIF sequences.

Sequence	Coding Gain
IRENE	53%
MOBILE&CALENDAR	58%
PARIS	42%
STUDENTS	45%
TEMPETE	41%
Average gain	49.2%

Table 6.2: Coding gain of H.264 over H.263 Baseline
Profile for various QCIF sequences.

Sequence	Coding Gain
AKIYO	51%
CAR PHONE	40%
CLAIRE	48%
COAST GUARD	38%
CONTAINER	41%
FOREMAN	42%
IRENE	50%
MISS AMERICA	44%
MOBILE&CALENDAR	48%
PARIS	56%
STUDENTS	52%
TEMPETE	37%
Average gain	45.6%

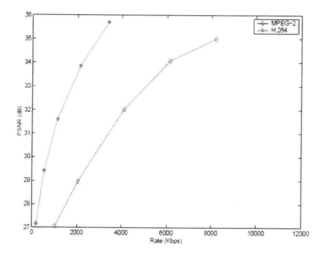

Figure 6.1:. Rate-PSNR curves of CIF PARIS sequence encoded
using H.264, H.263 Baseline and H.263 CHC encoders.

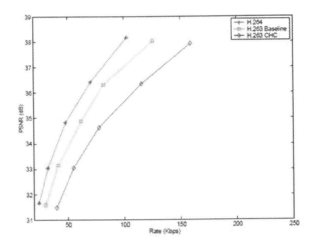

Figure 6.2: Rate-PSNR curves of QCIF FOREMAN sequence
encoded using H.264, H.263 Baseline and H.263 CHC encoders.

we presented an evaluation of the emerging H.264 video coding standard in terms of coding bit rate savings compared to existing most common video coding standards. We performed encoding tests at a wide range of rates for both low- and high-latency application.According to our test results,the future H.264 standard achieves 50% average coding gain over MPEG-2, 47% average coding gain over H.263 baseline, and 24% average coding gain over H.263 high profile encoders.

6.3 Comparison of h.264 with vp8

For the performance comparison, we utilized the _mpeg version of the initial VP8 release and the H.264 SVC refer- ence software encoder (ver. 9.19.9). For both encoders, we furthermore used only the basic encoding settings without additional optimizations. A GoP length of 16 frames was used with only I and P frames, resulting in a GoP pattern of IPPPPPPPPPPPPPPP for both encoders. We used the same quantization scale settings for I and P frames in both encoder settings, namely 10, 16, 22, 24, 28, 34, 38, 42, and 48. All encoded video sequences were in the CIF (352_288) resolution. We illustrate the different produced video bitrates for VP8 and H.264 SVC with comparable average video sequence PSNR values as in Equation 5 (approx. difference of 0.3 dB) on a two-GoP level (32 frames). We observe that overall, the two diffrent encodings follow the same trends in terms of the resulting bitrate, but with H.264 SVC being significantly lower for most of the encoded video. we illustrate the video bitrates on a two-GoP level for VP8 and H.264 SVC encodings of the *Terminator* video sequence with both encodings at a quantization scale setting of 28 and H.264 SVC having an approximately 51 kbps higher bitrate overall and a 1.66 dB higher average PSNR. We observe that both encodings exhibit a fairly sim- ilar behavior of the encoded video data bitrate over time. We note, however, that the H.264 SVC encoded video hasoverall slightly more pronounced 'peaks' of the encoded traffic, which attributes to the higher overall bitrate of the en-coding, but also has periods where the traffic produced is slightly lower than for VP8.The differences in the encodedbitrates we observe here in turn must be attributed to the individual encoder's e_ciency to encode different types of content. e.g.. high or low motion.

Rate-Distortion

Initial performance evaluation for video codecs typically investigates the rate-distortion performance, i.e., the video quality (distortion) as a function of the bitrate. We illus- trate the rate-distortion (RD) curves for the three evaluated video sequences *Sony Demo* and *Die Hard*, in Figures 6.3 & 6.4, respectively. We observe for all encod- ings the typical logarithmic increase of the PSNR quality as the bitrate increases. For the *Sony Demo* video sequence, we observe the smallest difference in PSNR values for similar bitrate values, with the average PSNR value produced by H.264 SVC outperforming the one obtained for VP8 by approximately 1{2 dB. For the *Die Hard* and *Terminator* video sequences, this spread is larger at approximately 3{4 dB. Overall. we note that the quality and bandwidth rangesproduced by VP8 are signi_cantly smaller than those produced by H.264 SVC and content-dependent.}

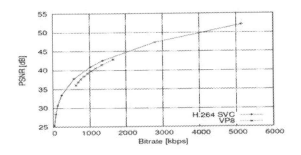

Figure 6.3: Rate-Distortion (RD) for the Sony Demo video sequence

Additionally,we note that the performance in terms of average PSNR values obtained for our evaluated long video sequences for a given bitrate are overall significantly smaller for the VP8 encoded videos.

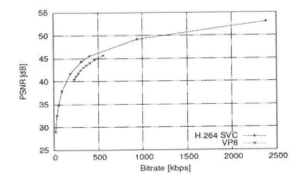

Figure 6.4: Rate-Distortion (RD) for the *Die Hard* video sequence.

6.4 Performance comparison of Dirac, Theora and H.264

In this section, Dirac and Theora are compared to each other performance-wise, and to Motion JPEG-2000 and H.264 as reference codecs and international state-of-the-art video compression standards (ISO/ IEC, 2001; ITU-T, 2003).To the author's knowledge, only a single independent evaluation of Dirac has been undertaken previously (Onthriar et al., 2006), where the authors found that H.264 outperforms the at that time emerging Dirac both in PSNR and SSIM value, especially at low bit rates. Theora remains untested in that respect. All encoders are operated in rate distortion optimization (RDO) mode or near RDO mode (if provided) and identical or near identical parameter sets required for fair codec comparisons. The involved motion compensation implies 250 P- or B-frames between I-frames and a single pass.

To assess the quality of Dirac 2.1.0, the version 0.9.1 of the reference implementation is used, which complies with the standard. The encoder is quality controlled by setting a quality factor similar to that of the JPEG standard. Near RDO is accomplished by requiring a full ME search with an area of 32×32 pixels. Concerning Theora I, version 0.19 of the reference implementation with the name libtheora is used.The software is quality controlled like Dirac with a quality parameter and is operated in RDO mode. For compressing video material compliant with H.264, the implementation named x264 is used.

The encoder is rate controlled but operated without any particular RDO due to a lack of such an option. Two B-frames are inserted between two P-frames, for which the ME process is based on a single reference frame. The search area is of the size 32 square pixels and has a hexagonal form. All video sequences used in the experiment comprise 8bpp image material and a YUV color space with 4:2:0 subsampling. AKIYO is a 300-frame headandshoulder sequence in QCIF resolution with little motion, MOBILE has SD/PAL resolution and consists of 220 frames with a moderate amount of motion, while CREW comprises HD 720p material with flashing effects.

Compression Ratio Test

Figure 6.5 and 6.6 shows a comparison of how Dirac and H.264 perform in compression. Compression is linked to bitrate. When there is high compression there is less bitrate and vice versa.This can be easily seen in Figure where the QCIF compression curve is near enough the inverse of the QCIF bitrate curve. Dirac achieves slightly higher compression ratios for lower bitrates than H.264. The compression achieved by Dirac out performs H.264, however this is only until a limit (approximately QF 10). Figures 6.5 and 6.6 follow the same trend whereby Dirac achieves better compression upto to Quality Factor 10 thereafter H.264 provides better compression. Again the CBR feature within H.264 has a great advantage, as H.264 can be seen to attempt to constrain its bitrate which in turn affects it compression.

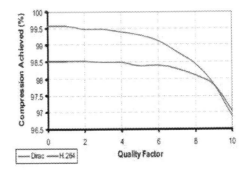

Figure 6.5: Compression ratio comparison of Dirac and H.264 for "Container" QCIF sequence

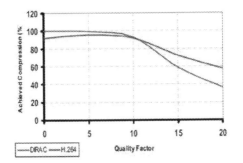

Figure 6.6: Compression ratio comparison for "Riverbed" HD sequence[269]

Theora is obviously designed for low to moderatebit rates. The container overhead is measured to be around 1% and is hence without influence on the final result. The efficiency of the involved implementations is measured in Table 6.3.[270]The respective software is invoked 20 times on a single general-purpose CPU with2:2GHz clock frequency, and the CPU time needed for encoding (in seconds) is averaged over all runs. This comparison has to be interpreted with care, as implementations like the one for Dirac are for a proof of concept only and not optimized for speed. However, the comparison serves as a pointer for a rough assessment of the encoders' complexity.

Table 6.3: Implementation efficiency, in fps.

sequence	Dirac	Theora	H.264
Akiyo	21	319	323
Mobile	2	9	13
Crew	0.03	0.3	8

The Dirac implementation appears to be the most inefficient software of the three measured implementations. Dirac's frame processing frequency is lowest in all cases, while the Theora and H.264 implementations are alternately best. However, it is of advantage that the processing frequency of Dirac's software is almost constant at varying bit rates, or in other words, its standard deviation sDirac is much smaller than 1. The standard deviation sTheora equals roughly 31, 1, and 0.07 with AKIYO, MOBILE, and CREW, respectively, and sH.264 is roughly equal to 49, 5, and 2, respectively. Summarizing, the frame processing frequency of Theora's implementation varies most.

It is concluded that Theora and H.264, which both deploy a transform instead of a filter bank like Dirac, can be operated much faster than the latter mentioned codec, despite the lifting structure as described in the Dirac specification. Dirac is close to real-time performance with QCIF-size video, while Theora and H.264 are way above this requirement. Neither of the mentioned codecs is capable of encoding in real time with SD-size video or larger (i.e., without additional implementation optimization and without extra hardware). Concerning Dirac, it should be mentioned that a high-performance implementation named Schr"odinger is being developed, and that specialized hardware exists for coding of HD signals in real time (Borer, 2007).

A visual comparison of all involved codecs at a very low bit rate reveals significant artifacts with both Dirac and Theora[271]. Fig. 6.7& Fig.6.8 shows a single decoded frame of the AKIYO & CREW video. All videos were encoded as described previously. The bit rates of Theora and H.264 are 17:8Kbps and 17:0Kbps, respectively, while the for the reference

SELVARAJ SARAVANAN

implementationlowest possible bit rate with Dirac is 67:2Kbps. It can easily be seen that, despite the significant higherbit rate, Dirac is the codec which performs worst, i.e. which introduces much more compression artifacts than the two competing codecs. The artifacts are mainly ringing along edges and blurred areas, which can be attributed to the use of a filter bank instead of a transform as with Theora and H.264.With Theora, the decoder outputs a slightly blurred picture when compared to H.264, and also minor blocking can be observed (in the women's face). Dirac and Theora yield 26:5dB and 30:5dB with the frame of concern, respectively, whereas H.264 achieves a PSNR of 34:3dB. Here, the decoded picture is slightly blurred compared to the original, but no blocking artifacts are found, despite the approach of block-based MC and a block-based transform.The explanation lies in the good performance of H.264's in-loop deblocking filter, which obviously outperforms the filter employed in Theora.

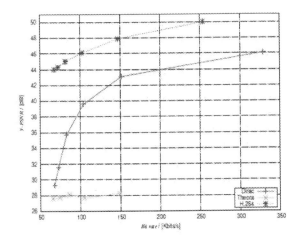

Figure 6.7: RD comparison for AKIYO (QCIF).

Note finally that, while the visual comparison (exemplified by a single frame) suggests that Theora is superior to Dirac at very low bit rates, the RD points in Figure 6.8 are averaged over the entire sequence.The Table 6.4 gives the Comparison of H.264, VC-1, AVS china, Dirac and Table 6.5 explains the Basic features of International video coding standards.

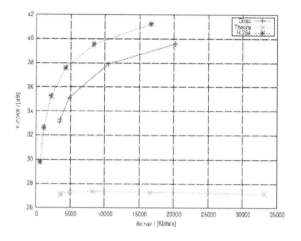

Figure 6.8: RD comparison for CREW (HD)

Table 6.4: Comparison of H.264, VC-1, AVS china, Dirac

Algorithmic Element	H.264 (MPEG-4 AVC)	SMPTE VC-1 (WMV 9)	AVS China Part 2	Dirac
Entropy coding	CAVLC, CABAC	Adaptive VLC	2D variable length coding.	Arithmetic coding
Transform	integer DCT, Hadamard	integer DCT	DCT	Wavelet transform

Table 6.5: Basic features of International video coding standards

	MPEG-1 (1993)	MPEG-2 (1995)	MPEG-4 (2000)	H.261 (1993)	H.263 (1993)	H.264/MPEG-4 AVC (2002)
Transform	8x8 DCT	8x8 DCT	8x8 DCT	8x8 DCT	8x8 DCT	4x4
MC Block Size	16x16	16x16 8x8	8x8,16x6	16x16	8x8,16x16	16x16,16x8,8x8 8x4,4x4
MC Accuracy	_Pel	_Pel	_Pel	1_Pel	_Pel	1/8_Pel
Additional Motion Prediction modes	B_Frames	B_Frames Interlace	B_Frames Interlace GMC (Globbal MC) -SPRITE Coding	-	B_Frames	B_Frames _Long Term Frame ,memory -in loop deblocking filter CAVLC/CABAC

Table 6.6: Encoder Operating System Support

Codec	Mac OS X	other Unix &Unix-like	Windows
3ivx	Yes	Yes	Yes
Blackbird	Yes	Yes	Yes
Cinepak	Yes	No	Yes
DivX	Yes	No	Yes
FFmpeg	Yes	Yes	Yes
RealVideo	Yes	Yes	Yes
Schrödinger (Dirac)	Yes	Yes	Yes
Sorenson Video 3	Yes	No	Yes
Theora	Yes	Yes	Yes
x264	Yes	Yes	Yes
Xvid	Yes	Yes	Yes
Elecard	No	No	Yes

Table 6.7: Network Bit Rate vs. Compression Ratio[273]

Frame Rates		Image compression		Video compression		Adv.Video Compression	
		Compressed10:1		Compressed30:1		Compressed60:1	
Network	Kbps	Frames/second		Frames/ second		Frames/ second	
GSM Digital cellular	14	1	7	1	2	1	1
56K Modem(PSTN)	56	1	2	2	1	4	1
DSLor Cable Up-link	128	1	1	4	1	8	1
Cellphone Tv	300	3	1	9	1	18	1
DSL Downlink	768	8	1	23	1	45	1
Wireless LAN (802.11)	11,000	109	1	326	1	652	1
		Ex: JPEG		Ex:MPEG-4		Ex:H.264	

The Table 6.6 dicuss the encoder support for the video coding standards and Table 6.7 gives the comparison of Network Bit Rate and Compression Ratio. In the video compressuion research,Marko Hebar and Peter Planinšič included the latest objective and subjective quality assessment of digital video sequences encoded by using the standard older H.261, H.263+ and newer H.264 codec. Experiments show clearly that when assessing a high quality, high definition and high frame rate video sequence, the human visual system fails to assess small quality degradation and for which reason assessment must be done using objective methods.The Table 6.8 gives the Maximum theoretical frame rates for transmitting generic VHS-quality digital video data and Table 6.9 Compares the video coding standards.

Table 6.8: Maximum theoretical frame rates for transmitting generic VHS-quality digital video data (352x240 frames) using various networks and compression techniques

Video Format	Y size	Color sampling	Frame rate (Hz)	Raw data rate(Mbps)
HDTV Over air,Cable, sateelite,MPEG-2 video,20-45 Mbps				
SMPTE 296M	1280x720	4:2:0	24p/30p/60p	265/332/664
SMPTE 295M	1920x1080	4:2:0	24p/30p/60I	597/746/746
Video production,MPEG-2,15-50Mbps				
BT.601	720x480/576	4:4:4	60/50I	249
BT.601	720x480/576	4:2:2	60/50I	178
High quality video distribution (DVD, SDTV),Mpeg-2,4-10Mbps				
BT.601	720x480/576	4:2:0	60/50I	124
Intermediate quality video distribution (VCD,WWW),MPEG1,1.5Mbps				
SIF	352x240/288	4:2:0	30p/25p	30
Video conferencing over ISDN/Internet,H.261,H.263/MPEG-4/128-328Kbps				
CIF	352x288	4:2:0	30p	37
Video telephony over wired/wired Modem,H.263/MPEG4,20-64Kbps				
QCIF	176x144	4:2:0	30P	9.1

Table 6.9:Comparison of standards [273]

Standard	Application	Video format	Raw data rate	Compress data rate
H.230 (H.261)	Video conferencing over ISDN	CIF QCIF	37Mbps 9.1Mbps	>=384Kbps >=64Kbps
H.323 (H.263)	Video conferencing over Internet	4 CIF/CIF/ QCIF		>=64Kbps
H.324 (H.263)	Video over phone lines/wireless	QCIF	9.1Mbps	>=18Bps
MPEG-1	Video distribution on CD/WWW	CIF	30Mbps	1.5Mbps
MPEG-2	Video Distribution on DVD/digital TV	CCIR601 4:2:0	128Mbps	3-10Mbps
MPEG-4	Multimedia distribution over Inter/Intranet	QCIF/CIF		28-102Kbps
GA-HDTV	HDTV Broadcasting	SMPTE296/295	<=700Mbps	18—45Mbps

In our experiments, the PSNR method was used for being a well-known and widely used method. The newest SSIM method was also used for obtaining more correlated results with human visual assessment, because the structural information from the images is considered in evaluation.The SSIM method at these bit rates more agree with the subjective grades than the PSNR method. The codec H.264 outperformed both the older standard codecs H.261 and H.263+. The codec encodes video almost at half of the size of that obtained by the H.263+ codec and consumes four times more processing time. The new generation codec H.264 has therefore a great potential for future use, from new mobile phones to HDTV video and even digital cinema. However, the capabilities of this codec are at this stage not yet fully exploited because of to low processing power currently available.

6.5 Comparison of standards - Experimental results

In general, it is essential to include critical sequences, especially when interpreting results,which are impossible to extrapolate from non critical sequences. The sequences "Foreman" and sequence from the movie Matrix Revolutions were chosen for our assessment experiment. The sequence "Foreman" is in resolution 352x288, the number of frames 300, color space YUV 4:2:0, source uncompressed progressive. The sequence Matrix is from DVD "Matrix Revolutions" including frames 120252 to 120552, coded in Motion Pictures Expert Group 2 (MPEG-2) known as H.262 [3], aspect ratio 2,40:1, NTSC, number of frames 300 of half the NTSC resolution. This sequence Matrix is very difficult to code. The main reasons for the difficulty are frequently brightness changes, very quick motion and frequent changes of scene.

The Table 6.10 gives subjective assessment of video sequences.With H.261,the sequences were encoded with no annoying impairment over an average bit rate of 2000 kbit/s. The assessment results show that H.261 and H.263+ failed to code the "Matrix" sequence well under 2000 kbit/s and the impairments became annoying or even unwatchable.

Table 6.10: Subjective assessment of video sequences

Average bit rate (kbit/s)	512	1024	2048	4096
Video sequence foreman	Grade	Grade	Grade	Grade
H.261	2,13	3,18	4,14	4,47
H.263+	3,04	3,64	4,32	4,53
H.264	3,82	4,35	4,56	4,82
Video sequence matrix	Grade	Grade	Grade	Grade
H.261	1,12	1,82	3,25	3,67
H.263+	1,47	2,26	4,01	4,28
H.264	2,49	3,24	4,29	4,45

In Figure 6.9. Every graph shows sequences coded H.261, H.263+ and H.264 through different bit rate coding. The left column shows grades of the SDSCE method. The middle column shows result of the PSNR method. The right column shows result of the SSIM method.In Figure 8.Upper row shows the capture from the sequence Matrix Revolutions coded with H.261, H.263+ and H.264 at 512 kbit/s and Lower row shows Capture from the reference sequence "Foreman" coded with H.261, H.263+ and H.264 at 512 kbit/s. Results of the objective measurement using the PSNR and SSIM methods show that, for the test sequence "Foreman" coded over approximately average bit rates of the 1024 kbit/s with, H261, and H263+, there is no perceptual gain in quality. At high-bit rates, both objective methods gave similar results.

Finally, we can see that codecs H.261 and H.263+ are quite good for the video sequence "Foreman" but are far from capabilities of the new generation codec H.264.

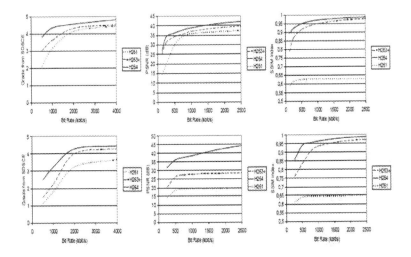

Figure 6.9: Upper row graphs show results from the "Foreman" video sequence. The lower row shows results from the "Matrix" video sequence.

The very complex sequence "Matrix" shows that old codecs H.261, H.263+ were unable to efficiently encode it in the quality-bit rate sense, because of the intensive motions and high-speed changes in the scene. All sequences coded with H.264 had low loss in quality for the human visual system. Codec was used in the main profile with single pass encoding. The new H.264 codec has high encoding efficiency, but needs four times more processing time than H.263+. The codec encodes video almost at half of the size of that obtained by the H.263+ codec and consumes four times more processing time.

The new generation codec H.264 has therefore a great potential for future use, from new mobile phones to HDTV video and even digital cinema.The Figure 6.10 shows the comparison of H.261,H.263+ and H.264 using Matrix and Foreman sequences at 512 kbit/s.

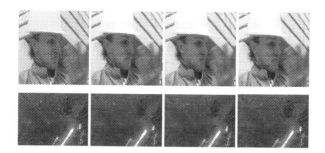

Figure 6.10: Lower row: capture from the sequence Matrix Revolutions coded with H.261, H.263+ and H.264 at 512 kbit/s. Upper row: Capture from the reference sequence "Foreman" coded with H.261, H.263+ and H.264 at 512 kbit/s.

we investigated the behavior of three major streaming applications — RealPlayer, Windows MediaPlayer,and Quicktime. We chose a straightforward test environment as a basis for comparison. It could be characterized by similar network conditions in all tests and particularly no traffic artifact caused by uncontrollable influences from the network. While it did not have the greatest throughput, no streaming media application lost less than Quicktime. We believe the loss ratio to be the best indicator of how closely a mechanism is able to follow the available bandwidth; from this point of view RealPlayer and Windows MediaPlayer must be judged as poorly performing.Our data concur with our subjective impression: the video stream looked best in all cases with Quicktime.They are evaluated these major streaming applications within our straightforward test environment.

The Table 6.11 gives used streaming software.It uses the same video clip (a trailer of Matrix Reloaded) for all tests in order to obtain comparable results. The original movie was encoded with DivX 5.02 using a bit rate of 863 kbps. We chopped the video to 2 minutes and saved it as an uncompressed AVI file. RealPlayer and Windows MediaPlayer required the stream to be saved in different scaled-down versions in order to be able to react to bandwidth fluctuations.We tried to keep all settings as close to their default values as possible and selected unaltered original templates for those video streams (variants with 43, 58, 282 and 548 kbps for Windows MediaPlayer and the templates 0 – 20 kbps, 20– 34 kbps,34– 225 kbps, 225– 450 kbps and above 450 kbps for RealPlayer). In the case of Quicktime, we activated the options prepare for Internet streaming, stream with control track and optimize control track for server. All servers and players were set to use UDP only.

Table 6.11: Used streaming software

Encoder	Server	Player
Real player		
Helix producer(v9.0.0.972)	Helix universal server basic(v9.03)	Real player(v10 Beta)
Windows media player		
Windows media Encoder (v9.0)	Helix universal server basic	Windows media player(v9.0)
Quick time		
Quick time player pro(vD-6.5)	Darwin streaming server(v5.0.1.1	Quick time player (vDE-6.5)

The Table 6.12 gives cumulative results of Real player,Windows media player and Quicktime player.The fact that the gap between the graph of the sender rate and the throughput of TCP overlap almost perfectly indicates that there was no loss. On the other hand, the streaming applications experienced loss with different magnitudes, whereby the number of lost packets in the RealPlayer and the Windows MediaPlayer setup is much higher than in the Quicktime.

Table 6.12: Cumulative results

Scenario with cross traffic	Sent (kb)	Received(kB)	Lost (KB)	Loss(%)
FTP Download				
no	13977.9	13977.9	0.0	0.00
Little	10433.0	10433.0	0.0	0.00
medium	8069.7	8069.7	0.0	0.00
heavy	6314.6	6303.7	10.8	0.17
burst	13833.8	13833.8	0.0	0.00
Real player				
no	8301.8	8301.8	0.0	0.00
little	5669.3	5546.4	122.9	2.17
Medium	3965.2	3414.7	550.4	13.88
heavy	4291.8	3172.1	1131.7	26.37
burst	4637.5	4637.5	0.0	0.00

CONCLUSION:

A growing number of video compression standards offer increasing compression efficiency and a wider variety of tools that can be tailored for specific end applications. JPEG and MPEG compression techniques will continue to be used for low-cost computer compression requirements and wherever editing is needed in professional television. MPEG-2 has become the international standard for video compression for any signals that are to be simply stored, distributed, and viewed. CDROMs are being developed employing MPEG-2 compression methods.

MPEG-2 has been adopted worldwide as the compression standard for satellite delivered DTH television and for future cable and digital terrestrial television (DTTV), including high-definition television (HDTV). H.264 is a huge step forward for not only the video surveillance world but for video compression in general. The ISO/IEC/MPEG ITU-T/VCEG AVC/H.264 standard is very successful video coding scheme because it reduces bit rate requirements by approximately 50% in comparison to MPEG-4 and H.263 standards.Ifeel H.264 is hugely important compression format for the security industry. The claims it makes about reduced bitrates are confirmed and we can say that the image quality is superior to MPEG-4 and even comes close to JPEG quality it's that good. H.264 will be a key differentiator between various system solutions and for those who choose to ignore this new standard.The H.264 standard with a wide range of tools and profiles defined for maintaining pristine quality.

Today's state of the art video compression such as H.264 and WMV9 deliver good quality at around 60:1 compression which represents about a 2ximprovement over the previous generation of video codecs. The proliferation of multiple standards and proprietary algorithms make it difficult to select one standard especially since hardware decisions are often made far in advance of the product deployment. Also, the growing trend toward networked connectivity means that many products will increasingly have to support more than one standard. As the number of standards that must be supported increases, there is a growing trend toward flexible media processors in digital video systems.

The newly introduced video codec VP8 is compared with H.264 in terms of bandwidth and video quality. While VP8 has the advantage of currently being license free, H.264 seems to over lower bandwidth usage and better video quality. In stark contrast to the announcement that VP8 would use half the bandwidth offfering twice the video quality compared to H.264, our findings show that H.264 outperforms VP8 in terms of rate-distortion performance by 1{4 dB for a given bit rate. VP 8 employs adaptive mixing strategy for creating Artificial reference frames which is aimed at providing improved coding efficiency for low-bit rate coding.Overall Dirac seems to be a very promising codec.According to BBC R&D the aim of Dirac was developed with not only performance be it compression ratio and perceptual quality at the forefront of its aim, but also its simplistic nature provides robustness which is a very beneficial feature; therefore to a certain extent Dirac has succeeded in its aim.

The SSIM indicates that H.264 is slightly greater improvement. However the question remains whether the enormous cost in royalty fees justify the additional increase in quality. The Dirac codec at low bit rates seems less stable than H.264It is stressed that the assessment is by no means exhaustive, but rather must be interpreted as a starting point for further research. The experiments showed that the reference system H.264 outperforms the two codecs significantly, both in the objective and the subjective/visual evaluation.

The variation in the bitrate can be achieved by changing the QP or QF for H.264 and dirac respectively. In an another research cumulative results of Real player,Windows media player and Quicktime playerare discussed. On streaming applications RealPlayer and Windows MediaPlayer must be judged as poorly performing than that of Quicktime player.The DCT gives higher performance compared to that of Quicktime player.We performed encoding tests at a wide range of rates for both low- and high-latency application. According to our test results, the H.264 standard achieves 50% average coding gain over MPEG-2, 47% average coding gain over H.263 baseline, and 24% average coding gain over H.263 high profile encoders. so H.264 adoption will move forward there.The H.264 is to be the video format of choice for the full range of applications it promises to support, it must have a significant impact on the digital video industry.So I am going to research on the Topic named High performance and Low power architecture for H.264.The next section deals with different types of Transform and their comparison. From the Literature review,The Transform block is a major part which determines most of the performance and power required for the architecture of H.264.Hence improving the transform will increase the performance and lower the power.

7

SHORT SURVEY ON H.264 BLOCKS

1. High Performance Architecture of the double – mode Binary – Coder for H.264 AVC

This paper presents binary coder which is based on pipeline arrangement. The architecture saves a considerable amount of hardware resources since two coding modes share the same logic and storage elements. It describes the architecture design for the high profile H.264/Avc binarization. The design supports all chroma formats, MB adaptive frame/field coding and the 8x8 transform. It explains the algorithm, architecture and comparison in terms of throughput and resource utilization. The binarization unit embeds four pipeline stages. The pipeline stage increases the throughput by about 40% where as enhanced bypass mode improves it by up to 20% for typical video sequence. The architecture enables to process two regular symbols and bypass mode symbols in the same clock cycle, and it is the most efficient in terms of throughput/resources ratio.

2. Fast motion estimation for H.264/AVC in walsh – Hadamard domain

This paper explains the Fast Walsh Search in Variable Block Size (FWS-VBS). It performs motion estimation in Walsh – Hadamard (WH) domain. It uses Partial Sum –of-Absolute Difference(PSAD) to eliminate most mismatches in the early stage so as to reduce computations. The adaptive threshold scheme which determines suitable threshold for each target block. The authors proposed a method called mea n rejection to reduce number of remaining candidates by half. The candidate is discarded if its PSAD is larger than a threshold. The SAD for 4x4 block is Number of SAD(NSAD)=16(15+16+32)+25=1033. The maximum search distance is 16 with full pixel accuracy. The rate – distortion performance of FWS-VBS is very close to full search but the computation time reduces by 90% It is faster than all fast Variable Block Size Motion Estimation (VSBME) algorithm.

3. Energy minimization of probable video communication devices based on power – rate distortion optimization

This paper explains Power- Rate- Distortion(P-R-D) optimization Which minimize the energy for delay tolerant video communication over portable devices. The power is highly coupled with the rate enabling us to trade bits for joules and perform energy minimization through optimum bit allocation. The P-R-D models are developed and on – line resource allocation is performed for real- time video encoding. The P-R-D model has two major parameters λ and σ^2 The authors evaluated resource allocation and energy minimization. The energy saving ratio at different variance of scene activity is plotted.It achieves encoding energy savings of 30% - 50% where per-bit energy cost of wireless transmission is relatively low.

4. H.264 Based compression of Bayer pattern video sequences

This power presents two methods for compressing Bayer pattern Color Filter Array (CFA) Video prior to demosaicking. In the first method, the CFA video is compressed using 4:2:2 sampling and in the second method modified Motion Compensation (MC) scheme is used. This paper explains demosaicking, aliasing and pixel rearranging & modified MC scheme. The bit rate at which the proposed methods outperforms demosaicking first approach. The advantage of first method is easier to incorporate into new applications. The bit-rate reduction achieved relative to range from 68% to 83% for the first method and from 76% to 90% for the second method using modified MC. Only few interpolations operations are required in both methods.

5. Case study of Reliability – Aware and Low – Power design

This power explains reliability characterization model and Novel design methodology and low-power design. Low power and reliable SRAM cell design, reliable Dynamic Voltage Scaling(DVS) algorithm design, voltage island partitioning and floor planning in System-On-a-Chip (SOC) were used as a case studies.The SRAM cells of different types will be discussed and it is experimented using transistor level and circuit level. The comparison of seven different SRAM cells designs under two temperatures are tabulated. The reliability enhancement and tradeoff problem is presented. The results of two algorithms on SOC are tabulated. The reliability-aware low power design will be the methodology for low power system design.

6. Optimal Post process/In-Loop filtering of Improved Video compression performance

This paper presents optimal filter approach to minimize and the filtered reconstructed frame. It aims to improve the overall compression quality in an optimal way by minimizing the error. The encoder multiplexes the filter co-efficients into the bit-stream for decoder access. A total of 25 filter co-efficients need to be encoded per frame as side information. The unrolled implementation of iterative preconditioned conjugate gradients algorithm is implemented. It improves the Peak Signal to Noise Ratio(PSNR) performance by more than 1 dB for low – bit rates and 0.5 dB for higher bit rates for foreman sequences at lower computational decoder complexity. In-loop optimal filtering shows in overall superior performance compared to post-process filtering.

7. High performance VLSI implementation for H.264 Inter/ Intra prediction

This paper describes hardware implementation of Motion Compensation and reconstruction (MCR) module of H.264. The MCR module takes the prediction modes and its parameters as input from bit-stream parser and residual data from Inverse discrete cosine Transform (IDCT) module. IN the proposed design inter prediction has fetched unit, a compute unite and a cache. The author assign 9 cycles for fetch unit and 4 cycles for compute unit.Intra prediction has three phases.1) init phase 2) compute phase 3) final phase. In the final phase, data passed on to deblocking filler. They used UMC [3] library in 0.13µ technology. MCR requires 95597 gates at 250 MHZ requires 128 K biks of RAM. The maximum no of cycles required per macro block is 172 and minimum is 100 cycles.

8. Low –power partial distortion sorting fast motion estimation algorithms and VLSI implementations

This paper presents low power oriented fast Motion Estimation (ME) algorithms. The Partial distortion sorting (PDS) and Local PDS (LPDS) were discussed. The idea of proposed PDS algorithm is to disable search points which have larger partial distortions and keep the smaller ones. It is realized in 1-D systolic array in verilog Hardware description language (HDL) and synthesized in synopsys. Full search Block Matching Algorithm (FSBMA) is used because of its regularity and stable performance. The PDS and LPDS is implemented and compared with FSBMA. The PDS algorithm can reduce 33.3% power consumption with 4.05k gates extra hardware cost and LPDS can reduce 37.8% power with 1.73k gates hardware overhead.

9. Priority-Based heading one detector in H.264/AVC decoding

This paper presents priority-based one detector for Exp-Golomb/context-Adaptive Variable Length Coding (CAVLC) decoding of H.264. The key idea is to exploit the statistical characteristics of the heading one position among various code words. It describes exponential Golomb codes. CAVLC entropy coding, system C modeling and proposed architecture. Output is Compared with JM 9.4 software to verify correct function. The Statistical position of 1 will be discussed. It is most likely around second input bit (position=1). The power consumption is achieved by blocking some sub-bocks.It achieves more than 3 times power reduction while maintaining area & speed performance. The authors suggest the effective method to reduce power by exploiting statistical characteristics.

10. A Novel High performance Architecture for H.264/AVC deblocking filtering

This paper proposes novel deblocking filler architecture based on two identical filtering units, allowing simultaneous on-the-fly filtering of vertical and horizontal edges. It also consists of temporal buffer, RAM neighbors and Boundary Strength(BS) units. All the data paths are 32 bits (4 pixels) wide. This architecture takes less clock cycles to filter an MB with lower on-chip memory requirements. The filtering process consumes 104 cycles, with foul additional clock cycles required to transfer the last transposed block and two cycles to register at the output of filter. So, total cannot be

110 cycles to filter 1 MB. The proposed architecture is able to process an HDTV -1080P (1920x1080 pixels @ 30 fps) video sequence at a frequency as low as 36.45MHZ without increase in design hardware cost.

11. A novel algorithm and architecture of combined direct 2-D transform and quantization for H.264

This power proposes direct 2D transform and quantization architectures for H.264. The four blocks are direct 2D-Integer transform, direct 2D forward-Hadamard transform, AC quantization and DC quantization. The proposed architecture is designed to perform pipelined operations. It computes direct transform with just additions/subtractions and a minimal number of shifts, but no multiplications. It also reduces memory resources and improves the throughput. It increases the data processing rate and eliminates transform multiplication and transpose memory. This architecture is implemented in Altera cyclone II and synthesized with simplify pro. It takes 20 clock cycles to process a 4x4 block of data, 2 clock cycles for integer transform & 7 clock cycles for quantization are needed.

12. Algorithmic and architectural design for real-time and power efficient Retinex image/Video processing

This paper presents some effective image enhancement techniques based on the separation of the illumination and reflectance components of the image. The dynamic range of input image is controlled by applying a suitable non-linear function to the illumination, while the details enhanced by processing the reflectance. After algorithimic optimization, the design of Application-Specific Instruction set Processor(ASIP) has been addressed. It will be synthesized with Synopsys in a 0.18 μm. 1.8v CMOS standard-cell technology. The maximum achievable clock frequency is 100MHz, which permits maximum throughput of about $1.9x10^6$pixels/s. When compared to DSP implementation, the ASIP achieves best trade-off between performance, power consumption and flexibility of Retinex filtering class.

13. A Wavelet VQ system for real-time video compression

This paper presents image compression using Bidirectional Discrete Wavelet Transformation(2D-DWT), and vector quantization (VQ) has been developed and implemented on an FPGA device. The 2D-DWT works in a non-separable fashion with distributed control to compute two resolution levels. Wavelet coefficients are quantized using multi-resolution code book and entropy coded. VQ is carried out by Self-Organizing Feature Map(SOFM) neural nets Book(MRCB), 2D-dWT stage, SOFM structure and statistical encoder. The result achieves real-time performance when coding 512x512 gray scale image frames at a rate of 30fps. The PSNR is 34.78 dB inside the training set and 31.28dB outside at a compression rate of 0.62 bpp.

14. Multiplier less and fully pipelined JPEG compression soft IP targeting FPGAS

This paper presents the design of soft Intellectual Property (IP) of a high performance FPGA based JPEG compressor. The JPEG architecture design is thoroughly detailed in this paper. An IP is a reusable hardware block that can be used in many different designs. JPEG compression involves 2D-DCT, quantization and entropy coding. The input image is divided into 8x8 matrices of pixels. The quantization was designed as a pipeline of four stages and the latency is of 4 clock cycles. The JPEG soft IP when mapped to FLEX 10KE FPGA, reaches a minimum period of 25.1 ns, allowing a processing rate of 39.8M pixels per second. This is higher than Standard – Definition TeleVision(SDTV) frames with 720x480 pixels. This device is able to process 39.8 millions of pixels per second. This performance allows procession of 115 SDTV frames per second, a real time throughput in video applications.

15. Adaptive block – size transform based on extended integer 8x8/4x4 Transforms for H.264/AVC

The 8x8 transform is extended from the original 4x4 transform and it is applied as Adaptive block – size transform (ABT) to reduce the complexity efficiently. The intermediate results can be strictly limited within 16 bits. It explains the extension transform. The scale matrices of core transforms are merged into the quantizer. The scale and quantization can be done together. As a result, the transform units and storage resources can be effectively saved in both encoder and decoder. This method needs fewer transforms but also saves more storage resources. It saves 1920 bytes storage resources for encoder and 960 bytes for decoder.

16. Zero Quantized DCT prediction technique for video encoding

The paper presents Zero Quantized DCT(ZQDCT) model is proposed to skip redundant DCT, Q, IQ & IDCT computations. The efficient model is presented to predict ZQDCT co-efficients before DCT and Q. In addition, fast DCT/inverse DCT algorithms are presented. The DCT coefficients in blank positions are predicted as ZQDCT coefficients whose calculations are skipped where as shadow ones are non-ZQDCT coefficients which require computations. The results shows that the proposed model reducing the computational complexity of DCT, Q, IQ & IDCT. The real time performance is better than previous models. The experimental results demonstrate that the analytical model can achieve higher coding efficiency without degrading video quality.

17. Low complexity deblocking method for DCT coded video signals

The paper presents an algorithm for the reduction of blocking artefacts in a block-based video coding. In smooth regions, it needs stronger filtering to improve visual quality and in non-smooth regions, the filter is applied to remove undesired artefacts. It includes three frequency related modes, one special mode and a refined mode. It describes overview of the algorithm and it explains all the modes.The Common Intermediate Format(CIF) comparison and PSNR is tabulated. The PSNR of proposed algorithm is lower than MPEG-4 by 0.05 to 0.1 dB. It demonstrate the elimination of blocking artefacts not only in the intra coded frames but also in inter-coded frames.Objective and Subjective imagequalities are both improved and the complexity is much lower than deblocking filters in MPEG-4 and H.264.

18. A variable block size motion estimation algorithm for rent – time H.264 video encoding

This paper explains the algorithm for enhancing the performance of H.264 video encoder. It is named as Variable Block Size-3D Recursive Search(VBS-3DRS). The algorithm uses the previous mode information and previous motion vector information in the current and preceding frames to determine the best motion vector and the mode for current macroblock. It is divided into two stages (i) Initial mode and motion vector selection (coarse search) (ii) Local search refinement (fine search). When a fine search is employed, there is a 1-9% reduction in bit-stream size over reference Full

Search(FS) and Fast Motion Estimation(FME) algorithms. The encoding time is 45-55% decreased compared to FME and 80-85% decreased when compared to FS reference algorithm. The complexity of software is reduced with the decrease in bit-stream size.

19. An improved H.246/AVC video encoding based on a new syntax element

This paper proposes the efficient coding method based on new single combined syntax element of mb-skip-run and mb-type. The length of each codeword in each category is 2K+2 bits. The symbols are assigned according to their probabilities. The 549 symbols are obtained using four test sequences: Container, Fore man, News and silent. The coding gain of MB type syntax data are up to about 23-55% for complex sequences or at low QP ranges. The proposed method removes many redundant bits describing 0 symbol of mb-skip-run occurring in complex sequences or low QP ranges. This method is simple to implement without degrading the image quality.

20. Applications and Improvement of H.264 in Medical video compression

This paper presents H.264 in medical video compression, and also presents hoe to improve the rate control algorithm. It explains Motion complexity measure (MC). H.264 rate control, perceptual, bit allocation and comparison between H.264 and MPEG-4 and H.264 rate control and proposed algorithm using experimental results. The proposed scheme estimating target bit at scene changes and high motions, and updating the Legrangian multiplier adaptively according to perceptual characteristics of the video contents.

8

TRANSFORM CODING

Transform coding constitutes a fundamental component of modern image/ video processing applications. Transform coding depends on the fact that pixels in an image exhibit a certain level of correlation with their neighboring pixels. Similarly in a video transmission system, adjacent pixels in successive frames are used to show very high correlation. Consequently, these correlations can be exploited to find the value of a pixel from its respective neighbors. A transformation is, therefore, defined to map this spatial (correlated) data into transformed (uncorrelated) coefficients. Clearly, the transformation should utilize the fact that the information content of an individual pixel is comparatively small i.e., to a large extent visual contribution of a pixel can found using its neighbors. The purpose of the source encoder is to exploit the redundancies in image data to offer compression. In other words, the source encoder reduces the entropy, which is none other than decrease in the average number of bits required to represent the image. On the converse, the channel encoder adds redundancy to the output of the source encoder in order to improve the reliability of the transmission.

8.1 Discrete Cosine Transform

Discrete Cosine Transform (DCT) is a mathematical tool which will have a lot of electronics applications, from audio filters to video compression hardware. A discrete cosine transform (DCT) expresses a chain of finitely many data points in terms of a sum of cosine functions fluctuating at different frequencies. [301]

DCT transforms the information from the time or space domains to the frequency domain, such that other tools and transmission media can be run or used more efficiently to reach application goals: compressed representation, fast transmission, memory savings, and so on. DCTs are essential to abundant applications in science and engineering, from lossy compression of audio and images(where small high-frequency components can be discarded), to spectral methods for the numerical solution of partial differential equations.

The use of cosine rather than sine functions is serious in these applications: for compression, it turns out that cosine functions are much more proficient (as explained below, fewer are needed to estimated a typical signal), whereas for differential equations the cosines express a particular choice of boundary conditions. In particular, a DCT is a Fourier-related transform analogous to the discrete Fourier transform (DFT), but using only real numbers. DCTs are comparable to DFTs of almost twice the length, working on real data with even symmetry (since the Fourier transform of a real and even function is real and even), where in some variants the input and/or output data are shifted by half a sample.

There are eight standard DCT variants, of which four are same. Like other transforms, the Discrete Cosine Transform (DCT) attempts to decorrelate the image data. After decorrelation, each transform coefficient can be encoded separately without losing compression effectiveness. This section describes the DCT and its important properties.

8.1.1 Properties of DCT

Discussions in the preceding sections have developed a mathematical base for DCT. However, the intuitive insight into its image processing application has not been presented. This section overviews (with examples) some properties of the DCT which are of particular value to image processing applications.

1.Decorrelation

As discussed previously, the principle advantage of image transformation is the deletion of redundancy between neighboring pixels. This leads to uncorrelated transform coefficients which can be encoded separately.

Let us consider our example from Figure 2 to overview the decorrelation characteristics of the 2-D DCT. Clearly, the amplitude of the autocorrelation after the DCT function is very small at all lags. Hence, it can be inferred that DCT exhibits excellent decorrelation properties.

2.Energy Compaction

efficiency of a transformation scheme can be directly measure by its capacity to pack input data into as few coefficients as possible. This allows the quantizer to remove coefficients with relatively small amplitudes without introducing visual distortion in the reconstructed image. DCT exhibits outstanding energy compaction for highly correlated images. Hence, from the preceding discussion it can be inferred that DCT renders excellent energy compaction for correlated images. Studies have shown that the energy compaction performance of DCT approaches optimality as image correlation approaches one i.e., DCT provides (almost) best possible decorrelation for such images.

3.Separability

The DCT transform equation **(4)** can be expressed as,

$$C(u,v) = \alpha(u)\alpha(v)\sum_{x=0}^{N-1}\cos\left[\frac{\pi(2x+1)u}{2N}\right]\sum_{y=0}^{N-1}f(x,y)\cos\left[\frac{\pi(2y+1)v}{2N}\right] \qquad (8.1)$$

for $u,v = 0,1,2,\ldots,N-1$.

This property, known as *separability*, has the principle benefit that $C(u, v)$ can be computed in two steps by consecutive 1-D operations on rows and columns of an image. This idea is graphically illustrated in Figure 8.1. The point of view presented can be identically applied for the inverse DCT calculation.

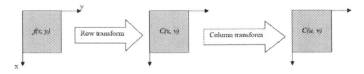

Figure 8.1: Computation of 2-D DCT using separability property.

4.Symmetry

Another look at the row and column operations in Equation reveals that these operations are functionally identical. Such a transformation is called a *symmetric transformation*. A divisible and symmetric transform can be expressed in the form [10]

$$T = AfA, \tag{8.2}$$

where A is an $N \times N$ symmetric transformation matrix with entries $a\ (i, j)$ given by

$$a(i,j) = \alpha(j) \sum_{j=0}^{N-1} \cos\left[\frac{\pi(2j+1)i}{2N}\right] \tag{8.3}$$

and f is the $N \times N$ image matrix. This is an tremendously useful property since it implies that the transformation matrix5 can be precompiled offline and then applied to the image thereby providing orders of magnitude improvement in calculation efficiency.

5.Orthogonality

In order to enlarge ideas presented in the previous section, let us denote the inverse transformation of 2.41 as,

$$f = A^{-1}TA^{-1}. \tag{8.4}$$

As discussed before, DCT basis functions are orthogonal. Thus, the inverse transformation matrix of A is equal to its transpose i.e. $A^{-1} = A^{t}$. Therefore, and in addition to its decorrelation characteristics, this property renders some decrease in the pre-computation difficulty.

Figure 8.2 and 8.3 shows the images reconstructed by performing the inverse DCT function on the quantized coefficients. Clearly, DCT (25%) introduces blurring effect in all images since only one-fourth of the total numbers of coefficients are used for restoration. However, DCT (50%) provides almost identical reconstruction in all images except Figure 8.2(Trees). The results of Figure 8.2 (Trees) can be explained by the fact that the image has a lot of uncorrelated high-frequency facts. Therefore, removal of high frequency DCT coefficients results in quality degradation.

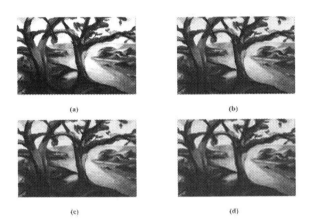

Figure 8.2: Inverse DCT of Trees; (a) DCT(100%); (b) DCT(75%); (c) DCT(50%);(d) DCT(25%).[291]

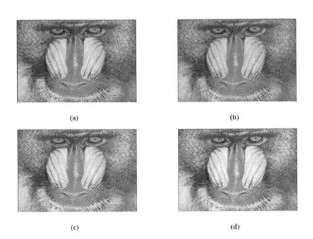

Figure 8.3: Inverse DCT of Baboon:a)DCT (100%) b)DCT(75%) c)DCT(50%) d)DCT(25%)

Nevertheless, DCT (75%) provides outstanding reconstruction for all images excluding the sine wave. This is a very appealing result since it suggests that based on the (heterogeneous) bandwidth requirements of receivers, DCT coefficients can be removed by the quantizer while rendering good enough quality.

The results presented in this file show that the DCT exploits inter pixel redundancies to render excellent decorrelation for most natural images. Thus, all (uncorrelated) transform coefficients can be encoded separately without compromising coding efficiency. In addition, the DCT packs energy in the low frequency regions. Therefore, some of the high frequency content can be removed without significant quality degradation. Such a (course) quantization system causes more reduction in the entropy (or average number of bits per pixel).Finally, it is concluded that consecutive frames in a video transmission show high temporal correlation (mutual information). This correlation can be engaged to improve coding efficiency. The aforementioned attributes of the DCT have led to its widespread exploitation in practically every image/video processing standard of the last decade, for example, JPEG (classical), MPEG- 1, MPEG-2, MPEG-4, MPEG-4 FGS, H.261, H.263 and JVT (H.26L). Nevertheless, the DCT still offers new research directions that are being explored in the current and upcoming image/video coding standards.

8.1.2 The One-Dimensional DCT

The most common DCT definition of a 1-D sequence of length N is

$$C(u) = \alpha(u)\sum_{x=0}^{N-1} f(x)\cos\left[\frac{\pi(2x+1)u}{2N}\right] \qquad (8.5)$$

for $u = 0,1,2,\ldots,N-1$. Similarly, the inverse transformation is defined as

$$f(x) = \sum_{u=0}^{N-1}\alpha(u)C(u)\cos\left[\frac{\pi(2x+1)u}{2N}\right] \qquad (8.6)$$

for $x = 0,1,2,\ldots,N-1$. In both equations (2.44) and (2.45)$\alpha(u)$ is defined as

$$\alpha(u) = \begin{cases} \sqrt{\dfrac{1}{N}} & for \quad u = 0 \\[2ex] \sqrt{\dfrac{2}{N}} & for \quad u \neq 0 \end{cases} \tag{8.7}$$

It is clear from (8.5) that for $u = 0, C(u = 0) = \sqrt{\dfrac{1}{N}} \sum_{x=0}^{N-1} f(x)$. Thus, the first

transform coefficient is the average value of the sample sequence. In literature, this value is referred to as the *DC Coefficient*. All other transform

coefficients are called the *AC Coefficients4*. The plot of $\sum_{x=0}^{N-1} \cos\left[\dfrac{\pi(2x+1)u}{2N}\right]$

for $N = 8$ and varying values of u is shown in Figure. In accordance with our previous observation, the first the top-left waveform ($u = 0$) renders a constant (DC) value, whereas, all other waveforms ($u = 1,2,...,7$) give waveforms at gradually more increasing frequencies. These waveforms are called the *cosine basis function*. Note that these basis functions are orthogonal. Hence, multiplication of any waveform in Figure 3 with another waveform followed by a summation over all sample points yields a zero (scalar) value, whereas multiplication of any waveform in Figure 3 with itself followed by a summation yields a constant (scalar) value. Orthogonal waveforms are self-governing, that is, none of the basis functions can be represented as a combination of other basis functions. If the input sequence has more than N sample points then it can be divided into sub-sequences of length N and DCT can be applied to these chunks separately. Here, a very important point to note is that in each such calculation the values of the basis function points will not change. Only the values of $f(x)$ will change in each sub-sequence. This is a very important property, since it shows that the basis functions can be pre-computed offline and then multiplied with the sub-sequences. This reduces the number of mathematical operations (i.e., multiplications and additions) thereby exposé computation efficiency. The DCT scale is corrected with a post-processing that is added to the quantization calculation pace. Since the quantization operation and the scale correction are multiplications by constants, these operations can be performed in a single operation. The Table 8.1 lists the steps for implementing 1-D DCT algorithm.

Table 8.1: 1-D DCT algorithm

Step1		
$b_0=a_0+a_7$	$b_1=a_1+a_6$	$b_2=a_2-a_4$
$b_3=a_1-a_6$	$B_4=a_2+a_5$	$B_5=a_3+a_4$
$b_6=a_2-a_5$	$b_7=a_0-a_7$	
Step2		
$c_0=b_0+b_5$	$C_1=b_1-b_4$	$C_2=b_2+b_6$
$C_3=b_1+b_4$	$C_4=b_0-b_5$	$C_5=b_3+b_7$
$C_6=b_3+b_6$	$C_7=b_7$	
Step 3		
$d_0=c_0+c_3$	$d_1=c_0-c_3$	$d_2=c_2$
$d_3=c_1+c_4$	$d_4=c_2-c_3$	$d_5=c_4$
$d_6=c_5$	$d_7=c_6$	$d_8=c_7$
Step 4		
$e_0=d_0$	$e_1=d_1$	$e_2=m_3xd_2$
$e_3=m_1xd_7$	$e_4=m_4xd_6$	$e_5=d_5$
$e_6=m_1xd_3$	$e_7=m_2xd_4$	$e_8=d_8$
Step5		
$f_0=e_0$	$f_1=e_1$	$f_2=e_5+e_6$
$f_3=e_5-e_6$	$f_4=e_3+e_8$	$f_5=e_8-e_3$
$f_6=e_2+e_7$	$f_7=e_4+e_7$	
Step 6		
$S_0=f_0$	$S_1=f_4+f_7$	$S_2=f_2$
$S_3=f_5-f_6$	$S_4=f_1$	$S_5=f_5+f_6$
$S_6=f_3$	$S_7=f_4-f_7$	

8.1.3 3D DCT for Low-power Video Codecs

The 2D-DCT is a dominant tool for reducing the spatial information redundancy in 2D images: *intraframe* coding of still images and videos in JPEG, MPEGx and H.26x standards. The 3D version expands the DCT energy compaction properties to integral 3D images (used in 3D face recognition techniques [1], watermarking, or 3D TV systems and to the spatial-temporal coding of video sequences.The latter application includes time as the third dimension: beside *intraframe* coding the 3D-DCT allows also the decline of temporal information redundancy (*interframe*) removing the need of motion vector assessment and reparation. Fig. 1 shows the architectures of a 3D DCT/IDCT-based video codec. While in the conventional MPEGx/H.26x hybrid scheme (using 2D transforms) each picture of the input video is separated into blocks of NxN pixels, in the 3D codec of Fig. 1 each block becomes a cube: a cube of size NxNxN pixels is made up of the NxN-pixel blocks belonging to N consecutive frames of the input video sequence. At the encoder side the 3D-DCT unit of Fig. 1 replaces the following units of the MPEGx/H.26x hybrid scheme: the 2D-DCT for *intraframe* coding plus 2D-IDCT, motion estimation and compensation in the *interframe* forecast loop. At the decoder side the 3D-IDCT in Figure 8.4 replaces the 2D-IDCT plus the motion reparation loop of the MPEGx/H.26x schemes.

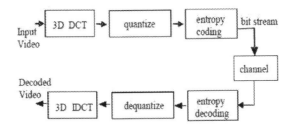

Figure 8.4: Block diagram of the 3D-DCT/IDCT video codec

3D DCT Transformation

The 3D Forward Discrete Cosine Transformation used in the planned 3D DCT image coder is based on the following formulas:

$$F(u,v,w) = \frac{C(u)C(v)C(w)}{8} \sum_{x=0}^{7} \sum_{y=0}^{7} \sum_{z=0}^{7} f(x,y,z)\cos\_prod \qquad (8.8)$$

where cos_prod and C(u), C(v), and C(w) are defined as:

$$\cos\_prod = \cos\left(\frac{(2x+1)u\pi}{16}\right)\cos\left(\frac{(2y+1)v\pi}{16}\right)\cos\left(\frac{(2z+1)w\pi}{16}\right)$$

$$C(i) = \frac{1}{\sqrt{2}}, if\ i = 0; C(i) = 1, if\ i > 0; \quad i \in \{u,v,w\} \qquad (8.9)$$

From the equations present above, x,y,z are pixel indices in the time domain, u,v,w are coefficient indices in the frequency domain, $f(x,y,z)$ denotes a normalized pixel intensity value, and $F(u,v,w)$ is a DCT coefficient value.

The proposed 3D DCT image decoder employs the following 3D Inverse Discrete Cosine Transformation:

$$f(x,y,z) = \frac{1}{8}\left[\sum_{u=0}^{7} \sum_{v=0}^{7} \sum_{w=0}^{7} C(u)C(v)C(w)F(u,v,w)\cos\_prod\right] \qquad (8.10)$$

where *cos_prod* is defined as in the formula (3), *C(u)*, *C(v)*, and *C(w)* take the same values as in the formula (4), and *f(x,y,z)* and *F(u,v,w)* have the same meanings as in the formula (8.10).

The goals for implementing the 3D-DCT algorithm were three fold:

* Recognize the first real-time VLSI execution of this algorithm (to the best of our knowledge).
* Provide a flexible test-bed for the algorithm by leaving some degree of freedom to adjust different parameters and test their manipulate on the compression results in a real-time environment.
* Demonstrate that the 3D-DCT algorithm can in fact be realized with a very reasonable level of complexity.

8.1.4 Fourth Dimension.

Take the non-infinite cube and extrude it in yet another direction perpendicular to the first three. But how can we do this? It is impracticable to do within the restrictions of the third dimension (which will I refer to as realm space in this webpage). However, within the fourth dimension (which I call tetra space), it is possible. The shape that results from this extrusion of a cube into tetra space is called a tesseract, which is a 4-hypercube. All tesseracts fluctuate from other tesseracts in dimension by four measurements (equal to each other within a single tesseract) - width, length, height, and a fourth measurement, which I call strength. Looking back to the previous n-dimensional cubes, they all have the same strength, which is considerably small. Just like the cube and square, all of the edges within a single tesseract are the same length, and all of the angles are right angles. If you extended the tesseract considerably, it would cover four-dimensional space.

There are a number of ways to view the tesseract, and I three of them is discussed here. The first one is called an inner projection, and it is created from a projecting the tesseract into realm space with a viewpoint projection. The parts of the original tesseract that are farther away appear smaller in the inner projection. The original cube cell that is existed before the extrusion into a tesseract is in gray, the paths of the vertices are in teal, plus the stopping point of the extruded cube cell is in blue. The real tesseract isn't formed like the inner projection shown below - the inner projection is a very indistinct "image" of the original tesseract. All of the edges you see in the image are in fact the same length as each other, and all angles between edges are right angles. This is shown in Figure 8.5.

Figure 8.5: Inner projection

The second way to outlook a tesseract isn't actually a normal tesseract, but a parallel projection of a twisted tesseract. To make this shape, first you make a tesseract, then shift the top cube cell a short distance in a diagonal path, parallel to realm space. Since this shift is parallel to realm space, it can, in fact be in any path that you can point to. After the shift, you outline the shadow of the skewed tesseract's edges. The result is a shape that has two cubes with their vertices connected together. In the original shape, all of the edges within the cube cells are the same length and have right angles with each other. However, they don't have right angles with the teal connection edges, and the teal connection edges are somewhat longer than the cube cells' edges. This is shown in Figure 8.6.

Figure 8.6: Parallel projection of a skewed tesseract

The third way to view a tesseract is a parallel projection into realm space. It is the same as a twisted tesseract, but without the top cube cell shifted. Since the edges of the tesseract were extruded in a path perpendicular to realm space, when the shape is estimated back into realm space, the edges of the blue cube cell are projected straight back onto the gray cube cell's edges. The resulting projection is a simple cube. This didn't happen with the inner projection, because that projection was a perspective projection. This is shown in Figure 8.7.

Figure 8.7: Parallel projection into realmspace6

This last step of annoying to view a tesseract shows the difficulties in portraying objects from tetra space within the restrictions of realm space - there is an extra perpendicular direction that we can't portray within our own space without distorting the original object. Because of these problems, it takes many examples in order to initiate understanding the nature of the fourth dimension.

The properties of the fourth dimension are rotation, flatness, levitation, shapes, water, and many others.

8.1.5 Discrete Cosine Transform in H.264

The need for 4×4 DCT in H.264 appeared due to the use of changeable block size motion reparation with blocks as small as 4×4 pixels. In H.264, 4×4 forecast is also used to encode pixels without referring to pixels in an previous frame (intra-coding). After applying motion reparation or intra forecast, the remaining is processed using the new transform.

In order to make 4×4 DCT even simpler, only additions and shifting are used, avoiding multiplications. The matrixes for forward $(DCT(X) = H \cdot X \cdot Ht)$ and inverse $(iDCT (Y) = G \cdot Y \cdot Gt)$ transforms are shown in Equations 1 and 2.

$$H = \begin{bmatrix} 1 & 1 & 1 & 1 \\ 2 & 1 & -1 & -2 \\ 1 & -1 & -1 & 1 \\ 1 & -2 & 2 & -1 \end{bmatrix} \qquad (8.11)$$

$$G = \begin{pmatrix} 1 & 1 & 1 & \frac{1}{2} \\ 1 & \frac{1}{2} & -1 & -1 \\ 1 & \frac{-1}{2} & -1 & 1 \\ 1 & -1 & 1 & \frac{-1}{2} \end{pmatrix} \qquad (8.12)$$

In the way they are defined, the matrixes for DCT and IDCT are orthogonal, but the norm does not equal 1. As a result, additional scaling is required. This problem is simply solved at no cost during quantization. After transform, the resultant DCT coefficients are quantized by means of multiplying by a constant.

The scaling factor is combined with the quantization multiplier in such a way that only one multiplication is desired. For inverse DCT, the scaling factor is combined with dequantization constants.

$$X_q(i,j) = sign\{X(i,j)\}(|X(i,j)| + f(Q_s))/Q_s$$
$$X_r(i,j) = Q_s X_q(i,j)$$

A quantization and dequantization coefficient depends on the condition of the coefficient and the compression settings. For each level of quality, there are only 3 unique values as it can be seen in Equation above.

$$Q = \begin{pmatrix} a & c & a & c \\ c & b & c & b \\ a & c & a & c \\ c & b & c & b \end{pmatrix}$$

(8.13)

The value of a, b and c differs with the quantization control parameter according to a simple rule. The basic matrixes for quantization and dequantization are shown in Equations 5 and 6.

$$Q = \begin{pmatrix} a & b & c \\ \hline 13107 & 5243 & 8066 \\ 11916 & 4660 & 7490 \\ 10082 & 4194 & 6554 \\ 9362 & 3647 & 5825 \\ 8192 & 3355 & 5243 \\ 7282 & 2893 & 4559 \end{pmatrix}$$

(8.14)

$$Q^{-1} = \begin{pmatrix} a & b & c \\ 10 & 16 & 13 \\ 11 & 18 & 14 \\ 13 & 20 & 16 \\ 14 & 23 & 18 \\ 16 & 25 & 20 \\ 18 & 29 & 23 \end{pmatrix} \qquad (8.15)$$

8×8 integer DCT

The 8×8 transform was recognized in order to extend High Definition video compression as, in that case, motion compensation with 4×4 block size is less common. The complexity of this transform is only significantly higher than the 4×4 case [3] in spite of the coefficients are not powers of two in all the cases. The forward transform coefficients are shown in Equation 7.

$$\begin{pmatrix} 8 & 8 & 8 & 8 & 8 & 8 & 8 & 8 \\ 12 & 10 & 6 & 3 & -3 & -6 & -10 & -12 \\ 8 & 4 & -4 & -8 & -8 & -4 & 4 & 8 \\ 10 & -3 & -12 & -6 & 6 & 12 & 3 & -10 \\ 8 & -8 & -8 & 8 & 8 & -8 & -8 & 8 \\ 6 & -12 & 3 & 10 & 10 & -3 & 12 & -6 \\ 4 & -8 & 8 & -4 & -4 & 8 & -8 & 4 \\ 3 & -6 & 10 & -12 & 12 & -10 & 6 & -3 \end{pmatrix} \qquad (8.16)$$

8.2 WAVELET TRANSFORM

The wavelet transform is considered unconnectedly for different segments of the time-domain signal at diverse frequencies. Multi-resolution analysis: observe the signal at different frequencies giving diverse resolutions. Multi-resolution analysis is anticipated to give good time resolution and poor frequency resolution at high frequencies and good frequency resolution and poor time resolution at low frequencies. Good for signal having high frequency components for small durations and low frequency components for long duration, e.g. Images and video frames.

Wavelet Definition

A 'wavelet' is a small wave which has its energy concerted in time which has shown in figure 8.8.It has a fluctuating wavelike characteristic but also has the capacity to allow simultaneous time and frequency examination and it is a appropriate tool for transient, non-stationary or time-varying phenomena.

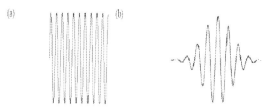

Figure 8.8: Representation of a (a) wave (b) wavelet

Wavelet Characteristics

The difference between wave (sinusoids) and wavelet is shown in Figure 8.9. Waves are smooth, expected and everlasting, whereas wavelets are of inadequate duration, irregular and may be asymmetric. Waves are used as deterministic basis functions in Fourier analysis for the extension of functions (signals), which are time-invariant, or stationary. The important characteristic of wavelets is that they can serve as deterministic or non-deterministic basis for creation and analysis of the most natural signals to offer better time-frequency illustration, which is not possible with waves using predictable Fourier analysis.

Wavelet Analysis

The wavelet analysis process is to accept a wavelet prototype function, called an 'analyzing wavelet' or 'mother wavelet'. Temporal analysis is performed with a constricted, high frequency version of the prototype wavelet, while frequency analysis is performed with a dilated, low frequency version of the same wavelet. Mathematical formulation of signal expansion using wavelets gives Wavelet Transform (WT) pair, which is similar to the Fourier Transform (FT) pair. Discrete-time and discrete-parameter version of WT is termed as Discrete Wavelet Transform (DWT).

Types of Transforms:

Fourier Transform (FT)

Fourier transform is a well-known mathematical tool to change time-domain signal to frequency-domain for proficient extraction of information and it is reversible also. For a signal x(t), the FT is given by

$$X(f) = \int_{-\infty}^{\infty} x(t)\, e^{-j2\pi ft}\, dt \qquad (8.17)$$

Though FT has a great capacity to capture signal's frequency content as long as x(t) is composed of a small amount of stationary components (e.g. sine waves). However, any sudden change in time for non-stationary signal x(t) is spread out over the whole frequency axis in X(f). Hence the time-domain signal sampled with Dirac-delta function is highly restricted in time but spills over entire frequency band and vice versa. The limitation of FT is that it cannot suggest both time and frequency localization of a signal at the same time.

Short Time Fourier Transform (STFT)

To overcome the limitations of the standard FT, Gabor introduced the early concept of Short Time Fourier Transform (STFT). The advantage of STFT is that it uses an random but fixed-length window g(t) for analysis, over which the actual non-stationary signal is assumed to be roughly stationary. The STFT splits such a pseudo-stationary signal x(t) into a two dimensional time-frequency representation S(τ, f) using that sliding window g(t) at different times τ.

Thus the FT of windowed signal x(t) g*(t-τ) yields STFT as

$$STFT_x(\tau, f) = \int_{-\infty}^{\infty} x(t)\ g^*(t-\tau)e^{-j2\pi ft}dt \qquad (8.18)$$

Wavelet Transform (WT)

Fixed resolution limitation of STFT can be determined by letting the resolution in time-frequency plane in order to obtain Multi resolution analysis. The Wavelet Transform (WT) in its continuous (CWT) form provides a flexible time-frequency, which narrows when observing high frequency phenomena and widens when analyzing low frequency behavior. Thus time resolution becomes randomly good at high frequencies, while the frequency resolution becomes randomly good at low frequencies. This kind of analysis is appropriate for signals consists of high frequency components with short duration and low frequency components with long duration, which is often the case in realistic situations.

8.2.1 Continuous wavelet transform

The continuous wavelet transform is defined as

$$X_{WT}(\tau, s) = \frac{1}{\sqrt{|s|}} \int_{-\infty}^{\infty} x(t)\ \Psi^*\left(\frac{t-\tau}{s}\right)dt \qquad (8.19)$$

The transformed signal XWT (τ, s) is a function of the both translation parameter τ and the scale parameter s. The mother wavelet is represented by the Ψ specifies that the complex conjugate is used in case of a complex wavelet. The signal energy is standardized at every scale by dividing the wavelet coefficients by 1/p|s|.

This guarantees that the wavelets have the same energy at every scale. The mother wavelet is constricted and dilated by changing the scale parameter s. The variation in scale s changes not only the central frequency fc of the wavelet, but also the window length. Therefore the scale s is used instead of the frequency for showing the results of the wavelet analysis. The translation parameter τ specifies the location of the wavelet in time, by varying τ the wavelet can be shifted over the signal. For stable scale s and varying translation τ the rows of the time-scale plane are filled, unstable the scale s and keeping the translation τ constant fills the columns of the time-scale plane. The elements in XWT (τ, s) are called wavelet coefficients, each wavelet coefficient is connected to a scale (frequency) and a point in the time domain. The WT also has an inverse transformation, as was the case for the FT and the STFT. The inverse continuous wavelet transformation (ICWT) is defined by

$$
x(t) = \frac{1}{C_\psi^2} \int\limits_{-\infty}^{\infty} \int\limits_{-\infty}^{\infty} X_{WT}(\tau, s) \frac{1}{s^2} \psi\left(\frac{t-\tau}{s}\right) d\tau ds \tag{8.20}
$$

Note that the acceptability constant C must satisfy the second wavelet condition. A wavelet function has its own central frequency fc at each scale and the scale s is inversely proportional to that frequency. A large scale corresponds to a low frequency, giving global information of the signal. Small scales write to high frequencies, providing detail signal information. For the WT, the Heisenberg inequality still holds, the bandwidth-time product $\Delta t \Delta f$ is constant and lower bounded. Decreasing the scale s, i.e. a shorter window, will boost the time resolution Δt, resulting in a decreasing frequency resolution Δf. This means that the frequency resolution Δf is proportional to the frequency f, i.e. wavelet analysis has a constant comparative frequency resolution [23]. The Morlet wavelet, shown in Fig. 3.2, is obtained using a Gaussian window, where fc is the center frequency and fb is the bandwidth parameter

$$
\psi(t) = g(t) e^{-j2\pi ft}, \quad g(t) = \sqrt{\pi f} e^{t^2/f_b} \tag{8.21}
$$

The center frequency fc and the bandwidth parameter fb of the wavelet are the tuning parameters. For the Morlet wavelet, scale and frequency are coupled as

$$
f = \frac{f_c}{s} \tag{8.22}
$$

The calculation of the continuous wavelet transform is typically performed by taking discrete values for the scaling parameter s and translation parameter τ. The resulting wavelet coefficients are called wavelet series. For analysis purposes only, the discretization can be done randomly, however if reconstruction is required, the wavelet limitations become important. The constant relative frequency resolution of the wavelet analysis is also known as the steady Q property. Q is the quality factor of the filter, defined as the center-frequency fc divided by the bandwidth fb.For a constant Q analysis (constant relative frequency resolution), a dyadic sample-grid for the scaling seems appropriate. A dyadic grid is also found in the human audible range and music. A dyadic grid discretizes the scale parameter on a logarithmic scale. The time parameter is discretized with respect to the scale parameter. The dyadic grid is one of the most simple and proficient discretization methods for realistic purposes and leads to the construction of an orthonormal wavelet basis. Wavelet series can be calculated as

$$X_{WT_{m,n}} = \int_{-\infty}^{\infty} x(t) \psi_{m,n}(t) dt, \quad with \quad \psi_{m,n} = s_0^{-m/2} \psi\left(s_0^{-m} t - n\tau_0\right) \qquad (8.23)$$

The integers m and n control the wavelet dilatation and conversion. For a dyadic grid, s0 = 0 and τ0 = 1. Discrete dyadic grid wavelets are chosen to be orthonormal, i.e. they are orthogonal to each other and normalized to have unit energy. This option allows the reconstruction of the original signal by

$$x(t) = \sum_{m=-\infty}^{\infty} \sum_{n=-\infty}^{\infty} X_{WT_{m,n}} \psi_{m,n}(t) \qquad (8.24)$$

The discretized CWT of the signal are analyzed with the Morlet wavelet, is shown in Fig.8.9. Both a surface and a contour plot of the wavelet coefficients are exposed. In literature, most of the time the contour plot is used for representing the results of a CWT. Note that in both figures large scales correspond to low frequencies and small scales to high frequencies. The CWT of Figure 8.10 gives a good frequency resolution for high frequencies (small scales) and a good time resolution for low frequencies (large scales). The different frequencies are detected at the correct time instants, the sharp peak at 0.2 s is noticed well as can be seen by the survival of the peak at small scales at 0.2 s.

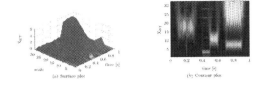

Figure 8.9: Continuous wavelet transform

8.2.2 The Discrete Wavelet Transform

Dilations and translations of [317,319] the "Mother function", or analyzing wavelet $\Phi(x)$ defines an orthogonal basis, our wavelet basis:

$$\Phi_{(sl)}(X) = 2^{\frac{-s}{2}} \Phi\left(2^{-s}x - l\right) \tag{8.25}$$

The variables s and l are integers that scale and dilate the mother function $\Phi(x)$ to generate wavelets, such as a Daubechies wavelet family. The scale index s indicates the wavelet's width, and the location index l gives its location. Notice that the mother functions are rescaled, or "dilated" by powers of two, and converted by integers. What makes wavelet bases particularly attractive is the self-similarity caused by the scales and dilations. Once we know about the mother functions, we distinguish everything about the basis.To span our data domain at different resolutions, the examining wavelet is used in a scaling equation:

$$W(x) = \sum_{k=-1}^{N-2}(-1)^k c_{k+1}\Phi(2x+k) \tag{8.26}$$

Where $W(x)$ is the scaling function for the mother function $\Phi(x)$, and c_k are the *wavelet coefficients*. The wavelet coefficients must gratify linear and quadratic constraints of the form

$$\sum_{k=0}^{N-1} c_k = 2 \quad , \sum_{k=0}^{N-1} c_k c_{k+2l} = 2\delta_{l,0} \tag{8.27}$$

Where δ is the delta function and l is the location index.

One of the most useful features of wavelets is the ease with which a scientist can choose the important coefficients for a given wavelet system to be modified for a given problem. In Daubechies' original paper, she urbanized specific families of wavelet systems that were very good for representing polynomial behavior. The Haar wavelet is even simpler, and it is often used for educational purposes.It is helpful to think of the coefficients $\{c_0,.............,.,.,.,c_n\}$ as a filter. The filter or coefficients are placed in a transformation matrix, which is applied to a raw data vector. The coefficients are planned using two dominant patterns, one that works as a smoothing filter (like a moving average), and one pattern that works to bring out the data's "detail" information. These two orderings of the coefficients are called a *quadrature mirror filter pair* in signal dealing out parlance. A more detailed explanation of the transformation matrix can be found elsewhere.

The Discrete Wavelet Transform

Dilations and translations of [317,319] the "Mother function", or analyzing wavelet $\Phi(x)$ defines an orthogonal basis, our wavelet basis:

$$\Phi_{(sl)}(X)=2^{\frac{-s}{2}}\Phi\left(2^{-s}x-l\right)$$ (8.28)

The variables s and l are integers that scale and dilate the mother function $\Phi(x)$ to generate wavelets, such as a Daubechies wavelet family. The scale index s indicates the wavelet's width, and the location index l gives its location. Notice that the mother functions are rescaled, or "dilated" by powers of two, and converted by integers. What makes wavelet bases particularly attractive is the self-similarity caused by the scales and dilations. Once we know about the mother functions, we distinguish everything about the basis.To span our data domain at different resolutions, the examining wavelet is used in a scaling equation:

$$W(x)=\sum_{k=-1}^{N-2}(-1)^k c_{k+1}\Phi(2x+k)$$ (8.29)

Where $W(x)$ is the scaling function for the mother function $\Phi(x)$, and c_k are the *wavelet coefficients.* The wavelet coefficients must gratify linear and quadratic constraints of the form

$$\sum_{k=0}^{N-1} c_k = 2 \quad , \sum_{k=0}^{N-1} c_k c_{k+2l} = 2\delta_{l,0} \tag{8.30}$$

Where δ is the delta function and l is the location index.

One of the most useful features of wavelets is the ease with which a scientist can choose the important coefficients for a given wavelet system to be modified for a given problem. In Daubechies' original paper, she urbanized specific families of wavelet systems that were very good for representing polynomial behavior. The Haar wavelet is even simpler, and it is often used for educational purposes.It is helpful to think of the coefficients $\{c_0,.,.,.,.,.,.,., c_n\}$ as a filter. The filter or coefficients are placed in a transformation matrix, which is applied to a raw data vector. The coefficients are planned using two dominant patterns, one that works as a smoothing filter (like a moving average), and one pattern that works to bring out the data's "detail" information. These two orderings of the coefficients are called a *quadrature mirror filter pair* in signal dealing out parlance. A more detailed explanation of the transformation matrix can be found elsewhere.

2-D Discrete-Wavelet Transform (2-D DWT)

The 2-D DWT block consists of three levels of disintegration as illustrated in Figure 8.10. Clearly, the specific disintegration used here results in 10 subbands.Specifically, A consists of low-pass and high-pass filtering (H and G) in the row direction and subsampling by a factor of two, pursued by the same procedure on each of the resulting outputs in the column direction, resulting in four subbands. The H and G filters (Image Coding Using Wavelet Transform are finite-impulse-response (FIR) digital filters. The exact input-output relationship for one level of DWT decomposition of a 1-D sequence X(n) can be represented as

$$X_l(n) = \sum_k h_1(2n-k)X(k)$$
$$X_h(n) = \sum_k g_1(2n-k)X(k) \tag{8.31}$$

In which Xl (n) and Xh (n) represent, respectively, the outputs of the low-pass and high-pass filters.The resulting 2-D subbands after the 2-D DWT operation are tagged subband1 through subband10. Due to the specific form of the degeneration, for a QCIF input sequence of size 176×× 144, subband1 through subband4 are of 22 ××18 pixel size, subband5 through subband7 are of 44 ××36 pixel size and subband8 through subband10 are of 88××72 pixel size in which Xl(n) and Xh(n) represent, respectively, the outputs of the low-pass and high-pass filters.

The resulting 2-D subbands after the 2-D DWT operation are labeled subband1 through subband10. Due to the specific form of the disintegration, for a QCIF input sequence of size 176××144, subband1 through subband4 are of 22××18 pixel size, subband5 through subband7 are of 44××36 pixel size and subband8 through subband10 are of 88××72 pixel size.

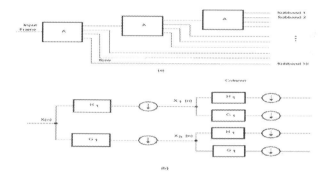

Figure 8.10: 2-D Discrete-Wavelet Transform

2-D Inverse DWT

To reconstruct a copy of the image frame, the dequantized and denormalized subbands are then fed into the 2-D IDWT block. Figure 8.11 shows the details of the 2-D IDWT operation. Specially, B consists of up-sampling by a factor of two and low-pass and high-pass filtering in the column direction followed by the same procedure on the outputs of this process in the row direction, integrating four subbands into one wider band. The filters used for reconstruction (Image Coding Using Wavelet Transform are FIR digital filters. The specific input-output relationship for the rebuilding of the sequence X (n) is represented by

$$X(n) = \sum_k h_2(2k-n)X_l(k) + g_2(2n-k)X_h(k) \qquad (8.32)$$

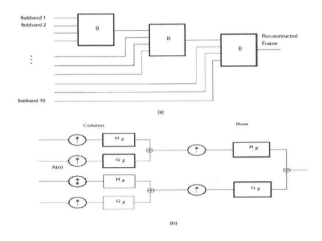

Figure 8.11: 2-D Inverse Discrete-Wavelet Transform

3D DISCRETE WAVELET TRANSFORM

DWT compression is executed on the resultant data using arithmetic coding. A 3D-DWT performs wavelet transform in the three x, y, and z directions on the image data. A 3D image is an extension of 2D images along the time axis whereby processing in 3D-DWT is carried out on the pixel values of the same location along the time axis. Figure 8.12 show one level of 3D-DWT where the H-pass and L-pass stand for the high pass filter and the low pass filters respectively. The down sampling of the filtered results is denoted as "↓2" which can be decomposed further into smaller data through multi-level image disintegration processes.

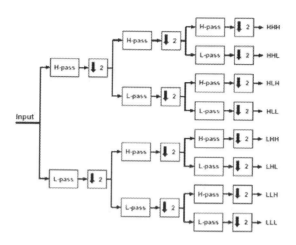

Figure 8.12: One level 3D-DWT

3D-DWT provides attractive possibilities and has been considered to decide the problem associated with compression of large size images, where compression of consecutive images becomes convenient within 3D-DWT algorithms [6][7]. This scheme, however, requires extremely longer processing time. Parallel computation algorithm implemented in VLSI (very large scale integration) is a talented candidate for such an execution and provides a sensible choice for technology mapping. Current activities on 3D-DWT are based on single chip planar VLSI architecture. The problems with single planar approach are consumption of large number of I/O circuitry.

Difference between Continuous Wavelet Transform and Discrete Wavelet Transform:

Wavelet transforms are classified into discrete wavelet transforms (DWTs) and continuous wavelet transforms (CWTs). Note that both DWT and CWT are continuous-time (analog) transforms. They can be used to signify continuous-time (analog) signals. CWTs operate over every potential scale and conversion whereas DWTs use a specific subset of scale and conversion values or depiction grid.

The Wavelet transform is in fact an infinite set of various transforms, depending on the merit function used for its calculation. This is the main reason, why we can hear the term wavelet transform in very different conditions and applications.

- Orthogonal wavelets are used to develop the discrete wavelet transform
- Non-orthogonal wavelets are used to develop the continuous wavelet transform

Applications of Discrete Wavelet Transform:

Generally, estimation to DWT is used for data compression if signal is already sampled, and the CWT for signal analysis. Thus, DWT estimation is commonly used in engineering and computer science, and the CWT in scientific research. One use of wavelet estimation is in data compression. Like some other transforms, wavelet transforms can be used to change data and then encode the transformed data, resulting in effective compression. For example, JPEG 2000 is an image compression standard that uses biorthogonal wavelets. An associated use is that of smoothing/denoising data based on wavelet coefficient thresholding, also called wavelet shrinkage. By adaptively thresholding the wavelet coefficients that correspond to undesired frequency components smoothing and/or denoising operations can be performed. Other applied fields that are making use of wavelets comprise astronomy, acoustics, nuclear engineering, sub-band coding, signal and image processing, neurophysiology, music, magnetic resonance imaging, speech discrimination, optics, fractals, turbulence, earthquake-prediction, radar, human vision, and pure mathematics applications such as solving partial differential equations.

8.2.3 Multi-Resolution Analysis using Filter Banks

Filters are one of the most extensively used signal processing functions. Wavelets can be realized by iteration of filters with rescaling. The resolution of the signal, which is a assess of the amount of detail information in the signal, is determined by the filtering operations, and the scale is determined by upsampling and downsampling (subsampling) operations.

The DWT is computed by consecutive lowpass and highpass filtering of the discrete time-domain signal as shown in Figure 8.13. This is known as the Mallat algorithm or Mallat-tree disintegration. Its importance is in the manner it connects the continuous-time mutiresolution to discrete-time filters. In the figure, the signal is indicated by the sequence x[n], where n is an integer.

The low pass filter is denoted by G_0 while the high pass filter is indicated by H_0. At each level, the high pass filter creates detail information; d[n], while the low pass filter associated with scaling function produces uncouth approximations, a[n].

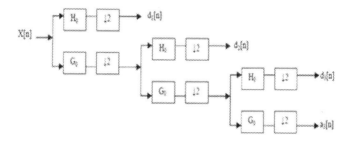

Figure 8.13: Three-level wavelet decomposition tree.

At each decomposition level, the half band filters produce signals spanning only half the frequency band. This doubles the frequency resolution as the uncertainity in frequency is condensed by half. In accordance with Nyquist's rule if the original signal has a highest frequency of ω, which requires a sampling frequency of 2ω radians, then it now has a highest frequency of $\omega/2$ radians. It can now be sampled at a frequency of ω radians thus disposing half the samples with no loss of information.

This decimation by 2 halves the time resolution as the whole signal is now represented by only half the number of samples. Thus, as the half band low pass filtering removes half of the frequencies and thus halves the resolution, the decimation by 2 doubles the scale. With this advance, the time resolution becomes randomly good at high frequencies, as the frequency resolution becomes randomly good at low frequencies. The time-frequency plane is thus determined. The filtering and decimation process is continued until the desired level is reached. The maximum number of levels depends on the length of the signal. The DWT of the original signal is then attained by concatenating all the coefficients, a[n] and d[n], starting from the last level of disintegration. Figure 2.3 shows the restoration of the original signal from the wavelet coefficients. Basically, the restoration is the reverse process of disintegration.

Conditions for Perfect Reconstruction

In most Wavelet Transform applications, it is necessary that the original signal be synthesized from the wavelet coefficients. To attain perfect reconstruction the analysis and synthesis filters have to assure certain conditions. Let $G_0(z)$ and $G_1(z)$ be the low pass analysis and synthesis filters, respectively and $H_0(z)$ and $H_1(z)$ the high pass analysis and synthesis filters respectively. Then the filters have to assure the following two conditions as given in [4]:

$$G_0(-z)G_1(z) + H_0(-z).H_1(z) = 0$$
$$G_0(z)G_0(z) + H_0(z).H_1(z) = 2z^{-d}$$

(8.33)

The first condition implies that the restoration is aliasing-free and the second condition implies that the amplitude distortion has amplitude of one. It can be observed that the perfect restoration condition does not change if we switch the analysis and synthesis filters. There are a number of filters which assure these conditions. But not all of them give perfect Wavelet Transforms, particularly when the filter coefficients are quantized. The accuracy of the Wavelet Transform can be determined after reconstruction by calculating the Signal to Noise Ratio (SNR) of the signal. Some applications like pattern detection do not need restoration, and in such applications, the above conditions need not apply.

Classification of wavelets

We can classify wavelets into two classes: (a) orthogonal and (b) biorthogonal. Based on the application, either of them can be used.

Features of orthogonal wavelet filter banks

The coefficients of orthogonal filters are real numbers. The filters are of the same length and are not symmetric. The low pass filter, G_0 and the high pass filter, H_0 are associated to each other by

$$H_0(z) = z^{-N} G_0(-z^{-1}) \qquad (8.34)$$

The two filters are alternated flip of each other. The alternating flip routinely gives double-shift orthogonality between the lowpass and highpass filters [1], i.e., the scalar product of the filters, for a shift by two is zero. i.e., $\Sigma G[k] H[k-2l] = 0$, where $k, l \in Z$. Filters that assure equation 2.4 are known as Conjugate Mirror Filters (CMF). Perfect restoration is possible with alternating flip. Also, for ideal restoration, the synthesis filters are identical to the analysis filters except for a time reversal. Orthogonal filters offer a high number of vanishing moments.This property is helpful in many signal and image processing applications. They have usual structure which leads to easy implementation and scalable architecture.

Features of biorthogonal wavelet filter banks

In the case of the biorthogonal wavelet filters, the low pass and the high pass filters do not have the same length. The low pass filter is forever symmetric, as the high pass filter could be either symmetric or anti-symmetric. The coefficients of the filters are either real numbers or integers. For ideal restoration, biorthogonal filter bank has all odd length or all even length filters. The two analysis filters can be symmetric with odd length or one symmetric and the other anti symmetric with even length. Also, the two sets of analysis and synthesis filters must be double. The linear phase biorthogonal filters are the most familiar filters for data compression applications.

Introduction to the Wavelet Families

From a theoretical viewpoint, wavelets are used to illustrate large sets of mathematical functions and are used in the study of operators connected to partial differential equations. From a practical viewpoint, wavelets are used in numerous fields of numerical analysis, making certain complex calculations easier to handle or more exact. There are a number of basic functions that can be used as the mother wavelet for Wavelet Transformation. Since the mother wavelet produces all wavelet functions used in the transformation through conversion and scaling, it determines the individuality of the resulting Wavelet Transform. Therefore, the details of the exact application should be taken into account and the appropriate mother wavelet should be selected in order to use the Wavelet Transform efficiently.

Complex Wavelets

Some complex wavelet families are available in the toolbox:

- Gaussian derivatives
- Morlet
- Frequency B-Spline
- Shannon

CURVELET TRANSFORM (CT):

Curvelet transform is a unique member of the multiscale geometric transforms. It is a transform with multiscale pyramid with many directions at each length scale.

Curvelets will be higher over wavelets in following cases:

1. Optimally sparse illustration of objects with edges
2. Optimal image restoration in strictly ill-posed problems
3. Optimal sparse illustration of wave propagators

Curvelets are primarily introduced by E.J. Candes and D.L. Donoho. Assume we have a function f which has a discontinuity across a curve, and which is smooth or else, and consider approximating f from the best m-terms in the *Fourier* expansion. The squarred error of such an m-term expansion obeys:

$$\left\| f - f_F \right\|^2 \quad \alpha 1 / \sqrt{m}, m \to +\infty \tag{8.35}$$

In a *wavelet* expansion, we have

$$\left\| f - f_W \right\|^2 \quad \alpha 1 / m, m \to +\infty \tag{8.36}$$

,($\sim fW$ is the approximation from m best *Wavelet* coefficients)

In a *curvelet* expansion (Donoho and Candes, 2000), we have

$$\left\| f - f_C \right\|^2 \quad \alpha m^{-2} \left(\log m \right)^3 , m \to +\infty, \tag{8.37}$$

(fC is the approximation from m best *Curvelet* coefficients.)

This shows that the mean squared error will be condensed in curvelets. A fast and precise discrete curvelet transform operating on digital data is necessary to use curvelet transform in a variety of applications. This is called Fast Discrete Curvelet Transform (FDCT). Figure 8.14 indicates the Curvelet tiling.

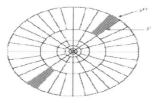

Figure 8.14: Curvelet Tiling of the Frequency Plane.
The shaded area represents such a generic wedge.

Curvelet transform obeys an anisotropy scaling relation,

$$length \approx 2^{-j/2} , width = 2^{-j}$$
$$width \approx length^2 \tag{8.38}$$

This is also called as a Curve scaling law. Fast digital curvelet transforms can be implemented via two methods 1) using Unquispaced FFTs 2) using Wrapping.

RIDGELET TRANSFORM (RT):

Ridgelet analysis was urbanized by E.J. Candes and D.L. Donoho, for solving significant problems such as constructing neural networks or approximating and estimating multivariate functions by linear combinations of ridge functions. Ridgelet transform is a new multiscale illustration for functions on incessant spaces that have some discontinuities along lines. Orthonormal version of the ridgelet transform for separate and finite-size images was proposed by Minh Do and M. Vetterli. It uses the fixed Radon transform proposed in and as a basic building block. The leads to a set of directional and Orthonormal bases for images.

The continuous ridgelet transform of an integrable bivariate function $f(x)$ is represented by

$$CRT_f(a,b,\theta) = \int_{\Re^2} \psi_{a,b,\theta}(x) f(x) dx \qquad (8.39)$$

where ridgelets $x \cos\theta + y \sin\theta = $ constant in 2-D, are defined from a wavelet type purpose in

$\psi(x)$ in 1-D, as
$$\psi_{a,b,\theta}(x) = \sqrt{a}\,\psi\left((x\cos\theta + y\cos\theta - b)/a\right) \qquad (8.40)$$

Wavelets are good to stand for the point singularities and ridgelets stand for line singularities. In Image Processing applications it is significant to notice singularities along edges. Ridgelets can be thought of a way of juxtaposing 1-D wavelets along lines. This results in a very efficient illustration of objects with singularities along lines.

Signal analysis

Signals are always the input for a wavelet analysis. The resulting wavelet coefficients can be influenced in many ways to attain certain results, these include denoising, compression, feature detection, etc.

Applications

The wavelet transforms enables high compression ratios with good quality of restoration. Wavelets find purpose in speech compression, which reduces communication time in mobile applications. They are used in denoising, edge detection, feature extraction, speech recognition, echo cancellation and others. They are very talented for real time audio and video compression applications. Wavelets also have many applications in digital communications. Orthogonal Frequency Division Multiplexing (OFDM) is one of them. Wavelets are used in biomedical imaging. For example, the ECG signals, calculated from the heart, are analyzed using wavelets or compressed for storage. The fame of Wavelet Transform is growing because of its capacity to decrease deformation in the reconstructed signal while retaining all the important features present in the signal.

8.3 WALSH-HADAMARD TRANSFORM

8.3.1.Walsh transform

Walsh basis functions write to local structure, in the form of positive or negative going horizontal or vertical edge, corner of a certain type, etc. Registration schemes based on wavelet coefficient corresponding do not present a general method of combining the matching results across different scales. Two images I1 and I2, I1 is assumed as reference image whereas I2 represent an image that has to be distorted to match I1. First, consider around each pixel, exclusive of border pixels, a 3X3 neighborhood and calculate from it, the nine Walsh coefficients (3X3 WT of a 3X3 image patch). If 'f' is the input image, the matrix of coefficients 'g' computed for it using equation,

$$g = \left(W^{-1}\right)^{T}.fW^{-1} \qquad (8.41)$$

Matrix contains the coefficients of the expansion of the image, in terms of the basis images as in Table 8.2(a) formed by captivating the vector outer products of the rows of matrix W. Coefficients are denoted by a00, a01, a02, a10, a11, a12, a20, a21, a22, in a matrix form as in Table 8.2(b) and take the value in the range. _ij is normalization given in equation (2.88) makes the method vigorous to global levels of change of enlightenment. a00 coefficient is the local average gray value of the image, aij constructs coefficients that describes the local structure.

$$\alpha_{ij} = a_{ij} / a_{00} \tag{8.42}$$

Table 8.2: Walsh Transformation (a). WTs basis images for a 3X3 images (b). Nine coefficients in matrix form

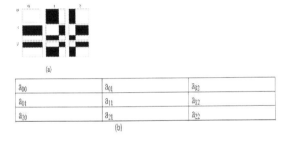

(b)

In Table8.2 (b), the coefficients along the first row and the first column are of equal significance, as they compute the existence of a vertical or a horizontal edge, respectively. The remaining four coefficients measure the existence of a corner. The following commanding of coefficients are used in images,

$$Ordering\ IA\ \alpha_{01}, \alpha_{10}, \alpha_{20}, \alpha_{02}, \alpha_{11}, \alpha_{21}, \alpha_{21}, \alpha_{22}$$

$$Ordering\ IB\ \alpha_{01}, \alpha_{10}, \alpha_{20}, \alpha_{02}, \alpha_{11}, \alpha_{21}, \alpha_{21}, \alpha_{22}$$

$$Ordering\ IIA\ \alpha_{22}, \alpha_{21}, \alpha_{12}, \alpha_{11}, \alpha_{02}, \alpha_{20}, \alpha_{10}, \alpha_{01}$$

$$Ordering\ IIB\ \alpha_{22}, \alpha_{12}\alpha_{21}, \alpha_{11}, \alpha_{20}, \alpha_{02}, \alpha_{01}, \alpha_{10}$$

(8.43)

8.3.2.Hadamard transform

urces of the Hadamard transform is the DC coefficients after quantization. The quantization of the DC terms in 16 x 16 intra mode is dissimilar to other modes. It conserves two extra bits comparing to other manner. The smallest quantization parameter (QP) has an equal upshot of dividing by 10, which reduces 3 bits of active range in the normal mode. Since two extra bits are conserved in 16 x 16 intra mode. The dynamic range of the data is 15-3+2=14 bits. The 1D Hadamard transform will improve dynamic range by 2 bits, *so* the transpose register array should be executed with 16 bits.

Walsh – Hadamard Transform

In this most general situation, we work in a ring R with unity 1. This includes R, C and Galois Field alphabets GF(p^a), though if we need to distinguish signal values x and −x, the ring must have characteristic # 2.

Definition 2.1: Suppose R is a ring with unity 1, category of units R*and that charR does not divide v. A square matrix M of sequence $v \geq 2$, with entries from a subset $N \leq R*$is a *Generalised Butson Hadamard (GBH)* matrix, if MM*= M*M = vIv, where M*is the transpose of the matrix of inverse component of M: m*ij = (mji) $^{-1}$. It is defined as *GBH*(N, v), or *GBH*(w, v) if N is finite of sequence w. A *GBH* matrix is always identical to a *normalised GBH* matrix, which has first row and column containing of all 1s.By considering the inner product of any non-initial row of a normalized *GBH* matrix M with the all-1s first column of M*, we see that the sum of the input in any row of M, other than the first, must equal 0, and likely for rows of M*(columns of the matrix of inverses M(−1) = [m^{-1}ij]). The tensor product of two *GBH* matrices over the same group N is a *GBH* matrix over N.

Generalised hadamard transform

In this most general condition, we operate in a ring R with unity 1. This includes R, C and Galois Field alphabets GF(pa), though if we need to differentiate signal values x and −x, the ring must have characteristic 6= 2.

Definition 2.1: Suppose R is a ring with unity 1, category of units R*and that charR does not divide v. A square matrix M of sequence $v \geq 2$, with entries from a subgroup $N \leq R*$is a *Generalised Butson Hadamard (GBH)* matrix, if

$$MM^* = M^*M = vI_v \qquad (8.44)$$

where M^* is the transpose of the matrix of inverse elements of M: $m_{ij}^* = \left(m_{ji} \right)^{-1}$. It is denoted GBH(N,v) or GBH(w,v) if N is finite of order w.

Definition 2.2: Let x be a signal of span n from R^* where n ε R^* and let b be a GBH(N,n).A generalised Hadamard Transform GHT of x is

$$\hat{x} = Bx \qquad (8.45)$$

and an Inverse Generalised Hadamard Transform of $\hat{x}$ is

$$x = n^{-1} B^* \hat{x} \qquad (8.46)$$

the next section explains the developement for GBh matrices of similar order and extra internal structure,consisting the WHT,even length DFT and reverse jacket transform matrices.In some real-time applications such as video conferencing with handheld machines, the algorithms detailed above may not be able to meet the time requirement. In this article, we introduce a fast full-pel VBSME algorithm, called fast Walsh search (FWS) for various block size (FWS-VBS), which does motion estimation in Walsh–Hadamard (WH) domain. FWS-VBS works several new techniques to decrease the computation burden without sacrificing the accuracy.

The merits of the proposed algorithm is that it is more efficient than most existing methods and can achieve a rate-distortion staging very close to FFS. We relate FWS-VBS with different fast block matching algorithms incorporated in the H.264 reference codec to exhibit the strength and weakness of FWS-VBS.

The Walsh Hadamard transform of a signal x of size $N=2^n$, is the matrix vector product WHT$_N\cdot^x$ where

$$WHT_N = \overset{n}{\underset{i=1}{\otimes}} DFT_2 = \overbrace{DFT_2 \otimes ...... \otimes DFT_2}^{n} \qquad (8.47)$$

The matrix

$$DFT_2 = \begin{bmatrix} 1 & 1 \\ 1 & -1 \end{bmatrix} \tag{8.48}$$

is the two point matrix and denotes tensor or Kronec ker product.

The tensor product of two matrices is gained by substituting each entry of the first matrix by that element multiplied by the second matrix. Thus.for instance,

$$WHT_4 = \begin{bmatrix} 1 & 1 \\ 1 & -1 \end{bmatrix} \otimes \begin{bmatrix} 1 & 1 \\ 1 & -1 \end{bmatrix}$$

$$= \begin{bmatrix} 1 & 1 & 1 & 1 \\ 1 & -1 & 1 & -1 \\ 1 & 1 & -1 & -1 \\ 1 & -1 & -1 & 1 \end{bmatrix} \tag{8.49}$$

Algorithms for computing the WHT can be derived using properties of the tensor product [8, 6]. A recursive algorithm for the WHT is obtained from the factorization

$$WHT_{2^n} = \left(WHT_2 \otimes I_{2^{n-1}}\right)\left(I_2 \otimes WHT_{2^{n-1}}\right) \tag{8.50}$$

This equation corresponds to the divide and conquer step in a recursive FFT. An iterative algorithm for computing the WHT is obtained from the factorization

$$WHT_{2^n} = \prod_{i=1}^{n}\left(I_{2^{i-1}} \otimes WHT_2 \otimes I_{2^{n-i}}\right) \tag{8.51}$$

which corresponds to an iterative FFT. More generally,

let $n = n1 + \cdots + nt$, then

$$WHT_{2^n} = \prod_{l=1}^{t} \left(I_{2^{n_1}} + ... +_{n_{l-1}} \otimes WHT_{2^{n_T}} \otimes I_{2^{n_{t+1} + ... + n_t}} \right) \tag{8.52}$$

This equation encompasses both the iterative and recursive algorithm and provides a mechanism for exploring different breakdown strategies and combinations of recursion and iteration.

Alternative algorithms are obtained through different sequences of the application of Equation 2.98. Each algorithm obtained this way can be represented by a tree, called a partition tree.

The root of the partition tree corresponding to an algorithm for computing **WHTN**, where $N = 2n$ is labeled with n. Each application of Equation 8.50 corresponds to an expansion of a node into children whose sum equals the node. Figure 8.15 shows the trees for a recursive and iterative algorithm for computing **WHT**16.we explore all WHT implementations corresponding to all possible partition trees. The total number of partition trees of size n is given by the recurrence

$$T_n = 1 + \sum_{n_1 + ... + n_k = n} T_{n_1} .... T_{n_k} \tag{8.53}$$

Table 8.3 lists the first few values of Tn. The generating function, $T(z)$, for Tn satisfies the functional equation

$$T(z) = z / (1 - z) + T(z)^2 / (1 - T(z)) \tag{8.54}$$

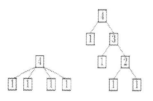

Figure 8.15: Partition Trees for Iterative and Recursive WHT Algorithms

Table 8.3: Number of Partition Trees for WHT$2n$

n	1	2	3	4	5	6	7	8
T_n	1	2	6	24	112	568	3032	17968

And consequently $T_n = \Theta(\alpha^n / n^{3/2})$, Where $\alpha = 4 + \sqrt{8} \approx 6.828427120$. Even if werestrict to binary partition trees,The number of trees is $\Theta(5^n / n^{3/2})$. Hence it isimpossible to Exhaustively search all possible trees for the optimal algorithm.

When we emboss an image onto the basis functions, all we required to do is multiply each pixel by ± 1 as shown in WHT equation assuming N×N image:

$$WH(u,v) = \sum_{r=0}^{N-1} \sum_{c=0}^{N-1} I(r,c)(-1)^{\sum_{i=0}^{n-1} [b_i(r)p_i(u) + b_i(c)p_i(v)]} \tag{8.55}$$

where $N = 2n$, the exponent on the (-1), and $b(r)i$ is found by taking r as a binary number and determining the ith bit, for example:n=3 (3 bits, so N=8), and r = 4.So r in binary is 100, giving

$$b_2(r) = 1, b_1(r) = 0, b_0(r) = 0$$

In addition, p (u) i is found as follows:

$$p_0(u) = b_{n-1}(u)$$
$$p_1(u) = b_{n-1}(u) + b_{n-2}(u)$$
$$p_2(u) = b_{n-2}(u) + b_{n-3}(u)$$

.

. (8.56)

.

.

$$p_{n-1}(u) = b_1(u) + b_0(u)$$

WHT is not grouped as a frequency transform, because the basis functions do not provoke the frequency concept in the way of sinusoidal functions. However, it considers the countings of zero crossings (or sign changes), this is a measure comparable to frequency, and is called order. The Hierarchal process explained for facial feature extraction received from WHT is as shown in Figure 8.16.

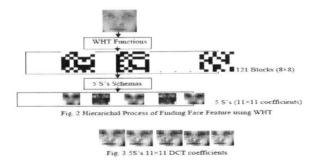

Figure 8.16: Hierarchal process described for facial feature extraction obtained from WHT

$$B(x, y, u, v) = \cos\left[\frac{(2x+1)u\Pi}{2N}\right]\cos\left[\frac{(2y+1)v\Pi}{2N}\right] \tag{8.57}$$

The concept of performing motion estimation in WH domain has been suggested in. Here we briefly explain the algorithm to make this article self-contained. The FWS algorithm uses a matching error called *partial SAD* (PSAD) instead of the common SAD. The remaining candidates are searched by more accurate matching error such as SAD or block pyramid match (BPM).This new criterion effectively eliminates most of the likely mismatch candidates and speed up the matching process considerably.

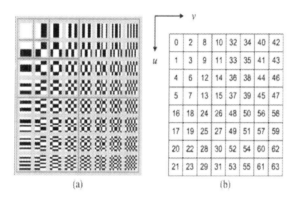

Figure 8.17: WHT basis pictures. (a) BPs of 8×8 images.
(b) Ordering of BPs for fast projection

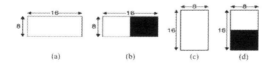

Figure 8.18: BPs for (a) first and (b) second WHT coefficients for 16 × 8 blocks and (c) first and (d) second WHT coefficients for 8 × 16 blocks.

The Figure 8.17(a) shows the BPs of 8×8 images.The first q indices shown in Figure 8.17(b).The Bps of two WHT co-efficient 8 × 16 and 16 × 8 are shown in Figure 8.18.

8.3.3 Fast WHT

A fast transform algorithm is seen as a scant factorization of the transform matrix, and directs to each factor as a stage.The proposed algorithms have a regular interconnection design between stages, and consequently, the inputs and outputs for each stage are named from or to the same positions, and the factors of the decomposition, the stages, have the property of being equal between them. The 2X2 Hadamard matrix is defined as H2 is given in equation (3)

$$H_2 = \begin{bmatrix} 1 & 1 \\ 1 & -1 \end{bmatrix} \tag{8.58}$$

A set of radix-R factorizations in terms of similar scant matrices rapidly obtained from the WHT property that links the matrix H with its inverse and is given in equation (4),

$$H_R^{\,n} = R^n (H_R^n)^{-1} \tag{8.59}$$

Where HR^n = radix-R Walsh Hadamard transform;
R^n = radix-R factorizations;
n = input element;

The FWHT is used to obtain the local outline of the images. This basis function can be efficiently used to obtain the digital numbers in the sense of coefficients. If these coefficients are normalized by the dc coefficient of the expansion, i.e., the local average gray value of the image, then they measure purely the local outline independent of modality. These numbers are then normalized to obtain the unique number that is used as feature for image registration. The execution of FWHT readily decreases the time consumption for medical image registration when relating the same with conventional WT technique for image registration.

Walsh-Hadamar and Haar transformations

The Walsh-Hadamar transformation (WHT) and the Haar transformation (HT) are two sim-plest orthogonal linear transformations of images. They are very similar, but their differences illustrate the different philosophies behind the classical transformations (such as DCT) and the wavelet transformations. Both WHT and HT are generalizations of the 45° rotation idea we have used in our examples before. The 2D transformations are separable.Let us start with the 1DWalsh-Hadamar transformation. It operates on the n-dimensional space Rn where n = 2k is a power of two.

The transformation matrix is defined recursively. The 2n = 2k+1 dimensional transformation matrix W2n is expressed in terms of the n dimensional transformation matrix Wn as follows:

$$W_{2n} = \frac{1}{\sqrt{2}} \cdot \begin{pmatrix} W_n & W_n \\ W_n & -W_n \end{pmatrix} \tag{8.60}$$

The starting point of the recursion is the familiar 2 × 2 matrix

$$W_2 = \frac{1}{\sqrt{2}} \cdot \begin{pmatrix} 1 & 1 \\ 1 & -1 \end{pmatrix} \tag{8.61}$$

Using tensor products of matrices we can write the recursion as

$$W_{2n} = W_2 \otimes W_n,$$

So that

$$W_{2^k} = \underbrace{W_2 \otimes W_2 \otimes \dots \otimes W_2}_{K\ times} \tag{8.62}$$

We do not need parenthesises as the tensor product is associative.

For example,

$$W_4 = \frac{1}{2} \cdot \begin{pmatrix} 1 & 1 & 1 & 1 \\ 1 & -1 & 1 & -1 \\ 1 & 1 & -1 & -1 \\ 1 & -1 & -1 & 1 \end{pmatrix} \tag{8.63}$$

The recursive definition above guarantees that W2n is orthogonal if Wn is orthogonal. Since the first matrix W2 is orthogonal, all WHT transformations are orthogonal. The two-dimensional version of WHT is obtained as the separable product of the vertical and horizontal one-dimensional versions of WHT. The transformation matrix for 2n × 2n WHT then has all elements } 12n. Therefore the transformation can be done by using only additions and subtractions, and dividing the coefficients in the end by 2n (=shifting n bits in binary). The following Table shows the 64 WHT basis vectors for 8 × 8 blocks. White represents 18 and black −18. The vectors are shown as 8 × 8 blocks.

Table 8.4: 2D basis vector

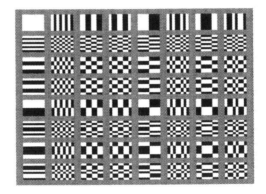

In the Table 8.4, the 2D basis vector in position (i, j) is the outer product of the i'th vertical and the j'th horizontal 1D basis vectors. The 1D vectors are ordered in the order in which they come out from the recursive formula (14). The basis vector in the upper left corner is the constant vector. It is commonly called the DC vector, while the other basis vectors are called AC vectors.

Example. Let us apply the 8 × 8 WHT transform on the test image "peppers". The image is divided into blocks of size 8×8, so there are 512/8×512/8 = 4096 non-overlapping image blocks, i.e., there are m = 4096 data vectors of the n = 64 dimensional space Rn. In the original data blocks the energy and variance are roughly evenly distributed in the 64 coordinates. In the transformed blocks most of the variance (88.4%) is packed into the DC coordinate.The 10 coordinates of highest variance contain over 97% of the total variance. The following Figure 8.19 shows the cumulative variance in the coordinates, when the coordinates are ordered from the highest variance coordinate to the lowest variance coordinate:

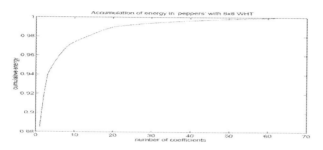

Figure 8.19: Cumulative variace in co-ordinates

The DC coefficient has the highest variance. The list of the nine highest variance basis vectors is shown in Figure 8.20.

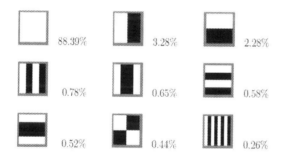

Figure 8.20: Nine highest variance basis vector

Note that more variance is packed in the basis vectors that have few changes between black and white. The variance in the rapidly changing basis vectors is typically small. Loosely speaking, the number of changes from black to white and back indicates the frequency of the basis vector. Smooth parts of images contain low frequencies, so the high frequency basis vectors capture less image energy than the low frequency ones. The WHT transformation itself is lossless and it produces little compression. In lossy compression the transform coefficients are quantized. The transformation is orthogonal so the MSE quantization error in the coefficients is the same as the MSE error in the reconstructed image.

Consider the 1D transform of size n = 2k. If we simply multiply the vectors by the transformation matrix Wn we need n2 operations. But using the recursive definition we get a faster algorithm: First divide the data vector x into two parts x1 and x2, both of size n/2.Then perform the WHT on both halves. Since

$$W_n\begin{pmatrix} \overline{x_1} \\ \overline{x_2} \end{pmatrix} = \frac{1}{\sqrt{2}} \cdot \begin{pmatrix} W_{n/2} & W_{n/2} \\ W_{n/2} & -W_{n/2} \end{pmatrix} \begin{pmatrix} \overline{x_1} \\ x_2 \end{pmatrix}$$

$$W_n\begin{pmatrix} \overline{x_1} \\ x_2 \end{pmatrix} = \frac{1}{\sqrt{2}} \cdot \begin{pmatrix} \overline{W_{n/2}x_1} & \overline{W_{n/2}x_2} \\ W_{n/2}x_1 & -W_{n/2}x_2 \end{pmatrix}$$

(8.64)

we only need to calculate the sum and the difference of n/2-dimensional vectors Wn/2x1 and Wn/2x2. This requires n/2 + n/2 = n operations. Let Sn be the total number of additions/subtractions for the n = 2k dimensional WHT. The analysis above shows that

$$S_n = 2.S_{n/2} + n.$$

(8.65)

Clearly S1 = 0. This recurrence equation has exact solution

$$S_n = n \log_2 n$$

(8.66)

In 2D, the following steps to take the WHT trans-form of an image:

(i)   Divide the image into 2×2 blocks
(ii) Transform each 2×2 block using the orthogonal transformation whose basis vectors are

$\frac{1}{2}$	$\frac{1}{2}$
$\frac{1}{2}$	$\frac{1}{2}$

$-\frac{1}{2}$	$\frac{1}{2}$
$-\frac{1}{2}$	$\frac{1}{2}$

"Low-low"   "low-high"

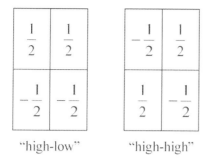

"high-low"   "high-high"

(iii) Collect the corresponding coefficients from the blocks together to form four quarter-sizeimages.
(iv) Recursively transform each quarter separately using WHT.

The quarters are called low-low (LL), low-high (LH), high-low (HL) and high-high (HH) frequency components, or subbands, of the image. The LL component contains most of the image energy. The LH (and the HL) component captures energy at vertical (resp. horizontal) edges of the image. Note that the whole image was transformed, not just 8×8 image blocks. All subbands except the LL subband contain large coefficients only along object bound-aries. Smooth areas of the image produce small coefficients. This means that the image energy is already well concentrated in the HL, LH and HH subbands. Consequently, apply-ing the WHT transformation recursively to all four subbands may not be such a good idea:The transformation spreads the localized large values into several coefficients.

A generalisation of Butson's Hadamard matrices determines a Generalised Hadamard Transform (GHT). The GHT along with the Fourier and Generalised Transform families (in particular the WHT and DFT) and the centreweighted Walsh-Hadamard, Complex Reverse Jacket and extended Complex Reverse Jacket Transforms. In the jacket case, GHT matrices can be permuted into tensor products of primary jacket matrices.

New primary jacket matrices may be constructed as tensor products of a Generalised Butson Hadamard matrix which is not a primary jacket matrix, and a primary jacket matrix. New examples in orders 8 and 12 have been given. Application of the GHT to image processing, error-control coding and decoding and sequence design are obvious directions for future research.

9

COMPARISON OF DIFFERENT TRANSFORMS

The compression staging of the DCT, DWT, and WHT are talked in this chapter by using various simulations which is refered from the journal. Discrete Wavelet Transform (DWT) and Discrete Cosine Transform (DCT) are the common methods used in signal and image compression. The hardware implementation for the DCT is simple; the noticeable blocking artifacts across the block boundaries cannot be rejected at higher compression ratio. In images having gradually shaded areas, the quality of reconstructed images is degraded by reel Contouring. In DWT based coding, has ability to project the images at various resolutions and also achieves higher compression ratio. The Forward Walsh Hadamard Transform (FWHT) is another choice for image and video compression applications which requires less computation as compared to DWT and DCT algorithms.

Discrete Cosine Transform (DCT) is one of the widely used image compression method and the Discrete Wavelet Transform (DWT) provides substantial improvements in the quality of picture because of multi resolution nature. Image compression decreases the storage memory of image and also maintains the quality information of the image. In this study the performance of three most widely used techniques namely DCT, DWT,FHT and Hybrid DCT-DWT are discussed for video compression and their performance is calculated in terms of Peak Signal to Noise Ratio (PSNR), Mean Square Error (MSE) and Compression Ratio (CR). The experimental results obtained from the study exhibits that the every transform technique for image compression has its own merits and demerits.

9.1 EXPERIMENTAL RESULTS

We are relating the images which are compressed by employing DCT and DWT using MATLAB.Figure 9.1(a) and Figure 9.2(a) shows peak signal to noise ratio graph of DCT and DWT, Figure 9.1(b) and figure 9.2(b) shows bit error rate graph of DCT and DWT.The Table 9.1 shows peak signal to noise ratio, bit error rate, compression ratio, Mean square error and time of the compressed images of DCT and DWT.

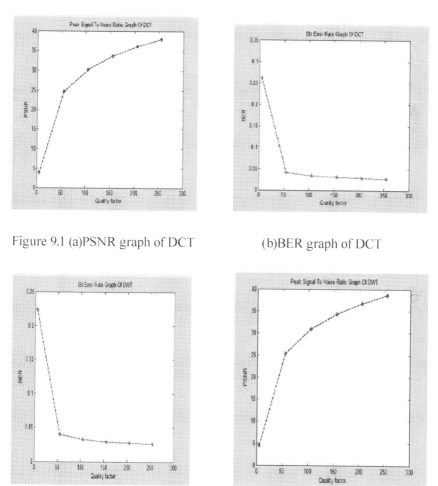

Figure 9.1 (a)PSNR graph of DCT   (b)BER graph of DCT

Figure 9.2 (a)PSNR graph of DWT   (b) BER graph of DWT

we are comparing the results of different transform coding techniques i.e. Discrete Cosine Transform (DCT) and Discrete Wavelet Transform (DWT) we see that DWT provides higher compression ratios & avoids blocking artifacts.

Table 9.1: Comparison of DCT and DWT

PARAMETERS	DCT	DWT
Compression ratio	20.1763	20.3955
PSNR	0.0263	38.6309
MSE	10.3820	8.9123
BER	37.9680	0.0259
TIME	7.4121	3.5139

Allows good localization both in spatial & frequency domain. Transformation of the whole image introduces inherent scaling. Better identification of which data is relevant to human perception higher compression ratio and we also see that DCT takes more time than DWT. For DCT technique we can achieve the Cr=20.1763 compression ratio.and for DWT technique we can achieve the Cr=20.3955 compression ratio.

In an another Research, DCT and DWT will be compared.The Table 9.2 gives MSE of output images by DCT technique and Table 9.3 gives MSE of output images by DWT technique.

Table 9.2: MSE of output images by DCT technique

Image name	MSE
Logo	15368176
Baby	10289294
Penguins	17012605

Table 9.3: MSE of output images by DWT technique

Image name	MSE
Logo	7.23 x 10
Baby	1.36 x 10
Penguins	8.05 x 10

Now using the table 2.42 and table 2.43 we draw two graphs for analyze the data. The Graph for DCT, DWT information loses and total information is shown in Figure 9.3.

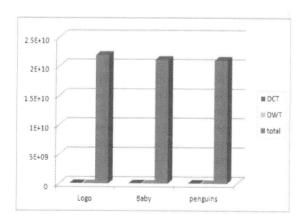

Figure 9.3: Graph for DCT, DWT information loses and total information

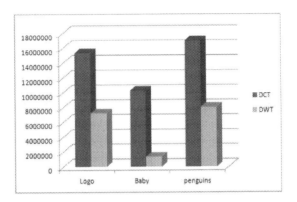

Figure 9.4: Graph for comparing DCT, DWT information lose

Figure 9.4 shows the comparison of DCT and DWT compressed image with its original information. We can confess that loss of information is quite negligible in both technique.From this we conclude that in DWT information loss is less than information loss in DCT. So quality wise the DWT technique is better than DCT technique, but in performance time wise DCT is better than DWT technique.Both techniques are quite efficient for image compression. We can get quite satisfactory compression ratio without loss of much important information. Though our experiments show that DWT technique is much efficient than DCT technique in quality and efficiency wise. But in performance time wise DCT is better than DWT.

The other research shows the estimating the energy compactness of a transform can not be estimate directly, and instead is ap-proximated by watching the reconstruction error of the transform when the number of components used for reconstruction is limited to less than the total number available. To measure this we need some measure to represent the reconstruction accuracy. For this we used standard Peak Signal to Noise Ratios(PSNR), calculated for the difference between the input and output images for each transform.

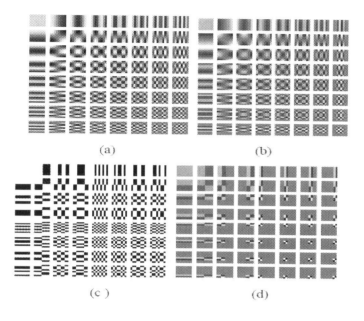

(a)   (b)

(c)   (d)

Figure 9.5: Comparison of (a) DCT(b) DTT(c) WHT (d) Haar

These results show that there is little difference between the DCT and Discrete Tchebichef Transform (DTT), and the Walsh-Hadamard Transform (WHT) gives significantly worse energy compactness than any of the other transforms.

The results also show that the Haar Transform is extremely biased towards images exhibiting rapid gradient changes. Figure 9.5 shows that both the DCT and DTT provide much poorer performance on the sharp changes of the 'Stripes' image, in this image the DTT output forms the DCT, the WHT provides relatable performance till approximately half of the components have been used, at which point it begins to fall behind dramatically. This implies that the low sequence moments of the WHT are less oriented on the image gradients than those of either the DCT or DTT. In this case the Haar Transform

Efficiently outperforms all the other transforms that they have studied.The results implies that the type of image being compressed has a significant effect on the performance of the transforms being used.

In another research they include only the evaluation results for the common 'Lenna' image, and a simple image with rapid intensity variation, 'ruler', these are shown in Figure 9.6 and 9.7. To compare the performance of each transform we measured the reconstruction error, as we improve the number of components used for the reconstruction of each block. The results are shown in Figures 9.6 and 9.7.

For images exhibiting rapid gradient variations the Haar Transform is clearly greatest of all the other transforms, how-ever it is less effective on continuous tone images. For such images either the DCT or DTT could be used, as they show very similar levels of performance. For continuous tone images the DCT is slightly more effective than the DTT, although for images showing rapid gradient changes the reverse is also true. The performance of the WHT is efficiently worse than any of the other transforms we have studied. In continuous tone images the level of performance is continually lower, for images exhibiting rapid gradient changes the performance level is erratic at best, and is still largely below that of the other transforms.

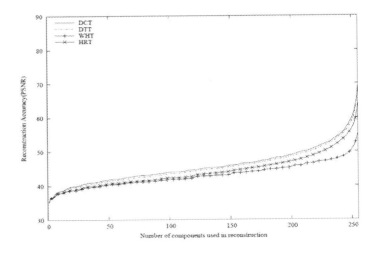

Figure 9.6: Reconstruction error for the 'Lenna' image.

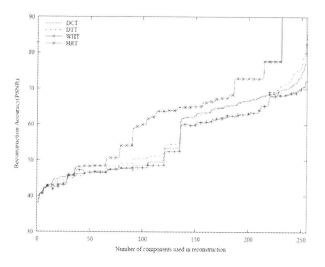

Figure 9.7: Reconstruction error for the `Stripes` image.

In this section the data compression performance of the DWT (Daubechies with 20 coefficients, i.e., Daub20, and Haar), DCT, and WHT is analyzed. The transform coefficients for a narrowband (NBW= 0.2) and a broadband (NBW= 0.5) ultrasonic echoes are shown in Figure 9.8. In this figure the transform coefficients have been ordered from largest to smallest energy, so that the first coefficient graphed is the most energetic one, and the last coefficient graphed is the least energetic.

The echo energy is normalized to 1.On contrast, if the echo has a longer time duration (narrowband), the WHT and DCT kernels will exhibits a higher correlation. The effect of this property is illustrated in Figure 9.9. In this figure the original echo is superimposed to the reconstructed signal using only the most energetic transform coefficient.

The broadband echo can almost be completely reconstructed using one DWT coefficient (Figure 9.9f and Figure 9.9h).On the contrary, more DWT coefficients are required to represent a narrowband signal (Figure 9.9b and Figure 9.9d). The DCT and WHT kernels have higher amplitude (i.e., higher energy) if the signal is narrowband (Figure 9.9a and Figure 9.9c), and lower energy if the signal is broadband (Figure 9.9e and Figure 9.9g). Since all the evaluated transforms are unitary, a high energy concentration of the transform coefficients means that a better data compression performance is achieved.

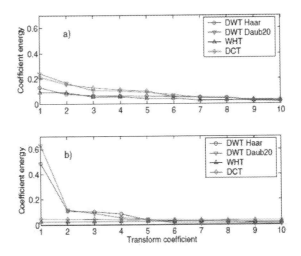

Figure 9.8: Ordered transform coefficientsof ultrasonic
echoes: a) narrowband and b) broadband.

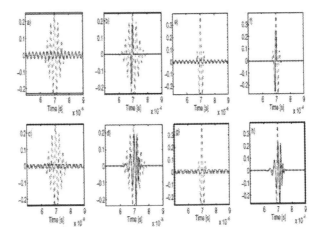

Figure 9.9: Narrowband original echo (dashed line) superimposed to most
energetic coefficient of a) DCT, b) DWT Haar, c) WHT, and d) DWT Daub20.
Broadband original echo (dashed line) superimposed to most energetic
coefficient of e) DCT, f) DWT Haar, g) WHT, and h) DWT Daub20

The compression performance of the DCT, DWT, and WHT as a function of the ultrasonic echo bandwidth (i.e.,NBW) is shown in Figure 9.10. This figure shows the total energy of the 5 most energetic transform coefficients. All signals are 512 16-bits samples long. For a broadband signal the DWT Daub20 outperforms the DCT and WHT, as the DWT coefficients are able to get back over 90% of the signal energy. The DCT and the WHT outperform the DWT for narrowband signals.

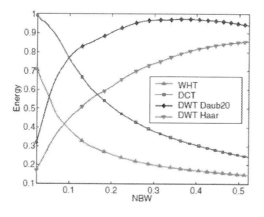

Figure 9.10: Relation between NBW and the
five most energetic transform coefficients.

In this study we have observed ultrasonic signal compression and denoising using the DWT, the DCT, and the WHT. The results acheived show that the DWT is better in the representation of broadband signals, while the DCT and the WHT are more apt in the representation of narrowband signals. For a narrowband ultrasonic signal the 5 most energetic coefficients of the DCT accumulate 95% of the total signal energy, while the DWT and the WHT accumulate 50% and 60% of the total signal energy respectively. On the contrary, for a broadband ultrasonic signal the 5 most dominant DCT coefficients accumulate 30% of the total signal energy, while the DWT and the WHT accumulate 97% and 15% of the total signal energy respectively. Thus, the discrete transform methods analyzed in this paper provide data compression and denoising capabilities for ultrasonic signals suitable for target detection, pattern recognition, and material characterization.

The another results shows the techniques DCT and DWT-SPIHT are compared by using two parameters such as Compressed Size, Compression Ratio, PSNR and MSE values from the reconstructed image. These compression algorithms provide a better performance in picture quality at higher compression ratio. These techniques are successfully tested on fishingboat.tif and crowd.tif images. It is observed that SPIHT provides a better result when compare to DCT. The SPIHT algorithm is coupled with the power of multiresolution analysis, yields significant compression with little quality loss.

The performance and robustness of watermarking algorithms based on DCT and FHT is measured in terms of PSNR and NCC. For that purpose different types of attacks have been implemented on the watermarked image and watermark is recovered using inverse watermarking algorithms based on DCT and FHT. Following attacks have been added to the watermarked image.

The Performace of DCT and FHT are evaluated by adding Gaussian noise. The Figure 9.11 shows DCT based watermarked image after addition of Gaussian noise and recovered watermark and Figure 9.12 shows FHT based watermarked image after addition of Gaussian noise and recovered watermark.

PSNR = 18.645 dB   NCC = 0.368

Figure 9.11: DCT based watermarked image after addition
of Gaussian noise andrecovered watermark

PSNR = 18.482 dB   NCC = 0.436

Figure 9.12: FHT based watermarked image after addition
of Gaussian noise andrecovered watermark

The efficient image watermarking schemes are proposed by using DCT and FHT. Experimental results shows that both schemes are very efficient and robust against various non-geometric attacks. But FHT technique is much better than DCT because in FHT technique imperceptibility is very good. The recovered watermark is also resembles with the original watermark and it can be seen easily from the test results that NCC values is greater in case of FHT as compared to DCT. The computation time for watermarking algorithm using FHT is also very low as compared to DCT.

Advantages of DWT over DCT Transformation of the whole image 1) introduces inherent scaling 2)Better determination of which data is similar to human perception 3) greater compression ratio. Performance Comparison of the DCT based embedded image coder and the SPIHT coder when a three level wavelet transform is used. The Comparison of SPIHT and Embedded DCT are given in Table 9.4.

Table 9.4: Comparison of SPIHT and Embedded DCT

Rate	SPIHT with 3-levelWavelet		Embedded DCT (8x8 DCT only)	
b:p	Lena	Barbara	Lena	Barbara
0.125	30.13	24.16	28.05	24.07
0.25	33.53	27.09	32.27	26.93
0.75	38.86	34.00	38.04	33.73
1.00	40.23	36.17	39.60	36.05

While the DCT-based image coders perform very well at moderate bit rates, at higher compression ratios, image quality degrades because of the artifacts resulting from the block-based DCT scheme.Waveletbased coding on the other hand provides substantial improvement in picture quality at low bit rates because of overlapping basis functions and better energy compaction property of wavelet transforms.

Because of the inherent multi resolution nature, wavelet-based coders initiate progressive transmission of images thereby permitting variable bit rates.The other research shows that the performance of camera man & Lena image in terms of MSE and PSNR values of DCT and DWT are given.

Figure 9.13 gives MSE and PSNR values of camera man with threshold=30 and Lena with threshold=40 for DCT and DWT.The Table 9.5 gives the list of MSE and PSNR values for camera man and Lena for different thresholds.

Figure 9.13: COMPARISON OF VISUAL IMAGE QUALITY OF RECONSTRUCTED IMAGE FOR DCT AND DWT FOR TEST IMAGES (A) CAMERAMAN FOR THRESHOLD 30 (B) LENA FOR THRESHOLD 40

Table 9.5: PSNR (in db) and MSE values at different
threshold values for different test images

IMAGE		CAMERAMAN		LENA	
Threshold	Transform type	DCT	DWT	DCT	DWT
10	PSNR	41.4616	41.8313	37.5321	37.7149
	MSE	4.6443	4.2654	11.4781	11.0050
20	PSNR	37.2135	37.5276	33.2485	33.4413
	MSE	12.3539	11.4901	30.7771	29.4409
30	PSNR	34.8173	35.0832	30.8452	31.1016
	MSE	21.4463	20.1727	53.5249	50.4369
40	PSNR	33.2627	33.4272	29.2907	29.5723
	MSE	30.6769	29.5368	76.5620	71.7549
50	PSNR	32.0103	32.2548	28.1364	28.3884

The comparison of PSNR values for 8*8 DCT and DWT is done using different images.DWT provides better quality than DCT,especially at higher threshld values.For lower threshold values,8*8 DCT gives similar results as DWT but for higfer threshold,the quality of images compressed using DWT slowly degrades,while the quality of 8* DCT compressed images deteriorates rapidly.At lower threshold DCT should be used at higher threshold DCT cannot be used because of poor image quality.There are noticable blocking artifacts in the DCT images at higher threshold values. However,DWT maintains good visula quality at high threshold.

10

QUANTIZATION

Quantization is of two types: scalar quantization and vector quantization. Scalar quantization is a phenomena on which, each pixel is quantized either by decreasing the number of gray levels or by decreasing the resolution. Vector quantization is one in which the entire image is divided into several blocks and a code vector replaces each block. The main principle involved in the vector quantization is the clustering technique, which is employed to generate an optimal codebook for the given training order. After quantizing the training order the authors obtain a codebook which optimally represents the probability distribution of intensities in images. This work mainly concentrates on vector quantization, based on a long training order of input. Methods are discussed to decrease computational complexity of the vector quantizer algorithm, thereby making the codebook pattern faster. The quantizer pattern in the authors' work reduces the psycho visual redundancy present in an image data by quantizing the data. This module can be used in the quantizer step of the overall image compressor.

Color quantization

Color quantization decreases the number of colors used in an image; this is important for displaying images on machines that support a restricted number of colors and for efficiently compressing certain kinds of images. Most bitmap editors and many operating systems have built-in support for color quantization. Popular modern color quantization algorithms include the nearest color algorithm (for fixed palettes), the median cut algorithm, and an algorithm based on octrees.It is common to mix color quantization with dithering to invent an impression of a larger number of colors and eliminate banding artifacts.

Frequency quantization for image compression

The human eye is fairly good at watching small differences in brightness over a relatively large area, but not so good at differentiating the same strength of a high frequency (rapidly varying) brightness variation. This fact allows one to decrease the amount of information needed by eliminating the high frequency components. This is done by simply dividing each component in the frequency domain by a constant for that component, and then rounding to the nearest integer. This is the main lossy operation in the entire progress. As a result of this, it is typically the case that many of the higher frequency components are rounded to zero, and many of the rest become small positive or negative numbers. As human vision is also more reactive to luminance than chrominance, further compression can be obtained by working in a non-RGB color space which divides the two (e.g., YCbCr), and quantizing the channels separately.

10.1 Quantization matrices

A typical video codec works by separating the picture into discrete blocks (8×8 pixels in the case of MPEG). These blocks can then be employed to discrete cosine transform (DCT) to estimate the frequency components, both horizontally and vertically. The resulting block (the same size as the original block) is then pre-multiplied by the quantisation scale code and divided element-wise by the quantization matrix, and rounding each resultant element. The quantization matrix is designed to provide more resolution to more perceivable frequency components over less perceivable components (usually lower frequencies over high frequencies) in addition to transforming as many components to 0, which can be encoded with greatest efficiency. Many video encoders (such as DivX, Xvid, and 3ivx) and compression standards (such as MPEG-2 and H.264/AVC) allow custom matrices to be used. The extent of the reduction may be varied by changing the quantizer scale code, taking up much less bandwidth than a full quantizer matrix.[1]This is an example of DCT coefficient matrix:

$$
\begin{bmatrix}
-415 & -33 & -58 & 35 & 58 & -51 & -5-15 & -12 \\
5 & -34 & 49 & 18 & 27 & 1 & 7 & 3 \\
-46 & 14 & 80 & -35 & -50 & 19 & 36 & -18 \\
-53 & 21 & 34 & -20 & 2 & 34 & 45 & 12 \\
9 & -2 & 9 & -5 & -32 & -15 & 4 & 37 \\
-8 & 15 & -16 & 7 & -8 & 11 & & 7 \\
19 & -28 & -2 & -26 & -2 & 7 & -44 & -21 \\
18 & 25 & -12 & -44 & 35 & 48 & -37 & -3
\end{bmatrix}
\tag{10.1}
$$

A common quantization matrix is:

$$
\begin{bmatrix}
16 & 11 & 10 & 16 & 24 & 40 & 51 & 61 \\
12 & 12 & 14 & 19 & 26 & 58 & 60 & 55 \\
14 & 13 & 16 & 24 & 40 & 57 & 69 & 56 \\
14 & 17 & 22 & 29 & 51 & 87 & 80 & 62 \\
18 & 22 & 37 & 56 & 68 & 109 & 103 & 77 \\
24 & 35 & 55 & 64 & 81 & 104 & 113 & 92 \\
49 & 64 & 78 & 87 & 103 & 121 & 120 & 101 \\
72 & 92 & 95 & 98 & 112 & 100 & 103 & 99
\end{bmatrix}
\tag{10.2}
$$

Dividing the DCT coefficient matrix element-wise with this quantization matrix, and rounding to integers results in:

$$
\begin{bmatrix}
-26 & -3 & -6 & 2 & 2 & -1 & 0 & 0 \\
0 & -2 & -4 & 1 & 1 & 0 & 0 & 0 \\
-3 & 1 & 5 & -1 & -1 & 0 & 0 & 0 \\
-4 & 1 & 2 & -1 & 0 & 0 & 0 & 0 \\
1 & 0 & 0 & 0 & 0 & 0 & 0 & 0 \\
0 & 0 & 0 & 0 & 0 & 0 & 0 & 0 \\
0 & 0 & 0 & 0 & 0 & 0 & 0 & 0 \\
0 & 0 & 0 & 0 & 0 & 0 & 0 & 0
\end{bmatrix}
\tag{10.3}
$$

For example, using -415 (the DC coefficient) and rounding to the nearest integer

$$\text{round}\left(\frac{-415}{16}\right) = \text{round}(-25.9375) = -26 \qquad (10.4)$$

10.2 Vector quantization

Vector quantization is a lossy compression that looks at an array of data, instead of individual datas. It can then generalize what it sees, compressing repeated data, while at the same time regaining the desired object or data stream's original intent. Vector quantization is a classical quantization technique from signal processing which permits the modeling of probability density functions by the distribution of prototype vectors. It was originally used for data compression. It works by dividing a large set of points (vectors) into groups having approximately the same number of points closest to them. Each class is represented by its centroid point, as in k-means and some other clustering algorithms.

The density matching property of vector quantization is effective, especially for determining the density of large and high-dimensioned data. Since data points are represented by the index of their closest centroid, commonly occurring data have low error, and rare data high error. This is why VQ is suitable for lossy data compression. It can also be used for lossy data valuation and density estimation. Vector quantization is based on the competitive learning paradigm, so it is closely compared to the self-organizing map model. A vector quantizer maps *k-dimensional* vectors in the vector space R^k into a finite set of vectors $Y = \{y_i: i = 1, 2, ..., N\}$. Each vector y_i is called a code vector or a *codeword*, and the set of all the codewords is called a *codebook*. Linked with each codeword, y_i, is a nearest neighbor region called *Voronoi* region, and it is defined by:

$$V_i = \{x \in R^k : \| x-y_i \| \le \| x-y_j \|, \text{ for all } j \ne i\}$$

The set of Voronoi regions partition the entire space R^k such that:

$$\bigcup_{i-1}^{N} V_i = R^k$$

$$\bigcap_{i=1}^{N} V_i = \Phi$$

(10.5)

for all $i \neq j$

As an instance we take vectors in the two dimensional case without loss of generality. Figure 10.1 shows some vectors in space. Associated with each cluster of vectors is a representative codeword. Each codeword resides in its own Voronoi region. These areas are separated with imaginary lines in figure 1 for illustration. Given an input vector, the codeword that is chosen to represent it is the one in the same Voronoi region.

The set of discrete amplitude levels is quantized jointly rather than each sample being quantized separately. Consider a K-dimensional vector $x_1, x_2, \dots x_k$ of amplitude levels. It is compressed by choosing the nearest matching vector from a set of N-dimensional vectors $y_1, y_2, \dots y_k$. All possible combinations of the N-dimensional vector $y_1, y_2, \dots y_k$ form the vector space to which all the quantized vectors belong. Only the index of the codeword in the codebook is sent instead of the quantized values. This conserves space and achieves more compression. Twin vector quantization (VQF) is part of the MPEG-4 standard dealing with time domain weighted interleaved vector quantization.

Use in Pattern Recognition

VQ was also used in the eighties for speech and speaker recognition. Recently it has also been used for on-line signature recognition. In pattern recognition applications, one codebook is constructed for each class (being each class a user in biometric applications) using training samples of this user. In the testing phase the quantization distortion of a testing signal is worked out with the whole set of codebooks obtained in the training phase. The codebook that provides the smallest quantization distortion indicates the identified user. The main advantage of VQ in Pattern Recognition is its low computational burden when compared with other techniques such as Dynamic Time Warping (DTW) and Hidden Markov Models (HMM).

The main demerit when compared to DTW and HMM is that it does not takes into account the temporal evolution of the signals (speech, signature, etc.) because all the vectors are combined. In order to rectify this problem a Multi-Section codebook approach has been proposed. The multi-section approach consists of modelling the signal with several sections (for instance, one codebook for the initial part, another one for the center and a last codebook for the ending part).

Measure of VQ performance

How does one rate the performance of a compressed image or sound using VQ? There is no better way to calculate the performance of VQ. This is because the noise that VQ incurs will be evaluated by us humans and that is a subjective measure. Don't despair! We can always resort to good old *Mean Squared Error* (MSE) and *Peak Signal to Noise Ratio* (PSNR). MSE is defined as follows:

$$\text{MSE} = \frac{1}{M} \sum_{i=1}^{M} (\hat{x}_i - x_i)^2 \qquad (10.6)$$

where M is the number of elements in the signal, or image. For instance, if we wanted to find the MSE between the reconstructed and the original image, then we would take the variation between the two images pixel by pixel, square the results, and average the results.

The PSNR is defined as follows:

$$PSNR[n] = 10.\log_{10}((2^n-1)^2/MSE[n])[dB] \qquad (10.7)$$

CONCLUSION

We are comparing the output of different transform coding techniques i.e. Discrete Cosine Transform (DCT) and Discrete Wavelet Transform (DWT) we see that DWT provides higher compression ratios & avoids blocking artifacts. Allows good localization both in spatial & frequency domain. we also see that DCT takes more time than DWT. By doing these experiments we conclude that both techniques have its' own merits and demertis. But, both techniques are quite efficient for image compression. We can get quite reasonable compression ratio without loss of much important information. Though our experiments show that DWT technique is much efficient than DCT technique in quality and efficiency wise. But in performance time wise DCT is better than DWT.

The performance of the WHT is signi cantly worse than any of the other transforms we have studied. In continuous tone images the level of performance is continually lower. for images exhibiting rapid gradient changes the performance level is erratic at best, and is still largely below that of the other transforms. On contrast, more DWT coefficients are required to represent a narrowband signal (Figure 2b and Figure 2d). The DCT and WHT kernels have higher amplitude (i.e., higher energy) if the signal is narrowband (Figure 2a and Figure 2c). and lower energy if the signal is broadband (Figure 2e and Figure 2g). Since all the observed transforms are unitary. a high energy concentration of the transform coefficients implies that a better data compression performance is obtained.

For a broadband signal the DWT Daub20 outperforms the DCT and WHT, as the DWT coefficients are able to regain over 90% of the signal energy. The DCT and the WHT outperform the DWT for narrowband signals.In other research,The DCT and DWT(SPIHT) are compared.It is observed that SPIHT provides a better result when compare to DCT.

The SPIHT algorithm is coupled with the power of multiresolution analysis, yields significant compression with little quality loss. efficient image watermarking schemes are proposed by using DCT and FHT. Experimental results shows that both schemes are very efficient and robust against various non-geometric attacks. But FHT technique is much batter than DCT because in FHT technique imperceptibility is very good. The recovered watermark is also resembles with the original watermark and it can be seen easily from the test results that NCC values is greater in case of FHT as compared to DCT. The computation time for watermarking algorithm using FHT is also very low as compared to DCT.

Hybrid DCT-DWT algorithm for image compression has improved performance as compared to the other standalone techniques, namely DWT and DCT. We observed that DWT technique is more efficient by quality wise than DCT and by performance wise DCT is much better than DWT. In transformation techniques, DCT and Walsh transforms are considered with all transform coefficients and partial transform coefficients For the first set of Georgia Tech Face Database i.e. with 350 test image set, when DCT is used, number of CPU units required is 37879807. With Walsh transform this number reduces to 9 times less than DCT. For Indian Face Database, KFCG algorithm requires 93267 CPU units which are 400 times less than required in DCT and Walsh transform. In KFCG, Codebook size at which highest accuracy is obtained varies as number of test images vary. It varies number of CPU units required in each case.

The comparison of PSNR values for 8*8 DCT and DWT is done using different images.DWT provides better quality than DCT,especially at higher threshld values.For lower threshold values,8*8 DCT gives similar results as DWT but for higfer threshold,the quality of images compressed using DWT slowly degrades,while the quality of 8*8 DCT compressed images deteriorates rapidly.At lower threshold DCT should be used at higher threshold DCT cannot be used because of poor image quality.

There are noticable blocking artifacts in the DCT images at higher threshold values.However,DWT maintains good visula quality at high tthreshold. The DCT based coder has lower complexity than its wavelet-based counterpart. The loss in performance for using DCT instead of the wavelet-transform is only about 0.7db for Lena at 1 b/p. DCT is used for mapping which reduces the inter pixel redundancies followed by quantization which reduces the psycho visual redundancies then coding redundancy is reduced by the use of optimal code word having minimum average length. In JPEG 2000 standard of image compression DWT is used for mapping, all other methods remaining same.They concluded that the existing conventional image compression technology can be developed by combining high performance coding algorithms in appropriate ways, such that the advantages of both techniques are fully exploited.

The coding tools of H.264/AVC when used in an optimized mode allow for bit savings of about 50% compared to previous video coding standards like MPEG-4 and MPEG-2 for a wide range of bit rates and resolutionsH.264 has taken a more pragmatic, focused approach to addressing the problems and needs of current and emerging multimedia applications.H.264 may become the technical leader that will drive the next generation of digital videoapplications. The encoder complexity depends largely on the algorithms for motion estimation as well as for the rate-constrained encoder control. However, before staking a reputation or a product development strategy on thelikely outcome of the 'MPEG-4 vs. H.264' debate, it is worth remembering a similar debatefrom the distant past: VHS *vs.* Betamax. We have proposed an H.264/AVC encoder for high-resolution video. H.264/AVC represents a number of advances in standard video coding technology, in terms of both coding efficiency enhancement and flexibility for effective use over a broad variety of network types and application domains.

On comparing all the Transforms,DCT is the best choice for giving High performance and Low power for H.264/AVC architecture.So, In this research DCT part is modified to get the highest performance and also low power for H.264/AVC in various applications.This research also includes video object detection and tracking of moving objects.It also dicuss about the techniques used for image watermarking and image compression based on wavelets.

LIST OF GLOSSARY & OPERATORS

GLOSSARY:

4:2:0 (sampling) Sampling method: chrominance components have half the horizontal and vertical resolution of luminance component

4:2:2 (sampling) Sampling method: chrominance components have half the horizontal resolution of luminance component

4:4:4 (sampling) Sampling method: chrominance components have same resolution as luminance component

ASO: Arbitrary Slice Order, in which slices may be coded out of raster sequence

CIF: Common Intermediate Format, a colour image format

Direct prediction: A coding mode in which no motion vector is transmitted

Entropy coding: Coding method to reduce redundancy

Error concealment: Post-processing of a decoded image to remove or reduce visible error effects

Exp-Golomb: Exponential Golomb variable length codes

Field: Odd- or even-numbered lines from an interlaced video sequence

Flowgraph: Pictorial representation of a transform algorithm (or the algorithm itself)

FMO: Flexible Macroblock Order, in which macroblocks may be coded out of raster sequence

GOP: Group Of Pictures, a set of coded video images

H.261: A video coding standard

H.263: A video coding standard

H.264: A video coding standard

Huffman coding: Coding method to reduce redundancy

HVS: Human Visual System, the system by which humans perceive andinterpret visual images

Inter (coding): Coding of video frames using temporal prediction or compensation

Interlaced (video): Video data represented as a series of fields

Intra (coding): Coding of video frames without temporal prediction

ISO: International Standards Organisation, a standards body

ITU: International Telecommunication Union, a standards body

JPEG: Joint Photographic Experts Group, a committee of ISO (also an image coding standard)

JPEG2000: An image coding standard

Latency: Delay through a communication system

Level: A set of conformance parameters (applied to a Profile)

Loop filter: Spatial filter placed within encoding or decoding feedback loop

Macroblock: Region of frame coded as a unit (usually 16×16 pixels in the original frame)

Motion prediction: Prediction of a video frame with modelling of motion compensation

Motion estimation: Estimation of relative motion between two or more video frames

Motion vector: Vector indicating a displaced block or region to be used for motioncompensation

MPEG: Motion Picture Experts Group, a committee of ISO/IEC

MPEG-1: A multimedia coding standard

MPEG-2:A multimedia coding standard

MPEG-4: A multimedia coding standard

Objective quality: Visual quality measured by algorithm(s)

Profile: A set of functional capabilities (of a video CODEC)

Progressive (video): Video data represented as a series of complete frames

PSNR: Peak Signal to Noise Ratio, an objective quality measure

Quantise: Reduce the precision of a scalar or vector quantity

Rate control: Control of bit rate of encoded video signal

Rate–distortion: Measure of CODEC performance (distortion at a range of coded bit rates)

SI slice Intra-coded slice used for switching between coded bitstreams (H.264)

Slice: A region of a coded picture

SMPTE: Ultra High Definition Television Image Parameter Values For Program Production.[377]

Subjective quality: Visual quality as perceived by human observer(s)

Test model: A software model and document that describe a reference

TSS Three Step Search, a motion estimation algorithm
VCEG Video Coding Experts Group, a committee of ITU
Video packet: Coded unit suitable for packetisation
YCbCr: Luminance, Blue chrominance, Red chrominance colour space
YUV: A colour space (see YCbCr)

OPERATORS:

1 Arithmetic Operators:
+ Addition.
− Subtraction
++ Increment.
− − Decrement.
// is also used as a comment marker in pseudocode and syntax tables.
Rest of the line is a comment.
| | Absolute value.
abs () Absolute value
$| x | = x$, when $x > 0$
$| x | = 0$, when $x == 0$
$| x | = -x$, when $x < 0$
$Sign(x) = 1$, when $x >= 0$
$Sign(x) = -1$, when $x < 0$
INT () Truncation to integer operator. Returns the integer part of the real-valued argument.
√ Square root.
log2 Logarithm to base 2.

2 Logical operators
| Logical OR.
&& Logical AND.
! Logical NOT
TRUE/FALSE Convention: The syntax uses the convention that a variable or expression evaluating to a nonzero value is equivalent to a condition that is TRUE and a variable or expression evaluating to a zero value is equivalent to a condition that is FALSE.

3 Relational operators
> Greater than.
>= Greater than or equal to.

< Less than.
<= Less than or equal to.
== Equal to.
!= Not equal to.

4 Bitwise operators

A twos complement number representation is assumed where the bitwise operators are used.

& AND
| OR
^ XOR.
>> Shift right with sign extension.
<< Shift left with zero fill.

5 Assignment

= Assignment operator.

6 Pseudocode operations[377]

The following operations are used in the pseudocode to define the decoding process.

- // is a comment to the line end
- /* this is a comment start and end */
- A group of statements enclosed in curly brackets is a compound statement and is treated functionally as a single statement.
- while (condition) (statement)
/* specifies repeated execution of statement until condition is no longer true. */
- for(initial statement; condition; subsequent statement) (primary statement)
/* specifies evaluation of intial statement followed by evaluation of condition, and if condition is true, specifies repeated execution of primary statement followed by subsequent statement until condition is no longer true */
- if(condition) (statement) else (alternate statement)
/* statement is executed if condition is true, alternate statement is executed otherwise */
- goto Label
/* jumps to the labeled statement represented as "Label: statement" */

LIST OF COMMONLY USED WEBSITES

S.NO	NAME OF THE WEBSITES REFERED
	http://www.iso.org/
	http://www.mpeg.org/MPEG
	http://www.itu.int/
	http://www.mpegla.com/
	http://www.smpte.org/
	http://mp4web.sourceforge.net/
	http://www.eetimes.com/
	http://www.dspguru.com/
	http://www.dspguide.com/
	http://www.eee.bham.ac.uk/woolleysi/links/datacomp.htm
	htttp://www.siggraph.org/education
	http://www.vcdhelp.com/
	http://bmrc.berkeley.edu/frame/research/mpeg/mpeg2faq.html
	http://www.thedigitalbits.com/articles/anamorphic/index.html
	http://mediasoftware.sonypictures.com/support/phonesupport.asp
	http://www.apple.com/quicktime/upgrade/
	http://www.sigmadesigns.com/products/MPEG4_video_encoder.htm
	http://mpeg.telecomitalialab.com
	http://mpeg.telecomitalialab.com/standards/mpeg-4/mpeg-4.htm

S.NO	NAME OF THE WEBSITES REFERED
	http://www.acm.org/sigs/sigmm/MM2000/ep/michelle/
	http://www.streamingmedia.com/tutorials/view.asp?tutorial_id=149
	http://www.everwicked.com/content/MPEG4IP_Guide/index.php
	http://www.extremetech.com/
	http://www.ivast.com/
	http://www.ncsu.edu/it/multimedia/380-kbs/IndianCrow320.mp4
	http://www.philips.com/
	http://www.francetelecom.fr/
	http://www.w3.org/AudioVideo/
	http://www.iec.org/
	http://www.isma.tv/
	http://www.ietf.org/

LIST OF REFERENCES

1. R. J. Clarke, "Digital compression of still images and video," Academic Press, San Diego, CA, 1995.
2. M. J. Riley and I. E. G. Richardson, "Digital video communications," Artech House Publishers, Boston, MA, 1997.
3. M. Tekalp, "Digital video processing," Englewood Cliffs, NJ: Prentice Hall, 1995.
4. HR Wu, W Lin, LJ Karam, "An overview of Perceptual processing for Digital pictures," IEEE conference on Multimedia and Expo Workshops (ICMEW),pp.113-120, 2012.
5. http://flylib.com/books/en/
6. Michal Irani*, P. Anandan, Jim Bergen, Rakesh Kumar, Steve Hsu, dang,"Efficient representations of video sequences and their applications," David Sarnoff Research Center, Princeton,U.S.A, pp.1-39, 1996.
7. M Ghanbari, "Video quality measurement", WO 2004/054274, Publication date 24 June 2004.
8. www.slideshare.net/ypnayak/video-enc-basicppttype
9. Philip Dang, "VLSI architecture for real-time image and video processing systems,", J Real-Time Image Proc,vol.1, pp.57-62, 2006.
10. Felipe Portavales Goldstein, "Video encoding: basic principles," International Journal of Image Processing (IJIP) Vol.3, Iss.6,
11. John G. Apostolopoulos, "Video Compression: Principles, Practice, and Standards", HP Labs, Palo Alto, CA.
12. http://en.wikipedia.og/wiki/HSL_and HSV/
13. http://www.huevaluechroma.com/071.php/
14. Dr.-Ing.Markus Rupp, "Vision and Image characteristics useful for compression," in 4F8 Image coding course, Nick Kingsbury
15. Ethan D. Montag,Mark D. Fairchild and Chester F. Carlson, "Gamut Mapping: Evaluation of Chroma ClippingTechniques for Three

Destination Gamuts," in Sixth Color Imaging Conference: Color Science, Systems, and Applications, pp.57-61, 1998.

16. E. R. Kretzmer, Bell System Tech. J. 31, 751-763 (1952). From Kretzmer, E.R., Bell Syst. Tech.

17. H. R. Wu K. R. Rao, "Digital video image quality and perceptual coding",

18. http://citeseerx.ist.psu.edu/viewdoc/

19. http://en.wikipedia.org/wiki/Data-compression/

20. V. Bhaskaranand K. Konstantinides, Image and Video Compression Standards: Algorithms and Architectures, Boston, Massachusetts, KluwerAcademic Publishers, 1997.

21. GökhanSimsek, "An approach to summarize video data in compressed domain," A Thesis Submitted to The Graduate School of Engineering and Sciences ofzmir Institute of Technology, 2007.

22. http://bbc.co.uk/rd/pubs/papers/

23. DR Bull, EJ Delp, S Takamura, "Introduction to the Issue on Emerging Technologies for Video Compression," IEEE Journal of Selected Topics in Signal Processing, vol.5, pp.1277-1281, 2011.

24. DjordjeMitroric, "Video compression", University of Edinburgh.

25. LA Rowe, "Video Compression", Lecture at the University of Berkeley, 1995.

26. S. J. Solari "Digital Video and Audio Compression", McGraw-Hill New York, 1997.

27. A. Bovik, (Ed), "Handbook of image and video processing," Orlando, FL: Academic Press, 2000. II Edition 2005

28. D.S. Peter, "Video compression: Fundamental compression techniques and an overview of the JPEG and MPEG compression systems", New York, NY: 1998.

29. Liming Mei, "A DWT Based Perceptual Video Coding Framework - Concepts, Issues and Techniques", A Thesis Submitted to RMIT university,2008.

30. ChamindaSampathKannangara, "Complexity Management ofH.264 AVC Video Compression", A Thesis Submitted to Robert Gordon University, 2006.

31. M Domański, "Image and Video Compression: Current Trends and Perspectives," in International conference on Signals and Electronic systems", pp 57-60, 2001.

32. http:en.wikipedia/wiki/HEVC/

33. Miguel Lobato de Faria Pereira Capelo, "Advances on Transforms for High Efficiency Video Coding",A Thesis Submitted to Jury University, 2011.

34. P. D. Symes, "Video compression,", McGraw-Hill New York, NY:, 1998.

35. David Strachan, Margarida DeBruinand RobertMarhong, "Video compression", Society of Motion Picture and Television Engineers, 1996.

36. ISO/IEC 10918-1, "Information Technology-Digital compression and coding of continueous tone still images:requirements and guidelines",Geneva,1994.

37. Yun Q.Shi,Huifang Sun, "Image and video comp for multimedia engineering", CRC press, Bocaraton,2008.

38. Sreejana Sharma M.S.,Dr.K.R.Rao, "Transcoding of h.264 bitstream to mpeg-2 bitstream" A Thesis Submitted to University of Texas at Arlington, 2007.

39. http://en.wikipedia.org/wiki/Bit-rate/

40. http://eetimes.com/design/signal-processing-dsp/4017518/How-video-compression-works

41. JörnOstermann, Jan Bormans, Peter List, DetlevMarpe, Matthias Narroschke,Fernando Pereira, Thomas Stockhammer, and Thomas Wedi, "Video coding with H.264/AVC: Tools, Performance, and Complexity," Circuits and systems magazine, IEEE,vol.4,no.1, pp.7-28,2004.

42. BG Haskell, PG Howard, YA LeCun, "Image and video coding-emerging standards and beyondTechnology," IEEE transactions on circuits and systems for video technology, vol.8, no.7, 1998.

43. I Ahmad, X Wei, Y Sun, "Video transcoding: an overview of various techniques and research issues," IEEE transactions on Multimedia, vol.17, pp.793-804, 2005.

44. K.R. Rao and J.J. Hwang, "Techniques and standards for digital image/video/audio coding," Englewood Cliffs, NJ: Prentice Hall, 1996.

45. Iain.E.G.Richardson, "H.264 and MPEG-4 video compression:Video Coding for Next-generation Multimedia", Johnwiley& sons ltd.,2003.

46. H.R. Wu and K.R. Rao (Editors), "Digital video image quality and perceptual coding", CRC press, 2006.

47. Chung-Tao Chu, DimitrisAnastassiou, Shih-Fu Chang, "Hybrid Object-Based/Block-Based Coding in Video Compression at Very Low Bitrate," Signal Processing: Image Communication, vol.10, pp.157-171, 1997.

48. MohammedGhanbari, "Standard Codecs: Image Compression to Advanced Video Coding.London, UK: IEE, 2003.

49. D Dalby,RJ Whiting, JM O'donnell,"Video coding", A R Leaning, 2002.

50. Thomas sikora, "Trends and perspectives In image and video coding," in Proceedings of the IEEE, vol. 93, no. 1, pp. 6–17, Jan 2005.

51. Bibhas Chandra Dhara, "Image and Video Compression using Block Truncation Coding and Pattern Fitting for Fast Decoding", Thesis, Jadavpur University,2008.

52. Luis Torres, Murat Kunt, Fernando Pereira, "Second generation video coding schemes and their role in MPEG-4" In European Conf. on Multimedia Applications, Services and Techniques, pp.799-824, Louvian-la-Neuve, Belgium, May 1996.

53. Michael Igarta, "A study of MPEG-2 and H.264 video coding",A Thesis Submitted toPurdue University, 2004.

54. http:en.wikipedia.org/wiki/H.261/

55. AlexandrosEleftheriadi and Arnaud Jacquin, "LOW BIT RATE MODEL-ASSISTED H.261-COMPATIBLE CODING OF VIDEO," Proceedings, 2nd IEEE International Conference on Image Processing (ICIP-95),pp. II.428-421, 1995.

56. http://www.itu.int/ITU-T/

57. Video codec for audio-visual services at p×64 Kbits/s,ITU-T. Recommandation,1990.

58. Jeremiah Golston, "Comparing Media Codecs for Video Content," in Embedded Systems Conference,San Francisco 2004.

59. www.ftp:ftp.imtc-files.org/jvt-experts

60. http://en.wikipedia.org/wiki/H.261

61. Recommendation H.261: Codec for audio visual services at n=38 Kbits/s,Melbourne,1988.

62. JVT,Testmodel software, http://bs.hhi.de/~suehring/tml/download

63. L Hanzo, P Cherriman, J Streit, "H.261: Video codec for audiovisual services at p x 64 kbit/s",Video compression and communications: from basics to H. 261, H. 263, H. 264, MPEG4 for DVB and HSDPA-style adaptive turbo-transceivers, ITU-T, 2007.

64. WS Chen, YY Peng, YT Chang, "Design and implementation of real-time software-based H. 261 video codec", in Proc. ICCE, 2001.

65. J.Kim, "System level modeling and Implementation of video codec" hostdb.ece.utexas.edu.

66. Tsuhanchen, "video coding for multimedia communication:H.261,H.263 and beyond",Video coding standards for Multimedia communication, pp.1-27, 2009.

67. http://www.uh.edu/~hebert/ece6354/H261-report.pdf

68. http://www.siggraph.org/education/materials/HyperGraph /.../H261.htm

69. C. M. Sharon I. Lambadaris M. Devetsikiotis A. R. Kaye, "Accurate Modeling of H.261 VBR Video Sources for Packet Transmission Studies," in Embedded Systems Conference, San Francisco, 2004.

70. D Brinthaupt, L Letham, V Maheshwari, "A video decoder for H. 261 video teleconferencing and MPEG stored interactive video applications," Technical Papers, 1993.

71. Den-Yuan Hsiau' and Ja-Ling Wu'r, "REAL-TIME PC-BASED SOFTWARE IMPLEMENTATION OF H.261 VIDEO CODE," IEEE Transactions on Consumer Electronics, Vol. 43, No. 4, 1997.

72. H.261 implementation application report.Texasinstruments,SPRA 161,1997.

73. H.261 Implementation on the TMS320C80 DSP, Texas Instruments (www.ti.com/general/docs/),1997.

74. http://www.bbc.co.uk/rd/pubs/papers/

75. http://computer.yourdictionary.com > Computer Definitions

76. http://en.wikipedia.org/wiki/H.262/MPEG-2_Part_2

77. http://en.wikipedia.org/wiki/H.262/MPEG-2_Part_2

78. http://www.tutorgig.net/t/Digicipher%2B2

79. "Generic coding of moving pictures and associated audio information – Part 2:Video," ITU-T Rec. H.262 and ISO/IEC 13818-2 (MPEG-2), Nov. 1994.

80. Pinnacle, "MPEG-2 White Paper", pp 2/2.2000.

81. http://iphome.hhi.de/wiegand/assets/.../DIC_vcs...

82. A. Puri, "Video coding using the MPEG-2 compression standard",in Proc. SPIE EI—Visual Communication and Image Processing, vol. 1199, pp. 1701–1713,1993.

83. http://www.itu.int/rec/T-REC-H.262-200011-S!Amd1/en

84. K. Konstantinides et al, "Design of an MPEG-2 codec", IEEE SP Magazine, vol.19, pp.32-41, July 2002.

85. "Video Test Model Editing Committee, MPEG-2 video test", ISO/IEC JTC1/SC29/WG11 N0400, April1993.

86. ITU-T, "H.262-Corrigendum1,2000.

87. B.G. Haskell, A. Puri, A.N. Netravali, "Generic Coding of Moving Pictures and Associated Audio Information", Introduction to MPEG-2,New York, May 1996.

88. Generic coding of moving pictures and associated audio information,ISO/IEC 13818-2:video(Mpeg-2),1996.

89. John Watkinson, "The MPEG Handbook (MPEG-1, MPEG-2, MPEG-4)" Focal press; 2 edition,2004.

90. http://www.bbc.co.uk/rd/pubs/papers/

91. http://trap.mtview.ca.us/~tom/tech/file/

92. http:// flylib.com/books/en/2.495.1.325/

93. http://en.wikipedia.org/wiki/Bit-rate/

94. SONY, "MPEG Encoding Overview: Using the Main Concept MPEG-2 plug-in", 2003.

95. T Demura, T Oto, K Kitagaki, S Ishiwata, "A single-chip MPEG2 video decoder LSI",TechnicalPapers,1994.

96. http://www.cs.washington.edu/education/courses/.../ garysullivansmall.pdf

97. K Kim, JS Koh, "An area efficient DCT architecture for MPEG-2 video encoder," IEEE Transactions on consumer electronics, 1999.

98. E Morimatsu, K Sakai, K Yamashita, "Development of a VLSI chip for real time MPEG-2 video decoder," Image Processing, 1995.

99. http://en.wikipedia.org/wiki/H.263

100. http://www.cmlab.csie.ntu.edu.tw/cml/dsp/training/coding] /h263/introduction/ html

101. http:// www.javvin.com/ protocolH263.html

102. http://www-mobile.ecs.soton.ac.uk/peter/

103. htttp://www.cmlab.csie.ntu.edu.tw/cml/dsp

104. Guy C^ot'e,BernaErol, Michael Gallant,andFaouziKossentini, "H.263+: Video Coding at Low Bit Rates",IEEE transactions on circuits and systems for video technology, Vol.8, no.7, pp 849-866, 1998.

105. MSRDN Tripathi, MAK Verma, A Shukla, "Designing and optimization of codec H-263 for mobile applications," IJCSNS, 2009.

106. http://www.itu.int/rec/T-REC-H.263/en

107. http://www.design-reuse.com/wiki/h.263

108. A Ben Atitallah, P Kadionik, F Ghozzi, P Nouel, "An FPGA implementation of HW/SW codesign architecture for H. 263 video coding",International Journal of Electronics & communication,vol.61,no.9pp 605-620, 2007.

109. M Freytes, CE Rodriguez, "Real-time H. 263+ video transmission on 802.11 wireless LANs Technology",IEEE, 2001.

110. L Hanzo, P Cherriman, J Streit, "Video compression and communications: From Basics to H.261, H.263, H.264, MPEG2, MPEG4 for DVB and HSDPA-Style AdaptiveTurbo-Transceivers",University of Southampton, UK, 2007.

111. ITU-T, "Transmission of non-telephone signals video coding for low bit rate communication:ITU-T Recommendation H.263, 1996.

112. http://www.h323forum.org/papers/: H.323 papers and documents

113. http:// www.javvin.com/ protocolH263.html

114. H.263: Video CODEC for Medium Quality Videoconferencing:http:// www.javvin.com

115. http://www.javvin.com/protoco/rfc2190.pdf: RTP Payload Format for H.263 Video Streams

116. http://online.movavi.com/format-h263.html

117. ITU-T, "Video coding for low bit rate communication," ITU-T Rec. H.263; v1: Nov. 1995, v2: Jan. 1998,v3: Nov. 2000.

118. ITU-T, "Video coding for low bit rate communication", Transmission of non-telephone signals, Geneva, 1996.

119. Jeremiah Golston, "Comparing Media Codecs for Video Content", Texas Instruments., in Embedded Systems Conference, San Francisco, 2004.

120. P Dang, "VLSI architecture for real-time image and video processing systems", Springer, 2006

121. http://en.wikipedia.org/wiki/H.263

122. http://www.itu.int/ITU-T/

123. T. Wiegand, G. J. Sullivan, G. Bjontegaard, and A. Luthra, "Overview of the H.264/AVC Video Coding Standard", IEEE Transactions on Circuits and Systems for Video Technology, Vol. 13, no. 7, pp. 560-576, 2003.

124. "Video Codec for Audio Visual Services at px64 kbits/s", ITU-TRecommendation H.261, 1990.

125. "Coding of Moving Pictures and Associated Audio for Digital storage Media at up to About 1.5 Mbits/s", ISO/IEC 1117-2: Video (MPEG-1), Nov. 1991.

126. "Generic Coding of Moving Pictures and Associated Audio Information", ISO/IEC 13818-2: Video (MPEG-2), May. 1996.

127. "Video Coding for Low Bit Rate Communication", Version 1,ITU-T Recommendation H.263, 1995.

28. "Coding of Audio-Visual Objects", Part 2: Visual,.ISO/IEC 14496-2 (MPEG-4 visual version 1), 1999.

129. M.MahdiGhandi and Mohammad Ghanbari, "The H.264/AVC video coding standard for the next generation multimedia communication," IAEE Journal., Vol. 1, No. 2, pp. 1–10, 2004.

130. Quicktime and Mpeg-4: Now featuring H.264. For more information www.apple.com/quicktime

131. ISO/IEC JTC 1/SC 29/WG 11 (MPEG), "Report of the formal verification tests on AVC/H.264", MPEG document N6231, Dec., 2003.

132. "Draft ITU-T Recommendation and Final Draft International Standard of Joint Video Specification (ITU-T Rec. H.264 | ISO/IEC 144496-10 AVC)", Joint Video Team of ISO/IEC and ITU-T, March 2003.

133. Chung-Ming Chen and Chung-Ho Chen Jian-Ping Zeng, Wan-Chug Hsu and Chao-Tang Yu, "Windows Processing for Deblocking Filter in H.264/AVC", in IEEE conference,IECON2006,paris,2006.

134. "H.264 video compression standard:New possibilities within video surveillance", White paper, Axis communications, 2008.

135. http://www.javvin.com/protocol/rfc3984.pdf

136. http://www.vcodex.com/h264.html

137. "Mpeg-4 AVC /H.264 video coding", wipro, 2004.

138. T. Wedi, "Motion compensation in H.264/AVC", IEEE Trans. Circuits Syst. Video Technol., vol. 13, pp. 577–586, Jul. 2003.

139. Nukhet OZBEK and Turhan TUNALI, "A survey on the H.264/AVC standard", in Turk j ElecEngin., vol. 13, pp. 287-302, 2005.

140. Gary J.Sullivan, pankajTopiwala and Ajay Luthra, "The H.264 /AVC Advanced Video Coding standard:Overview and introduction to the Fidelity Range Extensions", in Proc.SPIEXXVII., pp. 1–21, 2004.

141. Ahmed Abu-Hajar, "Introduction to H.264 video coding standard: Hardware challenges and oppurtinities," DIGITAVID,Inc, San Jose, CA.

142. http://spiedigitallibrary.aip.org

143. AtulPuri,XueminChen,AjayLuthra, "Video coding using the H.264/ MPEG-4 AVC compression standard", Elsivier Journal of signal processing: Image communication, Vol.19,pp. 793-849, 2004.

144. Iain E.G. Richardson, "H.264 and MPEG-4 Video Compression, Video Coding for Next Generation Multimedi",vol.6,2003.

145. http://www.slideshare.net/Videoguy/overview-of-the-h264avc-video-coding-standard-circuits

146. H. Malvar, A. Hallapuro, M. Karczewicz, and L. Kerofsky, "Low-Complexity transform and quantization in H.264/AVC", IEEE Trans Circuits Syst. Video Technol., vol. 13, pp. 598–603, July 2003.

147. "Generic coding of moving pictures and associated audio", ISO/IEC 13818-2, Draft International Standard, November 1994.

148. P. List, A. Joch, J. Lainema, G. Bjøntegaard, and M. Karczewicz, "Adaptive deblocking filter", IEEE Trans. Circuits Syst. Video Technol., vol. 13, pp. 614–619, July 2003.

149. Chung-Ming Chen and Chung-Ho Chen Jian-Ping Zeng, Wan-Chug Hsu and Chao-Tang Yu, "Windows Processing for Deblocking Filter in H.264/AVC", in IEEE conference,IECON2006,paris,2006.

150. T. Wiegand, G. Sullivan, A. Luthra, "Draft ITU-T Recommendation and final draft international standard of joint video specification (ITU-T Rec.H.264|ISO/IEC 14496-10 AVC)", JVT-G050rl, Geneva, May 2003.

151. http://en.wikipedia.org/wiki/context_adaptive_binary_arithmetic_coding

152. http://en.wikipedia.org/wiki/Context-adaptive_variable-length_coding

153. Iain E Richardson, "The H.264 Advanced Video Compression Standard", John Wiley & Sons, 2010.

154. D. Marpe, H. Schwarz, and T.Wiegand, "Context-adaptive binary arithmetic coding in the H.264/AVC video compression standard", IEEE Trans. Circuits Syst. Video Technol., vol. 13, pp. 620–636, Jul. 2003.

155. Alonso A. de A. Schmidt, Altamiro A. Susin, "CABAC Integration Into an H.264/AVC Intra-only Hardware Video Decoder." Symposium on Microelectronics,2011.

156. J.L. Chen, Y.K. Lin, and T.S Chang, "A low cost context adaptive arithmetic coder for H.264/MPEG-4 AVC video coding," In *Proc. ICASSP 2007*, vol. II, pp.105-108, 2007.

157. http://bradbury.informatics.indiana.edu/~daewkim/I500_Lab_Fall_11/Lab7/ Lab7.html

158. J. Ribas-Corbera, P.A.Chou, and Regunathan, "A generalized hypotheticalreference decoder for H.264/AVC", IEEE Trans. Circuits Syst.VideoTechnol, vol. 13, pp. 674–687, Jul. 2003.

159. JornOsterman,janBormans,PeterList,DetlevMarpe,MatthiasNarroschke,FernandoPereira, ThomasStockhammer,and Thomas Wedi "Video coding with H.264/AVC: Tools,Performance, and Complexity", IEEE Circuits and Syst. magazine., vol. 4, pp. 7–28, 2004.

160. M. Horowitz, A. Joch, F. Kossentini, A. Hallapuro, "H.264/AVC Baseline Profile Decoder Complexity Analysis", IEEE Transactions on Circuits and Systems for Video Technology, Vol. 13, no. 7, pp. 704-716, 2003.

161. A. Kaup, H. Mooshofer, "Performance and complexity analysis of rate constrained motion estimation in MPEG-4," in Proc.SPIE Multimedia Systems and Applications, pp. 202–211,1999.

162. V. Lappalainen, A. Hallapuro, T. D. Hamalainen, "Complexity of optimized H.26L video decoder implementation", IEEE Trans. Circuits Systems Video Technol. 13 (7), pp.717–723, Jul. 2003.

163. Limin Liu, Member, IEEE, Zhen Li, Member, IEEE, and Edward J. Delp, Fellow, "Efficient and Low-Complexity Surveillance Video Compression Using Backward-Channel Aware Wyner–Ziv Video Coding", IEEE transactions on circuits and systems for video technology, vol. 19, no. 4, April 2009.

164. G. J. Sullivan, J.-R. Ohm, W.-J. Han, and T. Wiegand, "Overview of the High Efficiency Video Coding (HEVC) standard," *IEEE Trans. Circuits Syst. Video Technol.*, vol. 22, no. 12, pp. 1648–1667, Dec. 2012.

165. http://www.vocodex.com/h.265.html

166. G. Sullivan, T. Wiegand, and K.-P. Lim, "Joint model reference encoding methods and decoding concealment methods," *Joint Video Team (JVT) of ISO/IEC MPEG and ITU-T VCEG, Doc. JVT-I049*, July 2003.

167. http://www.thefullwiki.org/D-frame/

168. http://en.wikipedia.org/wiki/MPEG-1/

169. John Watkinson, "The MPEG Handbook:MPEG-1,MPEG-2 and MPEG-4",focal press,Elsivier publications,2001.

170. "Coding of Moving Pictures and Associated Audio for Digital storage Media at up to About 1.5 Mbits/s",ISO/IEC 1117-2: Video (MPEG-1),November, 1991.

171. ISO/IEC JTC 1/SC 29/WG 11 (MPEG), "Report of the formal verification tests on AVC/H.264," MPEG document N6231, Dec., 2003.

172. Ketanmayer-patel,lawrence a. Rowe, "The Berkely software MPEG-1 video decoder",ACM Transactions on Multimedia Computing, Communications and Applications, Vol. 1, No. 1, pp 110–125, 2005.

173. A. Puri, "Video coding using the MPEG-1 compression standard", in Proc. the International Symposium of Society for Information Display, pp. 123–126,1992.

174. P.N.Tudor, "MPEG-2 video compression,electronics and communicatior engineering journal,December 1995.

175. http://boards.fool.com/quotphilipo-i-dou/

176. http://www.ee-techs.com/meeting/32.ppt

177. A. Puri, R. L. Schmidt, B. G. Haskell, "Performance evaluation of the MPEG-4 visual coding standard",in Proc. SPIE EI-Visual Communication and Image Processing, 1998.

178. K.R.Rao, "MPEG-4-the emerging multimedia standard", in Proc. Second IEEE,1988.

179. INTERNATIONAL ORGANISATION FOR STANDARDISATION, ISO/IEC JTC1/SC29/WG11,CODING OF MOVING PICTURES AND AUDIO,March 2002.

180. http://forum.digital-digest.com/f120/

181. MPEG-4 Industry forum, "MPEG-4 the media standard",The landscape of advanced multimedia coding,m4-out-20027-R3.pdf, 2002.

182. Prof. B. L. Evans, "System Modeling and Implementation of MPEG-4 Encoder under Fine-Granular-Scalability Framework:Final report",Embeeded software systems, 2002.

183. A Navarro, A Silva, J Tavares."MPEG-4 codec performance using a fast integer IDCT", ISCE'06. 2006.

184. F. Pereira and T. Ebrahimi, (Eds), "The MPEG-4 book," IMSC Press, Prentice Hall, Upper Saddle River, NJ, 2002.

185. Olivier Avaro, AlexandrosEleftheriadis, CarstenHerpel, Ganesh Rajan, Liam Ward, "MPEG-4 systems overview", Signal Processing: Image Communication, ELSIVIER, pp.281-298, 2000.

186. ISO/IEC JTC 1, "Coding of audio-visual objects – Part 2: Visual", ISO/IEC 14496-2 (MPEG-4 Part 2), Jan. 1999.

187. K. Panusopone, X. Chen, R. Eifrig, A. Luthra, "Coding tools in MPEG-4 interlaced video, IEEE Trans. Circuits" Systems Video Technol. 10 (5), (August 2000) 755–766.

188. http://mpeg.chiariglione.org/quality_tests.htm

189. AtulPuri a and AlexandrosEleftheriadisb,"An object-based multimedia coding standard supporting mobile applications", citeseerx, 2003.

90. PM Kuhn, W Stechele, Complexity analysis of the emerging MPEG-4 standard as a basis for VLSI implementation,in Proc. Photonics West,1998.

91. http://en.wikipedia.org.wiki/RealVideo/

92. http://wpedia.goo.ne.jp/enwiki/Realvideo/

93. http://www.smecc.org/real_media.htm/

94. http://www.streamingstar.com/streaming-m/

95. http://www.videoconverterfactory.com/glo./

96. http://www.ogg-converter.net/mkv/convert/

97. http://en.wikipedia.org/wiki/RealPlayer/

198. http://www.realnetworks.com/helix/download-streaming-media-products/

199. http://www.real.com/international/index.html/

200. http://www.siggraph.org/education/material/

201. http://www.real.com/

202. http://uk.real.com/realplayer/thank_you_for_downloading/

203. K Kosuge, "The Real Players",IEEE 15/100/6096005/06096021, 8 Dec 2011.

204. Sven Hessler,MichaelWelzl, "An Empirical Study of the Congestion Response of RealPlayer, Windows MediaPlayer and Quicktime", ISSC, 2005.

205. http://docs.real.com/docs/rn/rv10/RV10_Tech_Overview.pdf/

206. http://www.divx.com/

207. http://en.wikipedia.org/wiki/Digital_Video_ExpressDIVX/

208. http://www.divx-digest.com/

209. http://en.wikipedia.org/wiki/DivX/

210. http://en.wikipedia.org/wiki/Mayonnaisemayonnaise/

211. http://www.free-codecs.com/download/divx.htm/

212. M.Dreese, "A quick introduction to DivX recording",Terratec Electronic GmbH,2003.

213. www.divxmovies.com/codec/

214. www.divx.com/en/software/divx-plus/technologies/

215. http://www.sourceforge.net/projects/drdivx/

216. http://en.wikipedia.org/wiki/Windows_Media_Video/

217. http://support.microsoft.com/default.aspx?scid=kb;en-us;Q316992Media Player Formats

218. http://works.bepress.com/jzhang/

219. http://www.microsoft.com/windows/windowsmedia/player/wmcomponents.mspxPlay/

220. http://filext.com/file-extension/WMV/

221. http://www.tesionline.com/intl/

222. Sridhar Srinivasan, Pohsiang (John) Hsu, TomHolcom b KunalMukerjee,Shankar L. Regunathan, Bruce Lin, Jie Liang, Ming Chieh Lee, JordiRibas-Corbera, "Windows Media Video 9: overview and applications", Signal Processing: Image Communication, Elsivier pp.1-24, 2004.

223. http://en.wikipedia.org/wiki/WMV_HDWMV/

224. http://wiki.videolan.org/

225. http://www.theora.org/

226. http://free-electrons.com/community/videos/mini-howto/
227. http://people.xiph.org/~maikmerten/youtube/
228. http://theoradesign.com/
229. http://xiph.org/theora/
230. http://www.theora.org/doc/Theora.pdf/
231. http://www.ffmpeg2theora --deinterlace -o video.ogv video.dv/
232. http://www.students.ic.unicamp.br/~ra023772/images/
233. http://en.flossmanuals.net/ogg-theora/
234. http://v2v.cc/~j/SimpleTheoraEncoder/
235. TillHalbach," A performance assessment of the royalty-free and open video compression specifications Dirac, Dirac Pro, and Theora and their open-source implementations",2009.
236. http://en.wikipedia.org/wiki/Audio_Video_Standard/
237. Wen Gao1, Cliff Reader2, Feng Wu3, Yun He4, Lu Yu5,Hanqing Lu6, Shiqiang Yang7, Tiejun Huang1, Xingde Pan8," AVS - The Chinese Next-Generation Video Coding Standard", National Association of Broadcasters, Las Vegas, 2004.
238. L. Yu et al. "An Overview of AVS-Video: tools, performance and complexity", Visual Communications and Image Processing 2005, Proc. of SPIE, vol. 5960, pp.596021, July 31, 2006.
239. http://www.avs.org.cn/en/
240. Project on "Low Complexity AVS-China Part-2 video using data mining techniques" by Jennie Abraham: http://www- ee.uta.edu/Dip/Courses/EE5359/jennieproposal.doc
241. Swaminathan Sridhar, Dr.K.R.Rao and Dr.Zhang,"A LITERATURE REVIEW ON AVS CODEC", EE 5359 Multimedia Processing Project, 2009.
242. X. Wang et.al "Performance comparison of AVS and H.264/AVC video coding standards" J. Comput. Sci. & Technol., Vol.21, No.3, pp.310-314 J, May 2006.
243. Sharan K Chandrashekar," Overview, implementation and comparison of Audio Video Standard (AVS) China and H.264/MPEG -4 part 10 or Advanced Video Coding Standard",EE-5359 Class Project, Multimedia Processing, 2013.
244. Kaustubh Vilas Dhonsale, "Overview of H.264 and Audio Video coding Standards (AVS) China", Special issue on 'AVS and its Applications',Signal Processing: Image Communication, vol. 24, pp. 245-344, April 2009.

245. JBankoski,P Wilkins and Yaowu Xu, "Technical Overview OfVP8, An Open Source video codec for the web," static.googleusercontent. com/US/37073.pdf.

246. http://www.en.wikipedia.org/wiki/VP8

247. http://www.codecs.com/VP8_reviews.htm

248. http://www.free-codecs.com/download/VP8.htm

249. Google, "VP8 Reference Implemenation libvpx," 2011. http://webm. googlecode.com/files/libvpx-v0.9.6.zip.

250. http://www.webmproject.org/tools/

251. SA Cassidy, "An Analysis of VP8, a new Video Codec for the Web", Thesis submitted to Rochester Institute of Technology, Rochester,2011.

252. BasavaRaju S, B Siva Kumar, "Next Generation VP8 Video codecs for Mobile Multimedia Communications",inProc.IJCSIA, Vol 2: Issue 2,2012.

253. JBankoski,P Wilkins and Yaowu Xu, "Technical Overview OfVP8, An Open Source video codec for the web," static.googleusercontent. com/US/37073.pdf.

254. Patrick Seeling Frank H.P. FitzekGergöErtliAkshayPulipaka Martin Reisslein, "Video Network Traffic and Quality Comparison of VP8 and H.264 SVC", In: Proceedings of the 3rd workshop on Mobile video delivery. ACM Conference on Computer-Human Interaction, 2010.

255. F. D. Simone, L. Goldmann, J.-s. Lee, T. Ebrahimi, and E. P. F, "Performance analysis of VP8 image and video compression based on subjective evaluations," in SPIE Optics and Photonics, Applications of Digital Image Processing XXXIV, (San Diego), 2011.

256. http://www.sourceforge.net/projects/dirac/

257. T. Borer, and T. Davies, "Dirac video compression using open technology", BBC EBU Technical Review, July 2005

258. http://dirac.sourceforge.net/documentation/algorithm/algorithm/intro. htm/

259. AnuradhaSuraparaju,ChrisBowley,"Dirac video codec: A programmer's guide",BBC, September 2008.

260. www.bbc.co.uk/opensource/projects/dirac/

261. http://www.cs.sfu.ca/CourseCentral/365/li/material/notes/Chap4/ Chap4.3/Chap4.3.html

262. International Journal of Wavelets, "Multi resolution and Information Processing". World Scientific Publishing Company, 2003.

263. http://www.lib.fsu.edu/about/fsulibraries/dirac/

264. ARUNA RAVI,K. R. RAO, "Performance analysis and comparison of the dirac video codec with H.264 /MPEG-4 part 10 AVC",Journal of Visual ommunication and Image Representation, Elsevier,2009.

265. Saumya V Raval, "Implementation and Performance Analysis of Dirac Videocoding standard and comparison with AVS CHINA", EE-5359 Class Multimedia Processing Project, 2012.

266. T. Davies, "The Dirac Algorithm": http://dirac.sourceforge.net/documentation/algorithm/, 2008.

267. http://en.wikipedia.org/wiki/Dirac

268. http://www.diracvideo.org/

269. NejatKamaci, YucelAltunbasak, "Performance comparison of the emerging H.264 video coding standard with the existing standards" IEEE conference on Multimedia and Expo Workshops (ICME), vol.1, pp.345-348, 2003.

270. Jeremiah Golston, "Comparing media Codecs for Video Content",Texas Instruments., Embedded Systems Conference, San Francisco, 2004.

271. EmreBaykal andAygul Bulbul, "Alalysis and comparison of video coding techniques used by IPTV", ALCATEL LUCENT PROJECT.

272. Jennie G. Abraham, "Comparison and Performance Analysis of H.264, AVS-China, VC-1 and Dirac", EE5359 – Multimedia Processing, University of Texas at Arlington, Fall 2009.

273. Bhaskaran and K. Konstantinides, "Image and video compression standards: algorithms and architecture." II Edition, Kluwer Academic press,Norwell, MA, 1997.

274. K. Onthriar, K.K. Loo, Z. Xue, "Performance Comparison of Emerging Dirac Video Codec with H.264/AVC", Proceedings of the International Conference on Digital Telecommunications (ICDT '06), page 6, Washington (DC,USA). IEEE Computer Society.

275. VisheshKalra, Khan Wahid, and AnhDinh, "Video Codec Comparative Analysis between H.264 and DIRAC PRO/VC-2", in Proc. 24th IEEE Canadian Conference on Electrical and Computer Engineering (CCECE), pp. 951-955,2011.

276. Ryan Paul, "Ogg Theoravs H.264: A head to head omparison" ArsTechnica,2010.

277. Till Halbach, "COMPARISON OF OPEN AND FREE VIDEO COMPRESSION SYSTEMS". Norwegian Computing Center, 2009.

278. http://en.wikipedia.org/wiki/Comparison_of_video_codecs

279. T. Wiegand, H. Schwarz, A. Joch, F. Kossentini, G. Sullivan, "Rate-constrained coder control and comparison of video coding standards", IEEE Trans. Circuits Systems Video Technol.,vol.13, no.7, pp.688–703, 2003.

280. Daniel Alfonso, Daniele Bagni, Danilo Pau and Antonio Chimienti, "A Performance analysis of H.264 video coding standard" inProc. 23rd Picture Coding Symposium, pp. 23-28,2003.

281. EtitoOhwovoriole and YiannisAndrepoulous, "Rate –distortion Performance ofcontemporary video codecs" Rate-Distortion Performance Of Contemporary Video Codecs:Comparison of ofgoogle /Webm VP8, AVC/H.264 and HEVC TMuC, LENS 2010, 2010.

282. Marko Hebar, Peter Planinšič, "Comparison of video codecs and coded video sequences quality using the latest objective and subjective assessment methods", Elektrotehniški vestnik, vol.74, no.4, pp.171-176,2007.

283. SHorbelt, "Comparison of video codecs and coded video sequences quality using the latest objective and subjective assessment methods", Video Compression Comparison,1993.

284. C.T. Chen, "Video compression: standards and applications",inProc. VisualCommun. and Image Representation, vol.2, pp. 103-111,1993.

285. B. Girod, E. Steinbach, and N. Farber, "Comparison of the H.263 and H.261 Video Compression Standards," First International Symposium in Photonics Technologies and Systems for Voice, Video, and Data Communication, Pennsylvania, 1995.

286. Grzegerz pastuzak," A Highj performance architecture of the Dpouble-mode binary coder for H.264 AVC", IEEE Trans.cir.sys.for video tech. vol:18,no.7, pp949-960,July 2008.

287. Chun-man Mak, Chi-keung Fong and Wai-Kuen Cham, "Fast motion estimation for H.264 AVC in Walsh-Hadamard Domain", IEEE Trans. Cir.Sys.for video tech.vol:1.8, no.6, pp 735-745, June 2008.

288. Zhihai He, Wenye Cheng and Xi Chen, "Energy minimization o portable video communication devices based on Power-Rate-distortion optimization", IEEE Trans.Cir.Sys.for video tech., vol:18, no.5, pp 596 608, May 2008.

289. Colin Doutre, Panos Nasiopoulos and Konstantionos N.Plataniotis "H.264 based compression of Bayer pattern video sequences", IEEE Trans.Cir.Sys. for video tech. vol:18, no.6, pp 725-734, June 2008.

290. Shengqi Yang, Wenping Wang, Tiehan lu, Wayne Wolf, Vijayakrishnan and Yuan Xie, "Case study of Reliability –aware and Low power design" IEEE Trans.Cir.Sys. for video tech., vol:16, no.7, pp 861-873, July 2008.

291. Dong-Hwan Kim, Hwa-Yong Oh, Oguzhan Urzhan, Sarp Erturk and Tae-Gyu Chang, "Optional post process/In-loop filtering for improved video compression performance", IEEE Trans.Consumer Elec.,Vol:53, no.4, pp 1687-1693, Nov.2007.

292. Mythri Alle, J.Biswas, S.K. Nandy, "High peroformance VLSI implementation for H.264 Inter/Intra prediction", IISc, Bangalore.

293. Yang Song, Zhenyu Liu, Takeshi Ikenaga and Satoshi Goto, "Low-Power partial distortion sorting fast motion estimation algorithms and VLSI implementations", IEEE Trans. IF & Syst. Vol.E90-D, no.1, pp 108-117, Jan 2007.

294. Ke Xu, Chiu-Sing Choy, Cheong-Fat Chan & Kong-Pong Pun, "Priority based Heading one detector in H.264/AVC decoding", EURASIP Journal on embedded system, vol 2007, pp 1-7, Jan 2007.

295. Sebastian Lopez, Felix Tobajas, Gustaro M. Callico, Pedro A.Perez, Valentin de Armas, Jose F.Lopez and Roberto Sarmiento, "A Novel High performance architecture for H.264/AVC Deblocking filtering", ETRI Journal, vol.29, no.3, pp 396-398, June 2007.

296. Zhang Qi-dong, LI-JI, CAO XI-Xin, CAO Jian, "A Novel algorithm and architecture of combined direct 2-D transform and Quantization for H.264", Journal of China Universities of Posts and Telecommunications", vol.14, pp 79-83, Oct 2007.

297. Sergio Saponara, Luca Fanucci, Stefano Marsi, Giovanni Ramponi, "Algorithmic and architectural design for real-time and power-efficient retinex image/video processing", Real time image proc., vol.1, pp 267-283, May 2007.

298. Ausgustin Ramirez-agundis, Rafael gadea-Girones, Ricardo Colom-Palero, Javier diaz-Carmona, "A Wavelet-VQ system for real-time video compression", vol.2, pp 271-280, Nov.2007.

299. Luciano Volcan Agostini, Ivan Saraiva Silva and Sergio Bampi, "Multiplierless and Fully pipelines JPEG compression Soft IP targeting FPGAs", Microprocessor and Microsystems, Elsevier, vol.31, pp487-497, Feb 2006.

300. Honggong Qi, Wen Gao, Siwei Ma and Debin Zhao, "Adaptive block-size transform based on extended integer 8*8/4*4 transforms for H.264/AVC", International Conference on Image Processing/ICIP), 2006.

301. H.Wang, S.Kwong, C.W.Kok and M-Y Chan, "Zero quantized DCT prediction technique for video encoding", IEE Proc. Vis.Image Signal Process. Vol.153, no.5, pp 677-683, Oct 2006.

302. S-C-Tai, Y-R Chen, C-Y Chen, Y-H Chen, "Low complexity deblocking method for DCT coded video signals", IEE Proc. Vis.Image Signal Process. Vol.153, no.1, pp 46-56, Feb 2006.

303. N.A. Khan, S. Masud, A.Ahmed, "A variable block size motion estimation algorithm for real-time H.264 video encoding", Signal processing: Image communication, Elsevier, vol:21, PP 306-315, Nov 2005.

304. Seong Hak Back, Yong Ho Moon, Jae Ho Kim, "An Improved H.264/ AVC video encoding based on New syntax element "Vis.Co.Image., Elsevier, vol.17, pp 345-357, May 2005.

305. Hongtao Yu, Zhiping, Lin and Feng Pan, "Applications and Improvement of H.264 in Medical video compression", IEEE Cir. Sys.Sys., vol:52, no.12, Dec 2005.

306. http://en.wikipedia.org/wiki/Discrete_Cosine_Transform

307. Henrique S. Malvar, AnttiHallapuro, Marta Karczewicz and Louis Kerofsky, "Low-complexity transform and quantization in H.264/ AVC", IEEE Trans. Circuits Syst. Video Technol., vol. 13, July 2003, pp. 598- 603.

308. Syed Ali Khayam, "The Discrete Cosine Transform: Theory and Application", Department of Electrical & Computer Engineering Michigan State University.

309. Latha Pillai, "Application Note: Video Compression Using DCT", Virtex-II series, XAPP 610(v1.2),2002.

310. J Li, SL Lu, "Low power design of two-dimensional DCT", in IEEE Conf. on ASIC and Exhibit, pp. 309–312, 1996.

311. Rao, K. R., and Yip, P., "Discrete Cosine Transform: Algorithms Advantages and Applications", Academia Press,New York,1990.

312. G. A. Ruiz, J. A. Michell, and A. M. Buron, "Parallel-pipeline 8 × 8 forward 2-D ICT processor chip for image coding," IEEE Transactions on Signal Processing, vol. 53, no. 2 1, pp. 714–723,2005.

313. Ivan Saraiva Silva, Sergio Bampi and Luciano volcanAgostini "Pipelined Fast 2-D DCT Architecture for JPEG Image Compression",In proceeding of: Integrated Circuits and Systems Design, 2001.

314. Sergio Saponara, Luca Fanucci, "Context-Aware Fast 3D DCT/IDCT Algorithm for Lowpower Video Codec in Mobile Embedded Systems" Steaming Day 2010, University of Pisa,pp.1-5, 2010.

315. Xiuqi Li and BorkoFurht, "An Approach to Image Compression Using Three-Dimensional DCT",Proceedings ofthe Visual 2003 Conference. Miami, Florida, 2003.

316. Andreas Burg, Roni Keller, JuergenWassner, Norbert Felber, Wolfgang Fichtner, "A 3D-DCT Real-Time Video Compression System for Low Complexity Single-Chip VLSI Implementation", in Proceedings of the Mobile Multimedia Conference (MoMuC '00), p.1-6,Tokyo, Japan, November 2000.

317. http://www.teamikaria.com/hddb/classic/

318. http://www.divxmovies.com/software/

319. http://Tetraspace.com/ Fourth dimension

320. Ahmed, N., Natarajan, T., and Rao, K. R., "Discrete cosine transform", IEEE Trans. on Computers, C-23:90-3, 1974.

321. Javier D. Bruguera and Roberto R. Osorio, "A Unified Architecture for H.264 Multiple Block-Size DCT with Fast and Low Cost Quantization" In proceeding of: Ninth Euromicro Conference on Digital System Design: Architectures, Methods and Tools (DSD 2006), Dubrovnik, Croatia, 2006.

322. http://essaybank.degree-essays.com/educa/

323. R.J.E. Merry, "Wavelet Theory and Applications", A literature study, Eindhoven Un. Of Tech., Dept. of Mechanical Engineering, Control Systems Technology Group, Eindhoven, 2008.

324. http://www.amara.com/IEEEwave/IW_wave_an

325. http://eeweb.poly.edu/iselesni/WaveletSoftware/standard2D.html/

326. http://en.wikipedia.org/wiki/Discrete_wavelet_transform

327. Juyoung Kim and Taegeun Park, "High Performance VLSI Architecture of 2D Discrete Wavelet Transform with Scalable Lattice Structure", World Academy of Science, Engineering and Technology 30 2009.

328. H Khalil, AF Atiya, S Shaheen, "Three-dimensional video compression",IEEE transactions on Image Processing,vol.8, pp.762-773, 1999.

29. Kyung-Chang PARK, Yun-ki HONG, Sang-Jin LEE, Yeon-Ho KIM, Younggap YOU, Tae Won CHO, Kyoung-Rok CHO and Kamran ESHRAGHIAN, "Image Processor Using 3D-DWT as Part of Health Care Management System",Journal of Systemics, Cybernetics and Informatics ISSN 1690-4532, Vol.7, Iss.5, 2009.

30. Gregorio Bernabe' a,*, Ricardo Ferna´ndez a, Jose M. Garcı´aa,Manuel E. Acacio a, Jose´ Gonza´lez b, "An efficient implementation of a

3D wavelet transform based encoder on hyper-threading technology", Journal of Parallel Computing, vol.33,no.1, pp.54–72, 2007.

331. M. Janardan and dr. K Ashok babu, "An efficient architecture for 3-d lifting-based discrete wavelet transform",inInternational Journal of Computer Technology and Applications, vol.2, Iss.5, pp.1439-1458, 2011.

332. K. Wahid, V. Dimitrov, and G. Jullien, "Error-Free Arithmetic for Discrete Wavelet Transforms Using Algebraic Integers",in Proc.16th IEEE Symposium on Computer Arithmetic (ARITH), pp. 238-244,2003.

333. G. Strang and T. Nguyen, "Wavelets and filter banks," Wellesley, MA, Wellesley, Cambridge, MA, 1996.Companion, MATLAB ToolBox on wavelets.

334. http://etd.lib.fsu.edu/theses/available/etd-11242003-185039/unrestricted/09_ds_chapter2.pdf

335. R. Crandall, Projects in Scientific Computation, Springer-Verlag, New York, 1994

336. Y. Meyer, Wavelets: "Algorithms and Applications, Society for Industrial and Applied Mathematics", pp. 13-31, 101-105., Philadelphia, 1993

337. G. Kaiser, "A Friendly Guide to Wavelets",Birkhauser, pp. 44-45, Boston, 1994.

338. Uzun, Isa Servan, and Abbes Amira. "Real-time 2-D wavelet transform implementation for HDTV compression." *Real-time imaging* 11.2 (2005): 151-165.

339. M. Vetterli and C. Herley, "Wavelets and Filter Banks: Theory and Design," IEEE Transactions on Signal Processing, Vol. 40, pp 2207-2232.,1992.

340. I. Daubechies, "Orthonormal Bases of Compactly Supported Wavelets," Comm. Pure Appl. Math.,Vol 41, pp. 906-966.,1998.

341. V. Wickerhauser, Adapted Wavelet Analysis from Theory to Software AK Peters/CRC press,504 pages, 1996.

342. Michel Misiti, Yves Misiti, Georges Oppenheim, Jean-Michel Poggi "Wavelet Toolbox™ 4The MathWorks, Inc.,User's Guide, 1997-2001.

343. M.S. Joshi, R.R. Manthalkar and Y.V. Joshi, "Image compression using Curvelet,Ridgelet and Wavelet transform: A comparative study" ICGST-GVIP, ISSN 1687-398X, Vol. 8, Iss.(III), pp.25-34, 2008.

344. BibhuprasadMohanty,Pramod Kumar Verma and PrasantKumatPantra "A zero shifted SPIHT based SVC",International Journal of Engineering Science and Technology. Vol. 2, no.11, pp.6278-6283, 2010.

345. Tu-ChihWung, Yu- Wen Huang. Hung-Chi Fang, and Liang-Gee Chen, "Parallel 4x4 2D Transform and Inverse Transform Architecture for MPEG-4 AVC/H.264", Proc. IEEE Int'l. Symp. Circuits and Systems (ISCAS '03), pp.800-803, 2003.

346. http://en.wikipedia.org/wiki/Hadamard_transform/

347. http://en.wikipedia.org/wiki/Fast_Walsh–Hadamard_transform

348. K. J. Horadam, "A GeneralisedHadamard Transform",Hadamard Transform", in the proceeding of ISIT 2005, pp.1006-1008, 2005.

349. Jeremy Johnson and Markus p,.uschel. "In search of the optimal walsh-hadamard transform",in proc.ICASSP 2000, Philadelphia, 2000.

350. Hassan, M., I. Osman, and M. Yahia. "Walsh-Hadamard Transform for Facial Feature Extraction in Face Recognition." International Journal Of Computer And Information Science and Engineering 1, no. 3, 2007.

351. Chun-Man Mak, Chi-Keung Fong. and Wai-Kuen Cham, "Fast Motion Estimation for H.264/AVC in Walsh–Hadamard Domain", IEEE transactions on circuits and systems for video technology. Vol. 18, no. 6, pp.735-745, 2008.

352. users.utu.fi/jkari/compression/part2.pdf

353. D.Sasikala and R.Neelaveni, "Registration of Brain Images using Fast Walsh Hadamard Transform" International Journal ofComputer Science and Information Security, Vol.8, no.2, pp. 96-105, 2010.

354. RaÃ¬mondoTallia, PieroMorello, and Giancarlo CastellanoOspedale San Giovanni, "The Walsh-Hadamard Transform: An Alternative Means of Obtaining Phase and Amplitude Maps",J Nucl Med, vol.25, no.5, pp.608-612, 1984.

355. Y. Hel-Or and H. Hel-Or, "Real-time pattern matching using projection kernels." IEEE Trans. Pattern Anal. Mach. Intell., vol. 27, no. 9, pp.1430–1445, Sep. 2005.

356. Chun-Man Mak, Chi-Keung Fong, and Wai-Kuen Cham, "Fast Motion Estimation for H.264/AVC in Walsh–Hadamard Domain", IEEE transactions on circuits and systems for video technology. Vol.18, no.6, 2008.

357. Harry C.Andrews."Multidimensional rotations in feature selection", IEEE trans. Computers, vol.20, pp.1045-1051, 1971.

358. AmanjotKaurl, JaspreetKaur, "Comparision of Dct and Dwt of Image Compression Techniques", International Journal of Engineering Research and Development ISSN: 2278-067X, Vol.1, Iss.4,pp.49-52, 2o12.

359. AnilkumarKatharotiya,Swati Patel and Mahesh Goyani, "Comparative Analysis Between DCT & DWT Techniques of Image Compression, Journal of Information Engineering and Applicationx, ISSN 2224-5758 (print) ISSN 2224-896X (online),Vol 1, No.2, pp.9-17, 2011.

360. O. Hunt, and R. Mukundan, "A Comparison of Discrete Orthogonal Basis Functions for Image Compression",Akaroa: Image and Vision Computing New Zealand (IVCNZ-2004), pp.53-58, 2004.

361. Marko Hebar, Peter Planinšič, "Comparison of video codecs and coded video sequences quality using the latest objective and subjective assessment methods", Elektrotehniškivestnik, vol.74, no.4,pp.171-176, 2007.

362. Guilherme Cardoso and JafarSaniie, "Performance Evaluation of DWT, DCT, and WHT for Compression of Ultrasonic Signals", in Proc. IEEE Ultrason.,Ferroelectr., Freq. Control Symp., vol. 3, pp. 2314–2317, 2004.

363. Nivedita, Pardeep Singh, Sonika Jindal, "A Comparative Study of DCT and DWT-SPIHT", IJCEM International Journal of Computational Engineering & Management, Vol. 15, Iss.2, pp.26-31, 2012.

364. M. Ali Qureshi, Abdul Aziz, Bilal Ahmed, Ayesha Khalid, and HumeraMunir, "Comparative Analysis and Implementation of Efficient Digital Image Watermarking Schemes", International Journal of Computer and Electrical Engineering, Vol. 4, no. 4, pp.558-561, 2012.

365. V.Srinivasarao, DrP.Rajesh Kumar, G.V.H.Prasad, M.Prema Kumar, S.Ravichand, "Discrete Cosine Transform Vs Discrete Wavelet Transform: An Objective Comparison of Image Compression Techniques for JPEG Encoder", Published in International Journal of Advanced Engineering & Applications, pp.87-90, 2010.

366. KiranBindu, Anita Ganpati, Aman Kumar Sharma, "A Comparative Study of Image Compression Algorithms",International Journal of Research in Computer Science, vol.2, no.5, pp. 37-42, 2012.

367. Bhavana Tewari,Sonali Dubey,M.Nizamuddin, "Comparison analysis between DWT and DCT",Proceedings of 2nd international Conference on IT & Business Intelligence (ITBI-10),New delhi, INDIA, 2010.

368. W Y Ma and B. S. Manjunath, "A comparison of wavelet transform features for texture image annotation",in Proc. IEEE Int. Conf. on Image Proc., 1995

369. http://www.en.wikipedia.org/wiki/Quantization

370. A.Puri, R. Aravind, "Motion-compensated video coding with adaptive perceptual quantization", IEEE Trans. Circuits Systems Video Technol. 1 no.4, pp.351–361, 1991.

371. http://people.bu.edu/scott/chromatic.htm/

372. http://www.wave-report.com/blog/

373. G. Allen and M.G. Robert, "Vector quantization and signal compression", Boston, MA: Kluwer Academic Publishers, US, 1992.

374. http://en.wikipedia.org/wiki/Vector_quantization

375. Agustin Ramirez-Agundis, Rafael Gadea-Girones, Ricardo Colom-Palero, Javier Diaz-Carmona, "A wavelet-VQ system for real-time video compression", Journal of Real-Time Image Processing, Vol.2, Iss.4, pp 271-280, 2007.

376. Nicolaos B. Karayiannis and Yiding Li, "A Replenishment Technique for Low Bit-Rate Video Compression Based on Wavelets and Vector Quantization" IEEE Transactions on In Circuits and Systems for Video Technology, Vol. 11, Iss.5, pp. 658-663, 2001.

377. Siwei Ma, Wen Gao, Debin Zhao, Yan Lu, "A Study on the Quantization Scheme in H.264/AVC and Its Application to Rate Control" in Proc. Advances in Multimedia Information Processing - PCM 2004, pp. 192-199,2005.

378. http://www.mqasem.net/vectorquqntization/vq.html

379. ZHANG QI-dong, U Ji, CAO Xi-xin, CAO Jan, "A Novel algorithm and architecture of combined 2-D Transform and Quantization for H.264" The Journal of China Universities of Posts and Telecommunications", Vol.14, pp.79–83, 2007.

380. H. S. Malvar, A. Hallapuro, M. Karczewicz, L. Kerofsky, "Low complexity Transform and Quantization", IEEE Transactions on In Circuits and Systems for Video Technology.Vol. 13, No. 7, pp. 598-603, 2003.

381. En-hui Yang and Xiang Yu, "Soft decision Quantization for H.264 with main profile compatibility", IEEE transactions on circuits and systems for video technology, Vol.19, Iss.1, pp.122-127, 2009.

382. http://agocg.ac.uk/reports/mmedia

383. http://rfc-ref.org/RFC-TEXTS/

384. SMPTE Draft Standard for Television, SMPTE Technology Committee on video compression technology,http://www.smpte.org/

385. http://www.networkwebcams.com/ip-camera/

BIBLIOGRAPHY

1. Kibium Suh, Seongmo, park, and Hanjin cho "An Efficient hardware architecture of Intra prediction and TQ/IQIT Module for H.264 encoder," ETRI Journal, Vol.27, N).5,OCT 2005.

2. Antonio Nurez "Advances in Video coding for hand-held device implementation in networked electronic media," J.Real-time Image proc. Springer, PP 9-23, 10th Aug 2006.

3. Esra Sahin and Tlker hamzaoglu "A High performance and low power architecture for H.264 CAVLC Algorithm," Faculty of Engg.& natural sciences, Sabanci University', Turkey.

4. H.264 inverse integer transform, Pisil technology corporation, 4533 MacArthur Blvd. Newport Beach, CA 92660.

5. Woong Hwangbo, Jaemoon Kimard Chang-Min kyung, "A high-performance 2-D Inverse transform Architecture for the H.264/AVC decoder," Department of EECS, KAIST, Republic of Korea.

6. Min Wu, Bede Liu, "Watermarking for image Authentication", IEEE, 1998.

7. Yang song, Zhenyu Liu, "Enhanced partial distortion Sorting fast motion estiamation algorithm for low power Applications," IEEE, 2006.

8. Chi-Wang, Oscar C.Au, S.H. Gary chan, Shu-Keiyip and Hoi-Ming Wong, "Motion estimation for H.264 AVC using programmable graphics hardware" IEEE,2006.

9. Yen-Kuangchen, eric Q.Li,Xiasorg Zhol, and Steven Ge, "Implementation of H.264 Encoder and decoder on personal computers," Journal of Visual Communication and Image Represenataion, Corporate Technology group, Intel corp.

10. Christopher Cramer, "Neural networks for image and video Compression: A. review," European Journal of Operational research, ELSIVIER,PP 266-282,1998.

11. A.A. Kassim, F.K.Fong, K.S. Chua and S.Rangananth, "A DSP-basedvideo compression test-bed, Journal of Microprocessors and Micro systems," ELSIVIER, PP.541-551,1997.

12. Debnath Bhattacharyya, Samir Kumar Bandyopadhyay and poulami Das, "Handwritten signature Watermarking and Extraction Technique Inspired by principle of segregation," International Journal of Security and its applications, Vol.1, NO.1, JUL2007.

13. Yusuk Lim,chagsheng Xu and David Dagan Feng," Web based Image Authentication using Invisible Fragile Water mark," in Workshop on Visual Information processing (VIP),Sydney.

14. Kelvin Harper, "Projects in Watermarking and Image Authentication ", REU 2009 at Utah State University.

15. Shuiming Ye, Qibin Sun and Ee-chein chang," Error resilient content-based Image authentication over Wireless channel", IEEE, 2005.

16. MPEG-4 Part 10 AVC (H.264) Video encoding, 7007887 Rev B H.264.

17. MPEG-4 Part 10: Intra prediction, www.recodex.com, Jain E.G.Richard Son,2003.

18. M.Mahdi Ghandi, Mohammad Ghanbari, "The h.264/AVC Video Coding Standard for the next generation multimedia communication," IAEEE Journal.

19. Ahmed Abu-Hajar, "Introduction to H.264 Video codec standard: Hardware challenges and opportunities, DIGITAVID, Inc. San Jose, CA.

20. Anne Lorette/ Edouard Francois," H.264 /MPEG-4 AVC ",%th June 2003,Rennes.

21. Main Profile H.264 codec; A Low power implemenatation for consumer Application", by Yusuhiro Yamada, hitoshi Watanabe and Ming Ning Gu,Qpixel.

22. LIU Dong-Hua,CHEN YI-Qiang, "A New all zero 4x4 block determination rule for integer transform and quantization in AVS-M encoder," Journal of Zhjang university,SCIENCE A,PP 89-94,2006.

23. WWW.google.com

24. www.opencores.org

25. www.alma-tech.com

26. Jamil Khatib, Distributed Arithmetic Theory,May 23, 2000.

27. S.N.Merchant & B.V.Rao, "Distributed Arithmetic Architecture fo Image Coding", IEEE,1989.

28. Sungwook Yu and EarlE.Swarzlander, "DCT implementation with distributed Arithmetic," IEEE, 2001.

29. Ozgur Tasdizen and Ilker Hamzaoglu, "A high performance low cost hardware architecture for h.264 transform and quantization algorithms," Faculty of engineering and natural sciences,Sabanci University, TURKEY.

30. Khurram Bukhari,Georgi Kuzmanov and Stamatis Vassiliadis, "DCT and IDCT implementations on different FPGA technologies", computer engineering lab,Delft university of technology,Netherlands.

31. Hun-Chen Chen, Tian-Sheuan Chang and Chein-Wei Jen, "A Low Power and Memory efficient Distributed Arithmetic Design and its DCT application," Department of Electronics engineering and Institute of electronics,Tung University,Taiwan.

32. J.Ameye, J. Bursens, S. Desmet, K. Vanhoof, G. Tu, J. Rommelaere, and A. Oostevlinck, "ImageCoding Using the Human Visual System," in Int'l Workshop on Image Coding, August 1987, pp. 229-308.

33. Analog Devices Corporation, "ADSP-2106x SHARC User's anual", 1995.[AG78]W. Adams and C. Giesler, "Quantizing Characteristics for Signals Having Laplacian AmplitudeProbability Density Function," IEEE Transactions on Communication, Vol. 26, August 1978, pp.1295-1297.

34. K.B. Benson and D.G. Fink, "HDTV - Advanced Television for the 1990s",Mc-Graw Hill, 1991.

35. R.Boynton, "Human Color Vision", Optical Society of America, 1992.

36. Antonio Ortega and KannanRamchandran, "Rate-distortion methods for image and video compression," IEEE signal processing magazine, vol.15, pp. 23-50, 1998.

37. "Coding of audio-visual objects", ISO/IEC 14496-2, International Standard:1999/Amd1:2000,January 2000.

38. http://ce.sharif.edu/courses/83-/1/ce712/resources/root/.../H.263.pdf

39. http://docs.real.com/docs/rn/rv10/RV10_Tech_Overview.pdf

40. Ningxu, Haibing Yin, Bingqian Zhou, Jia Wang, LongshengGuo, "Study on rate-quantization models based on main DCT coefficient distribution models," Technology, ICMT, IEEE, China, pp.3681-3684, 2011.

41. IM Pao, MT Sun, "Approximation of calculations for forward discrete cosine transform," IEEE Transactions on Circuits and Systems for Video Technology, vol.14, no.4, pp.405-415,2004.

42. P.C. Yip and K.R. Rao, "The transform and data compression handbook," CRC press,Boca Raton, FL, 2001.

43. M.A. Cody, "The Wavelet Packet Transform," Dr. Dobb's Journal,Vol 19, pp. 44-46, 50-54., Apr. 1994.

44. J. Bradley, C. Brislawn, and T. Hopper, "The FBI Wavelet/Scalar Quantization Standard for Gray-scale Fingerprint Image Compression," Tech. Report LA-UR-93-1659, LosAlamos Nat'l Lab, Los Alamos, N.M. 1993.

45. D. Donoho, "Nonlinear Wavelet Methods for Recovery of Signals, Densities, and Spectra from Indirect and Noisy Data," in Proc. Symposia in Applied Mathematics,Vol 47, pp. 173-205,1993.

46. B. Vidakovic and P. Muller, "Wavelets for Kids," unpublished. Part One, and Part Two, 1994.

47. Scargle et al., "The Quasi-Periodic Oscillations and Very Low Frequency Noise of Scorpius X-1 as Transient Chaos: A Dripping Handrail", Astrophysical Journal, Vol. 411, L91-L94,1993.

48. M.V. Wickerhauser,"Acoustic Signal Compression with Wave Packets", 1989.Available by anonymous FTPat pascal.math.yale.edu, filename: acoustic.tex.

49. Dr. H. B. Kekre,Dr. T. K. Sarode,Prachi J. Natu,Shachi J. Natu, "Performance Comparison of Face Recognition using DCT and Walsh Transform with Full and Partial Feature Vector against KFCG VQ Algorithm", in 2nd International Conference and workshop on Emerging Trends in Technology (ICWET), vol.5, pp.22-29, 2011.

50. M.MahdiGhandi and Mohammad Ghanbari, "The H.264/AVC video coding standard for the next generation multimedia communication,' IAEE Journal., Vol. 1, No. 2, pp. 1–10, 2004.

51. Agostini, R.Porto, M.Porto, "Forward and Inverse 2-D DCT architecture targeting HDTV for H.264/AVC Video Compression," Latin American Applied Research, vol.37, no.11-16, 2007.

52. Roman C. Kordasiewicz, ShahramShirani, "ASIC and FPGA implementations of H.264 DCT and Quantization blocks", IEEE International Conference on Image Processing,Vol.3, no.11- 14, Sept 2005.

53. Luciano VolcanAgostini, Ivan Saraiva Silva, Sergio Bampi "Pipelined Fast 2-D DCT Architecture for JPEG Image Compression", in Proc 14th symposium on Integrated Circuits and Systems Design, PP. 226 231, 2001.

54. Arjun K Pai, KhaledBenkrid and Danny Crookes,"Embedded Reconfigurable DCT Architectures Using Adder-based Distributed Arithmetic",in Proc. Seventh International Workshop on Compute Architecture for Machine Perception (CAMP'05), Italy, pp. 4-6, 2005

55. Tu-Chih Wang, Yu-Wen Huang, Hung-Chi Fang, and Liang-Gee Chen, "Parallel 4x4 2-D transform and inverse transform architecture for MPEG-4 AVC/H.264", in Proc.2003 International Symposium on Circuits and Systems, vol. 2, pp. 800–803.2003.

56. M. Horowitz, A. Joch, F. Kossentini, and A. Hallapuro, "H.264/AVC Baseline Profile Decoder Complexity Analysis", IEEE Transactions on Circuits and Systems for Video Technology, vol. 13, Iss.7, pp.704-716, 2003.

57. Arturo Mendez Patino, M.M. Peiro, F. Ballester, and G. Paya, "2D-DCT on FPGA by polynomial transformation in two-dimentions",in Proc. 2004 International Symposium on Circuits and Systems, vol.3, pp. 365–368.2004.

58. Minyi Fu, G.A. Jullien, V.S. Dimitrov, and M. Ahmadi, "A low-power DCT IP core based on 2-D algebraic integer encoding" in Proc. 2004 International Symposium on Circuits and Systems, vol. 2, pp.765–768, 2004.

59. Fernando Pereira, "Video compression: Dicussing the next steps",in Proc. IEEE conference on Multimedia and Expo(ICME), pp. 1582-1583, 2009.

60. J. Ostermann, J. Bormans, P. List, D. Marpe, M. Narroschke,F. Pereira, "Video Coding with H.264/AVC: Tools,Performance, and Complexity", IEEE Circuits and Systems Magazine, vol.4,Iss.1, pp.7-28, First Quarter 2004.

61. T. Wiegand, G. Sullivan, G. Bjntegaard, A. Luthra, "Overview of the H.264/AVC Video Coding Standard", IEEE Transactions on Circuits and Systems for Video Technology,Vol. 13, No. 7, pp. 560-576, July 2003.

62. H. Schwarz, D. Marpe, T. Wiegand, "Overview of the Scalable Video Coding Extension of the H.264/AVC Standard", IEEE Transactions on Circuits and Systems for Video Technology, vol.17, Iss.9, pp.1103-1120, 2007.

63. A. Kubota, A. Smolic, M. Magnor, M.Tanimoto, T. Chen, C.Zhang, "Multiview Imaging and 3DTV", IEEE Signal Processing Magazine, Vol. 24, Iss.6, pp. 10 – 21, Nov. 2007.

64. E. Q. L. X. Zhou and Y. Chen, "Implementation of h.264 decoder on general purpose processors with media instructions", in Proc.SPIE Conf. on Image and Video Communications and Processing,US, pp. 224-235, 2003.

65. E. Y. Lam and J. W. Goodman, "A mathematical analysis of the dct coefficient distributions for images", IEEE Trans. Image Process., vol.9, no. 10, pp. 1661–1666, Oct. 2000.

66. A. N. N. T. R. K.R, "Discrete cosine transforms",.inIEEE transactions on computing, pp. 90-93, 1974.

67. S. B. Gokturk and A. M. Aaron, "Applying 3d methods to video for compression",.inDigital Video Processing (EE392J) Projects\Winter Quarter, 2002.

68. T. Fryza, "Compression of Video Signalsby 3D-DCTTransform", Diploma thesis, Institute of Radio Electronics, FEKT Brno University of Technology, Czech Republic, 2002.

69. G. M.P. Servais, "Video compression using the three dimensional discrete cosine transform",.inProc.COMSIG, pp. 27-32, 1997.

70. R.A.Burg, RoniKeller,JuergenWassner, Norbert Felber, and Wolfgang Fichtner, "A 3d-dct real-time video compression system for low complexity singlechip VLSI implementation" in Proceedings of the Mobile Multimedia Conference (MoMuC '00), p. 1B-5-1, Tokyo, Japan, 2000.

71. T.Fryza and S.Hanus, "Video signals transparency in consequence of 3d-dct transform",.inProc.Radioelektronika Conference, pp.127-130, 2003

72. Nikola Božinović and J. Konrad, "Motion analysis in 3d dct domain and its application to video coding",. Signal Processing:Image Communication, vol. 20, no. 6, pp. 510–528, 2005.

73. M. B. T. Q. N. A. Molino, F. Vacca, "Low complexity video codec for mobile video conferencing", in Proc. Eur. Signal Processing Conf. (EUSIPCO), pp.665-668, 2004.

INDEX

I

Image 4, 378,54,49

Insertion 190

Images 4, 378,54, 49

    Blurring/Sharpening 48,268,313

    Digital 1,12,356

    Human visual system (HVS) 31

    Registration 81,366

    Background 1,232,171

    Binary 35,363,300

    Blur 48,283,313

    Digital 1,12,351,46

    Gray scale 8,307

Intensity. 14,378

Image processing toolbox. See also

    MATLAB 346,429,373

Inset theory view

    PDF 411,418,409

Interpixel redundancy. See compression

    32,35,33,36

Interpolation 53,234

Intellectual property 176,179,180,307

Intellectual property identification (IPI)

Intellectual property rights (IPR)

International standard (IS)

Inverse DCT 75,228,247,313

Internet 167,287,169

ITU 37,45

ITU-T J83A

ITU-T J83B

ITU-T J83C

Interframe 34,84,250

ITU 37,45

ISO/IEC 5,38,81,111,141

Intra prediction 111,303

Interpolation 53,234

    Function 382,363,14,50

    Spline 350

Wavelets 54,266,362

Inwavelet bases

    Linear 23,76,270

    Thresholding 341

    Hierarchical block matching
    57,73,360

J

JPEG 1,38,279,306

JM Software 51,137

Joint video team (JVT) 110

Joint model (JM) 273

K

Kernel 380,401

L

Lightness 23,24

Lookup table 245,246

Luminance 18,390,270

Likelihood 207

Low pass 207,338,342

Transient 207,328

LCD 17

M

Motion vector 57,307,250

Motion 5,35,170,209

Multi resolution 330,373,386

Macro blocks 113,218

Motion vector 57,250,255

Macro block 113,218

Microsoft windows media 202

MPEG

    MPEG-1 4,208,266

    MPEG-2 5,315,390

    MPEG-4 88, 178

    MPEG-4 part 10 450

Macro block, 2

Printed in the United States
By Bookmasters

Signal processing can be broadly defined as the application of analog or digital techniques to improve the utility of a data stream. Analog techniques are applied to a data stream embodied as a time-varying electrical signal. While in the digital domain, the data are represented as an array of numbers. A video signal is represented as a sequence of frames of pixels. There exists vast amount of redundant information that can be eliminated with video compression technology. So that its transmission and storage becomes more efficient. Video and image compression is a complex and extensive subject, and this book keeps an offered limited focus, concentrating on the standards themselves and on video coding concepts that directly underpin the standards. The leading contenders are the International Standards known as MPEG-4 Visual and H.264. H.264/AVC, the result of the collaboration between the ISO/IEC Moving Picture Experts Group and the ITU-T Video Coding Experts Group, is the latest standard for video coding. H.264/AVC provides gains in compression efficiency of up to 50% over a wide range of bit rates and video resolutions compared to previous standards. There is therefore a need to develop low complexity implementations of H.264/AVC that offer the performance and flexibility advantages of the standard without an excessive computational cost.

Selvaraj Saravanan received B.E degree from university of Madras in 2000 and M.E. from Satyabama University. He has completed Ph.D in video compression in 2013. He joined as a Lecturer and became an assistant professor in saraswathi velu college of engineering. He is currently Associate professor in Maamallan institute of technology. There he teach graduate-level courses in digital image processing. He has been actively involved in research and development of signal processing. His research interest include Image processing, video compression, VLSI and digital signal processing. He is a formal reviewer of many standard journals. He was acted as a chairperson for many IEEE conferences. He thanks all the authors and companies for supporting this work.

PARTRIDGE
A Penguin Random House Company

ISBN 978-1-4828-425
900
9 781482 842593